One Man's Medicine

ARCHIBALD L COCHRANE
with MAX BLYTHE

One Man's Medicine

An autobiography of
Professor Archie Cochrane

in a 2009 edition celebrating the centenary of his birth
with original foreword by Sir Richard Doll FRS
and additional contributions by Sir Richard Peto FRS
and Sir Iain Chalmers

A Cardiff University Publication

First published 1989 by BMJ Books.
Published in paperback 2009 by Cardiff University, Cardiff CF10 3XQ, Wales.

ISBN 978 0 9540 8843 9

This book is printed on paper suitable for recycling and made from fully managed and sustained forest sources.

British Library Cataloguing-in-Publication Data.

A catalogue record for this book is available from the British Library.

Permissions
Plates 7–12: Crown Copyright and reproduced with the permission of the Controller of Her Majesty's Stationery Office. Plate 13: reproduced with the permission of the *Yorkshire Evening Press*. Plate 14: reproduced with the permission of Professor Michael Lichtenstein.

Printed and bound in Great Britain by CPI Antony Rowe, Chippenham, Wiltshire.

Contents

v

vi

2009 Edition Acknowledgements

Congratulations to Cardiff University on the decision to publish a paperback edition of *One Man's Medicine* as part of the University's celebration of the centenary of Archie Cochrane's birth. It is a fitting tribute to a man forever associated with Cardiff and South Wales in his research achievements, and an initiative principally of Vice-Chancellor Dr David Grant CBE, Professor Peter Halligan and Emeritus Librarian Steve Pritchard, who has admirably coordinated publishing arrangements, with support from the University's impressive Information Services team led by Mr Martyn Harrow. Along the way, the project has been generously assisted by Rosemary Soper, Librarian of the University's Archie Cochrane Library, and Karen Pritchard. Christopher Jones of CPI Antony Rowe, printers, arranged the book's production. By kind permission of publishers Wiley-Blackwell this edition has been produced by scanning the original publication of 1989.

To Sir Iain Chalmers and Sir Richard Peto, special thanks for contributions enhancing this commemorative edition.

Max Blythe

1989 First Edition Acknowledgements

Gratefully acknowledged is the assistance of many of Archie Cochrane's colleagues and friends during the completion of this text after his death. Their critical observations on various chapters of the biography and addition of data to Archie's sparkling, initial drafting of the work have enhanced its authenticity. Major contributors include Professors Charles Fletcher, Ian Higgins, Stewart Kilpatrick, Estlin Waters, Hubert Campbell, Peter Oldham, Richard Schilling, George Knox, Guy Scadding, Alan Williams, Archibald Duncan, Ken Rawnsley and Bryan Hibbard; Drs John Gilson, Bill Miall, Reginald Saxton, Peter Elwood, Max Wilson, Philip Hugh-Jones, Julian Tudor Hart, Jean Weddel, Neville Willmer, Joyce Landsman, Richard Mayon-White, Wilfrid Harding, Jeffrey Chapman and David Bainton, also Mr Fred Moore, Mr Peter Sweetnam, Miss Irene Calford and Mr Peter Nicholas. Artist Derek Whiteley supplied maps and charts. Special thanks to Sir Richard Doll and Dr Dick Cohen for introductory observations, and to Archie's family, particularly Helen, Joe and Maggie Stalker for supportive kindness.

2009 Foreword

During the 20 years since Archie Cochrane (1909–1988) died and this biography of him first appeared, a remarkable international collaboration has arisen, named after Archie and dedicated to making systematic reviews of all the properly randomised evidence in the world on any therapeutic question conveniently available to all doctors, patients and other interested parties. The Cochrane Collaboration, which began in 1992–3, was preceded by a systematic review in the late 1980s (which Archie himself lived to see and enjoy) of all the randomised evidence in just one area of medicine, pregnancy and childbirth.[1] From its relatively small beginnings, the international Cochrane Collaboration involved by 2009 more than 20,000 unpaid collaborators from 100 countries, had produced (and was disseminating and updating) systematic reviews of the randomised evidence in some 3600 different areas of medicine, was widely cited in high-impact journals, and was still growing rapidly in size and influence.[2] In times when an increasingly visible proportion of medical research is concerned more with profits and patents than with patients, the Cochrane Collaboration provides a nice reminder that many who are employed in health care are there not only for themselves but also for others. More importantly, it provides useful answers to many practical therapeutic questions, identifies big gaps where further research is needed,[3] helps foster that research and spreads rationality and integrity.

Archie would have been delighted, but utterly amazed; he would have expected to be largely forgotten by now (indeed, Max Blythe, Richard Doll and I were the only academics at his quiet cremation), but Cochrane posthumously became one of the iconic figures of twentieth-century medicine. He was not himself a particularly great medical research worker, but he was a great man, both as an individual living with unusual integrity and reserved charm in difficult circumstances, and as a questioner[4,5] who inspired others to doubt unjustified certainties and to seek scientific evidence. The 1993 decision by Iain Chalmers and others to name the international network that they were trying to establish the "Cochrane Collaboration" was a decision inspired by affection and respect for Archie; it was, however, also an inspired decision in another sense, because Archie's name helped emphasise the altruistic purposes of the enterprise, and helped attract hundreds, then thousands, then tens of thousands of enthusiastic voluntary collaborators from around the world. To see why it did so, read and enjoy this book about the man.

Richard Peto, Oxford 2009

NOTES

1 Chalmers I, The pre-history of the first Cochrane centre. Pp 242–253 in Bosch FX, Molas R. eds. Archie Cochrane: Back to the Front. Barcelona, Thau, SL, 2003. (Reprinted as Appendix C of this Edition).
2 Starr M, Chalmers I, Clarke M, Oxman A. The origins, evolution and future of the Cochrane Database of Systematic Reviews. In: Banta D, Johnsson E, eds. A history of Health Technology Assessment. *Int. J. HTA*, 2009.
3 Clarke L, Clarke M, Clarke T. How useful are Cochrane reviews in identifying research needs? Journal of Health Services Research and Policy 2007; 12: 101–103.
4 Cochrane AL. Effectiveness and efficiency: random reflections on health services. London: Nuffield Provincial Hospitals Trust, 1972.
5 Peto R, Chalmers I. Obituary: Archie Cochrane (1909-1988). *Controlled Clinical Trials* 1989; 10: 426-427 plus 428-433.

Original 1989 Foreword

Archie Cochrane was a man of the 1930s. His character and lifelong convictions were formed by the cataclysmic events that brought Hitler to power and plunged the greater part of the world into a devastating six-year war. In this he was not alone. What distinguished him from so many others of his generation was the depth of his emotional and intellectual reaction to these events and his fiery independence of mind, which prevented him from accepting any of the easy political solutions and kept him a rationalist to the day of his death.

Archie's personality was unique and so were his contributions to medicine. It is fortunate, therefore, that he not only had a mind to tell his story but that he chose a friend to help him complete it who had a zeal for accuracy and a gift for clear exposition. Max Blythe, a lecturer in epidemiology at the Oxford Polytechnic with a special concern for health education, came to know Archie in 1984, when he was seeking information for a biography of another leading British physician. They quickly became close friends and Archie, who was uncertain how long he had left to complete the account of his life, sought Blythe's assistance in its preparation. The result was a most happy partnership, which retains all of Archie's idiosyncrasies and wit and makes the dramatic events of his early life, his scientific contributions, and his later battle against obscurantist members of the medical establishment as pleasurable to read as a well constructed novel. For those who never had the good fortune to know Archie personally this autobiography will provide a worthy substitute.

Richard Doll, Oxford 1989

1 The tens and the twenties

EARLY DAYS

I was born on 12 January 1909 in Galashiels, a small town in the south of Scotland. (I would like to believe that I was conceived in Bamburgh, a lovely village on the Northumbrian coast, and there is some evidence to support the idea.) My background was industrial upper middle class. In spite of brief encounters with Evelyn Waugh and George Orwell, who had different views in different directions, I have never tried to conceal or change this. My father's family was industrial. My grandfather and great-grandfather became wealthy through textile manufacturing. They made Scotch tweeds. My father was a very successful managing director of his father's business. He was killed in the first world war at the Battle of Gaza when I was too young to know him well, but he was described in his obituary as "of sterling character, kind hearted and fair minded and he had the saving grace of human and genuine friendship." The Cochrane family was the wealthiest family and the biggest employer in the small town. My grandfather, to establish his position, built a large house, Abbotshill, overlooking Sir Walter Scott's Abbotsford on the other side of the Tweed. He had a wonderful garden in which we often played as children. It was the origin of my lifelong interest in gardening.

My mother's family was different. Both her father and grandfather were lawyers in a neighbouring town, Hawick. My mother was educated at a rather snob school, St Leonard's School at St Andrews, and later in Paris. She painted, and played hockey for Scotland, but gave up both activities when she married. Her family is examined in detail for another reason in chapter 5.

I have searched in vain for any sign of a scientist in my family. The only trace I could find is Lord Archibald Cochrane, ninth Earl of Dundonald, who was a first rate amateur scientist, a friendly rival of Watt, Cavendish, and Priestley. There is a suggestion that we were descended from some branch of that family – probably illegitimately. (I was strongly reminded of this possibility when I visited Jamaica in the 1960s. The beautiful black Jamaican girl at the desk kept my passport rather a long time and I asked why. She smiled and said, "My name's Cochrane too." The tenth Earl Dundonald, the famous admiral, was appointed Commander-in-Chief of the West Indian Station in 1848 and visited Jamaica in 1849. Unfortunately further research on my family in Galashiels made this hypothesis rather improbable.)

I had a happy early childhood. I had one elder sister, Helen, and two younger brothers, Robert and Walter. There were two nurses and three servants, but in spite of this we saw a great deal of our loving parents before the war. We were, I suppose, to some degree spoilt by regular seaside holidays at Easter and in the summer and expensive Christmas and birthday presents, but there was an underlying element of Calvinist discipline.

The general atmosphere of the larger family in which we grew up was more definitely Calvinist. The work ethic was installed early and the existence of a clear cut moral code, telling one what was right or wrong, was assumed. There were other minor strands. It was assumed that I would be wealthy when I grew up, but it was always made clear to me that I would have to start at the bottom and work my way up in my grandfather's business. The need for self sufficiency was stressed. Another minor strand was the need to treat the lower classes with fairness and politeness. The whole doctrine was probably dug in rather deeper when I was prepared for confirmation into the Presbyterian Church by the Reverend Dr Donald (later well known in Canada). I do not remember much about it, but I can guess what he said.

I do not know how much influence this early Calvinist background had on my life. I have certainly worked hard most of my life and am still working. I am, I think, rather conscientious, and if adaptability is one aspect of self sufficiency I certainly adapted quicker and better to sudden changes – such as life as a prisoner of war, the Spanish Civil War, and an unexpected presidency – than most people. I ought possibly to be more grateful to Calvin and John Knox than I usually am.

Our weekly pocket money was at first only one penny a week, and church attendance was obligatory. Our social contacts were limited at first. I think there were only five families in the town with whose children we were allowed to play. Later on we met a wider circle of the children of upper middle class families in the surrounding towns. We never met the "County." We had excellent relations with our servants. I learned to play whist, and later bridge, from our cook Jean and housemaid Grizzle (whom I recently visited just before her 90th birthday).

My whole world changed when war was declared in 1914. We were on holiday at Bamburgh at the time. I remember the hurried journey home in my father's car and a vague memory of my father explaining to my mother that he must join the Army at once, and her tears.

I saw little of my father after that. He came back occasionally on leave and all the children were very happy indeed. He was finally posted to Egypt with the King's Own Scottish Borderers. He came back once, at least, on leave from Egypt. I remember how determined I was to be the first to welcome him and how I dashed downstairs in my dressing gown to hug him. He was killed on 19 April 1917 at the battle of Gaza. I still remember my feeling of desolation and that of my whole family.

My family later sent money to Gaza to build a new wing to a hospital there, which contained a memorial to my father and a friend of his who was killed in the same battle – R R M Lumgair (my father was killed trying to rescue Lumgair). Many years later I decided to take my two nieces to see their grandfather's memorial and grave. I took advice from the Egyptian Embassy beforehand, but everything went wrong. We were arrested at El Arish. I got out of that by a speech in French, saying I was an elderly professor with one foot in the grave making his last visit to his father's grave. They let us through. We reached Gaza, tired and worried, had a wash and a meal, and then set off for the hospital. I knocked on the door and a lady with a middle-Western American accent eventually opened it. I stated my credentials – medical professor, my family's contribution to the hospital, and the memorial to my father. There was a curious pause. She looked at me carefully and then, to my utter astonishment, asked me if I was a Christian. I admit I hesitated for a moment. My nieces and I were tired, but I thought the question was so monstrous that I replied that I was agnostic and that I thought the question was irrelevant. The door was slammed in our faces! Later Arab officials forced our entry, but it is clear that Gaza is an inconvenient place for one's relations to be buried in. I still cannot guess how she diagnosed me.

The desolation caused by my father's death was not only a family affair. Many people in the town and neighbourhood were killed in the same battle, and there was an atmosphere of gloom in the town for a considerable time. I slowly noticed the repercussions of my father's death. Our own family slowly moved down in the family hierarchy. We were soon the only family in our circle who did not have a car. Another unfortunate possible result of my father's death was that I started fighting with my brother Robert. I have no idea why. (My psychoanalyst later had many theories, but I was never convinced.) Soon after we had another tragedy. My brother Walter died. In retrospect I am pretty sure he died of tuberculous pneumonia. It is clear that the whole family had been exposed to tuberculosis in the local milk. I remember the cows, which passed our windows every day from the filthy cowbyre in Church Street. I have as a result a large calcified tuberculous gland in my abdomen. My sister suffered from tuberculous glands in the neck. I think my sister and I were immunised against the second attack of tuberculous infection on the part of an undernurse, Violet, who died of tuberculosis (I remember seeing her having a haemoptysis). I am afraid my brother Walter had not got sufficient resistance from the milk.

It must have been hard on my mother. She had lost a husband and a son and she had to learn to run a family with reduced finances, in wartime. The advice available to her was not of a very high level. The only brother, or brother-in-law, of any intelligence was G P Thompson (later Rear Admiral and Sir), well known in the next war as the "Blue Pencil Admiral."[1] He, however, was busy on active service and rather alienated from my mother because of his unfaithfulness to my mother's only sister Betty. I imagine our local lawyer Mr Chapman was her main support, and possibly my uncle, Russell Cochrane. I think she did very well in difficult circumstances.

Education was started early at home. The first experiment was with a local friend of my mother's, who was rather stupid but enabled me to learn to read rather early. Then there was a short period at a dame's school in Hawick, which had no great effect; after that we returned to Galashiels under the daily tuition of a Miss Lowe. I remember nothing about her past, but she was certainly a remarkable woman. She taught us to read and write, do our sums, and draw. She told us about the United States and Ireland, introduced us to poetry in general, including the Border Ballads, Macauley's *Lays of Ancient Rome*, and Shakespeare. I had soon learned a lot by heart. She was weak on mathematics and biology; but I am very grateful to her. At that age I could have been described as precocious, imaginative, and rather quarrelsome. I was red haired and freckled, and rather overweight. My health was good, except for rather frequent attacks of migraine. We received a sort of minimal cultural exposure by other means. We were taken to Edinburgh to see Shakespeare, pantomimes, and the art gallery; and we heard Gilbert and Sullivan performed by the local operatic group.

I was sent off at the age of about 7 to a preparatory school at Rhos-on-Sea, North Wales. There are two theories as to why I went there. My mother had a friend, Mrs Hilton, who had been at school at St Leonard's with her and who had a son going to that school. Alternatively, I believe that the Cochrane family thought that my mother would spoil the eldest son of the eldest Cochrane son and that he should be sent outside Scotland. England was not far enough – it must be Wales or Ireland!

I spent about seven years at Rhos-on-Sea. It is fashionable now to describe the horrors of the preparatory schools of that period – the schools described by Evelyn Waugh and George Orwell – but I must admit that I was happy there. I was of course miserable at first, but I recovered quickly. It was a shock to hear Welsh spoken, but I adapted even to that, as I had to do again much later. There was little corporal punishment or bullying, and as far as I know no homosexuality. The headmaster, Mr Glover, aroused my interest in mathematics and I made rapid progress. He also had a fascinating book of "problems" and in later years gave me one a week to solve. I loved that. Then there was Mr Asche who taught me Latin. I do not altogether regret that. In addition I learnt some French and history. The curriculum was weak on science, but I can hardly complain as it enabled me to win a scholarship to Uppingham (a school of which I had scarcely heard except that Mr R R M Lumgair had been educated there). At this stage I imagine my reports would have described me as "intelligent, athletic, real ability in mathematics, with an interest in poetry."

I was frightened by the idea of going to Uppingham. The stories about public schools of that period had horrific accounts of corporal punishment and harsh discipline. I was not altogether disappointed. Uppingham at that time had the Reverend R H Owen as headmaster. In retrospect I see him as an unimaginative, uncultured disciplinarian. He believed firmly in the value of corporal punishment. I do not remember ever hearing that he said a kind word to anyone. (Because of the national strike in 1926 my brother and I arrived a day late for school after being driven from Scotland by an uncle through road blocks and stonings. The headmaster at first seized his cane, but then relented saying, "The greater the difficulty, the greater the importance of overcoming it.") The worst side of Uppingham was certainly the amount of corporal punishment that could be applied by house prefects, housemasters (on the advice of form masters), and the headmaster. It was painful and particularly humiliating having to "bend over" before people only a few years older than yourself (I must admit that, with cunning, I got off rather lightly).

On the other hand there were great advantages. The school had several excellent masters. V T Saunders, a physicist, was a bit of a bully, but he somehow got me to understand that new knowledge was obtained by testing hypotheses using reproducible measurements. I have no idea what more he could usefully have taught me at that age and I am really grateful to him. Then there was Mr Powell, who helped my mathematics, and T B Belk, who encouraged my interest in literature, helped later by S S Cameron. I wrote rather amusing essays during that period and acted quite well. It was also during this time that I read a large number of Victorian novels, because Uppingham had an excellent library.

There was another bad side to Uppingham – its overinterest in athletics. The headmaster told me that he had made me a school prefect because I was in the Rugby XV and not because I had won a scholarship to King's College Cambridge! Fortunately the worship of athleticism worked in my favour as I was reasonably athletic. I was in the Rugby XV, the 2nd XI in cricket and hockey, and I won the cup for Eton Fives. This helped me in two ways. Firstly, in a complicated way, it saved me some beatings; secondly, it gave me the freedom to be slightly eccentric.

There are two footnotes to add to my career at Uppingham. The first point was my loss of religious faith there. The story I usually tell is that the crucial event was a sermon in the chapel (attendance was compulsory) in which a muscular Christian speaker argued that Christ was an athlete, and probably "stroked the Gallilean eight"! My loss of faith was more likely to have been the product of a long term of intellectual growth, and the story, if true, was just the final straw.

The other point is a more general one. The decline of the United Kingdom as an industrial nation has often been associated with the fact that intelligent sons of industrialists abandoned industry and went into the Civil Service and research. I think there is a great deal of truth in this. In my case the explanation was simple. My grandfather, after my father's death, sold the business shortly after the end of the war – fortunately before the slump. So there was no opening for me there. One offer came from a wealthy childless uncle-in-law, also in textiles, who offered to make me his heir if I would go into his business. There was only one condition: that I should resign my scholarship to Cambridge and join him at once. I did not take long to make up my mind.

One last comment. The Reverend Reggie Owen sent me a telegram asking me to resign the scholarship, stay on as head boy, and try for a major scholarship the next year. Again I did not hesitate. I had had enough of Reggie Owen.

CAMBRIDGE

The change from Uppingham to Cambridge was a remarkable experience – no doubt exaggerated because it was King's College. (I probably went up too young. I would, in retrospect, have profited from a year in industry or abroad.) I suddenly found myself free in a land of plenty and I wanted to do everything. I wanted to learn more about science, to strengthen my new found love; I wanted to play rugby football, golf, tennis, and squash; I wanted to join play reading and debating societies; I wanted to act; I wanted to go to the theatre; I wanted to talk and argue and make friends and, more mundanely, to ride horses and play bridge. The curious thing about it was that I managed to do them all for the first year while never missing a lecture or laboratory session. I do not know how I did it, but I certainly enjoyed it.

I had a fascinating interview when I arrived at King's with someone who was a tutor, or someone like that (I do not remember his name), to decide what I should study. I mentioned first physiology, biochemistry, and zoology, and he nodded with approval. I then unfortunately mentioned a vague idea that I might later revert to medicine. "Cochrane," he said, "If you wish to study a trade, you must do that in your vacations. You have come here to be educated." And educated I was. We finally compromised on my reading physiology, comparative anatomy, and zoology, which was the routine for medical students in other less anti-trade colleges.

I found the teaching of science exciting, particularly in

physiology. I shall never forget the first time I stimulated a frog's nerve and saw the muscle contract. The teaching in zoology and comparative anatomy was not so experimental but of a high standard. I heard the distinguished Russian physiologist, Ivan Pavlov, lecture – translated by Dr Anrep. Pavlov looked like a prophet of the Old Testament and was too dogmatic.

I played in the freshmans' rugby match. I got a fair press, but not enough. I enjoyed playing for the college and was elected secretary for the next year. I joined the leading play-reading society; I frequented the Arts Theatre where I saw a wide range of productions including plays by Aeschylus, Shakespeare, Ibsen, and Shaw. I joined the Amateur Dramatic Company and acted in "The Servant of Two Masters" (Goldoni). Frank Birch[2] was the producer. I did not act well, but I enjoyed it enormously. However, the main experience of those years was what might be called the "family life" of King's, which I found entrancing. Briefly, everyone was willing to talk to everyone, and I found it wonderful. Scientists were few in number at King's and I had an uphill battle defending science, but everyone – undergraduates and dons – tolerated me and was willing to talk. The first year was a bit of a blur, but I did enough work to get a good first in my Mays and was given a major scholarship at King's.

A rugger accident in which I ruptured two muscles in my right leg, semi-membranous and the long head of biceps, was possibly my saving. I was operated on and warned I might never run again. This did not happen, but the accident did slow me down. I stopped rugby, acting, riding and golf, and concentrated on work and more social things. I think it was during this period that the main impact of Freud and Marx began to hit me, as it hit so many others of my generation. My only criticism of King's was that there was no don who could really put these new ideas into proper perspective. A Karl Popper at King's at that time would have been an enormous advantage, but one cannot expect everything. Even without a Popper in residence I still gained a great deal from being there. I settled down into the life of King's and began to make friends and learn from people. There are a large number to whom I am deeply indebted, particularly three remarkable Fellows of the College, "Goldie" Dickinson,[3] Vice-Provost Sheppard,[4] and Lay Dean Donald Beeves,[5] and a close circle of undergraduate friends, Patrick Wilkinson,[6] Donald Lucas,[7] Dickon Steele,[8] Dick Cohen,[9] Kenneth Mellanby,[10] Julian Bell,[11] and William Francis.[12]

I worked hard during the second year. I had my first tripos exam, as well as my 2nd MB exam in physiology and anatomy in December. I got a first in my natural science tripos and was first in anatomy in the 2nd MB.

Around about this time my grandfather died and I achieved a small, entirely independent private income. I then decided to take two years over the second part of my tripos in physiology and relaxed a little. The first year of those two years was most enjoyable. I started going to outside lectures, such as bio-chemistry (Gowland Hopkins and J B S Haldane) and English (I A Richards). I met some of the younger established scien-tists like C P Snow. My leg recovered and I was soon playing tennis and skiing again. In the vacations I travelled a lot in Europe and learnt about art and architecture. I became more interested in politics, called myself a socialist, but joined no party. I read widely and talked a lot.

I liked the way homosexuality was discussed and tolerated at King's, though I probably underestimated its prevalence. I did not know then, for instance, that Maynard Keynes had been homosexual or that David Prestwick, whom I knew well and was on my staircase, was one as well. I also did not know he was a communist until I met him in San Francisco many years later. I also knew very little about the "Apostles." I was surprised later to discover that two people whom I knew well, Alistair Watson and Julian Bell, had been members. I was clearly a bit of an innocent and though I am told that I met Blunt, I was too old to be involved by the "Traitors."

The peace of that year was disturbed by two family events – the death of my brother and the remarriage of my mother. Both upset me badly. My brother was killed on a motor cycle at the age of 20. We had started to get on well together in the latter years of his all too short life. My sister and I heard of my mother's intended remarriage when we were abroad, and fortunately met on the way home. We both liked the idea of our mother remarrying but strongly disliked the man she had chosen, whom we knew well. We realised that the marriage would be strongly disapproved of by the Cochrane family on the grounds that he had not fought in the war (he was in munitions) and was rather hard up. We decided to help our mother by pretending to support the marriage and we did it rather well, but it was a strain. My sister suffered more than I did. In order to re-establish some semblance of unity we decided that the four of us should go to winter sports together. We went to Samaden near St Moritz in Switzerland. As a family holiday it was not a great success, but it led to my meeting George Rink[13] and his family. They were an anglicised Austrian Jewish family. George was a very intelligent young barrister, with a most interesting father and a difficult mother. They were kind to Helen and myself during a rather difficult holiday. George was to become a loyal friend for the rest of our lives.

The second year started. I decided that if I got a double first I would try for a fellowship at King's (a bad decision as it turned out, but I had become very fond indeed of King's and found life there increasingly attractive). Time passed, and I became more and more worried about getting another first. In some ways it was understandable. If you got one first you were labelled for the rest of your life. If you failed to get your second you lost that distinction. If, however, you got a second first, a double first had greater snob value. I got neurotic about this, overworked and got ill. James (later Sir James) Gray was patient with me and kind. I got my double first, but at a price.

So, there I was – a young man, socially acceptable, with a double first in science, and a small private income, with admittedly a small "black cloud" in the background. Most people would have given me a good prognosis, but I regret to say I made a mess of it in the short term.

NOTES

1 Rear Admiral G P Thomson, *Blue pencil admiral*, London, 1948.
2 Francis Lyall Birch CMG, OBE, fellow of King's College, Cambridge, 1915–34, in which period he made a major contribution to the theatre in Cambridge. Later he acted on the London stage and in films and became a well known radio broadcaster. In addition to his career as a teacher of history there were important periods of war and government service. In the second world war he served as head of the naval section of the Government Code and Cypher School at Bletchley Park.
3 Goldsworthy Lowes Dickinson, distinguished author, historian, teacher, and philosopher.
4 Later Sir John Sheppard and provost of King's from 1933 to 1954.
5 Donald Beeves, fellow of King's and director of studies in modern languages.
6 Later fellow of King's, reader in Latin literature and Brereton reader in classics, Vice-Provost of King's and Public Orator.
7 Later fellow of King's and Lawrence reader in classics.
8 Later secretary, Schools' Broadcasting Council.
9 Later deputy chief medical officer, Medical Research Council, deputy chief medical officer, and first chief scientist, Department of Health and Social Security.
10 Later head of Department of Entomology, Rothamstead; first director of Monks Wood Experimental Station and first principal of University College, Ibadan.
11 Poet, professor, traveller, and son of Clive and Vanessa Bell. He died, when still in his twenties, while serving as an ambulance driver on the Republican side in the Spanish Civil War.
12 Later secretary of the Science Research Council.
13 A distinguished and most successful Chancery QC, who was to become Archie's life long friend and confidant.

2 The thirties

1931–34: YEARS OF MISTAKES

I nearly called them the "wasted years," because they were so
unproductive scientifically, but they were not altogether
wasted. They had some beneficial effects. I made a series of
serious mistakes for which I alone was responsible. The first
was to want to become a fellow of King's. This was
excusable, although I do not think I was at all suited to
become a fellow. What was inexcusable was my hurry. I
thought that I must write a first class thesis in two or three
years in order to get a fellowship. I am fairly sure, in retrospect,
that if I had gone to London, become medically qualified, and
possibly gone into social medicine and written a good thesis I
would have stood an excellent chance of a fellowship. On the
other hand, I might have ended up in Harley Street!

As I have said before, I was in a hurry and, to my shame,
looked around for a bandwaggon on which I could jump. I
found one with Dr Neville Willmer, who was a pioneering
figure in Cambridge[1] in the field of tissue culture. Tissue
culture was relatively new and clearly had possibilities – the
study of individual human cells and the reasons for their
growth. It was an exciting area for a pure scientist, but I
should have known by then that I was not a pure scientist. I
had already too much of a social conscience. At that time
there appeared to be no important general hypothesis to be
tested. Then tissue culture was a technical business: progress
depended upon glass blowing, electrical knowledge, and
mechanical ability. I lacked most of these skills. Certainly I
was not good with my hands, but I went ahead, and paid the
penalty.

13

After the kindly Neville Willmer had helped me to make a start on a research programme much of my time was spent working under the direction of Dr Field at the Strangeways laboratory on the outskirts of Cambridge, where tissue culture interests were then centred. Later I spent time with Professor Levi in Torino, where I was unhappy. I produced one good result: the effect of pH on the rate of growth of human nerve fibres in tissue culture. It was the outcome of many months of struggle about reproducibility. I thought the whole thing so trivial that I did not bother to publish the findings.

The difficulties about my research were unimportant, however, when compared with my psychological problems at this time. Sexually I had matured late and my first affairs were postgraduate ones revealing a disturbing problem. To my horrified surprise I discovered that I was incapable of ejaculation, despite desire and erection. I tried again and again but was forced to admit that I was definitely abnormal. I became very neurotic and finally turned to the medical profession for help. I found my original contacts with the profession singularly unsympathetic and unhelpful, although there did emerge the idea that psychotherapy might be worth trying. I tried it and found it superficial and rather unsympathetic.

In considerable despair I went to the Kaiser Wilhelm Institute in Berlin, which had a great reputation. I have unfortunately forgotten the name of the professor there who saw that I was in trouble and was kind. The next step was precipitated by a chance encounter with an American who was staying in Berlin at the same hostel as me. He was being psychoanalysed and we spoke at length about it. As I have mentioned earlier, I had been strongly influenced by Freud. I had found his hypotheses fascinating. The trouble was the lack of supporting, and, in particular, experimental, evidence. The main evidence in support of Freud's theories was the success of therapy. The idea became increasingly attractive to me to test his principal hypothesis by seeing if the technique could help my own troubles, while at the same time learning more about psychoanalysis and seeing whether the hypothesis could be tested in other ways. It seemed much more attractive than tissue culture; so I made my second mistake.

I was introduced to Dr Theodor Reik[2] by my now virtually

forgotten American friend. I told him of my troubles and interests. He impressed me by saying that he had already successfully psychoanalysed Richard Braithwaite, a fellow of King's, a man I had met and admired. We discussed terms, and I found that I could just afford his help if I cut my standard of living. We started out with a promise that I would resume medical studies as soon as possible, while he would recommend me to be accepted as a psychoanalyst if he found me suitable. It all seemed very reasonable.

In retrospect it was not so. I probably made a poor choice of psychoanalyst. This is not because he was not an able man. I still respect him, but he was the most intuitional analyst of them all, and I was always asking, "But what is the evidence?" This made transference, as they called it, difficult. At the same time, my memory suggests that this U-turn cheered me up a great deal.

The next problem arose because the year was 1933. Dr Reik was a Jew and he decided, reasonably enough, that he must move to Vienna. He asked me to go with him and study medicine there. In one way it was not a difficult decision to make. I had seen the growing political debacle in Berlin. I had seen the Nazi toughs beating up Jews. I had, also, my devotion to my new found interest, psychoanalysis, which I could not quickly abandon. So I went. Vienna had great advantages, not least reciprocal arrangements with Cambridge, which made it easy for me to study medicine there. It was also then very inexpensive. The opera, theatre, and skiing were cheap; thus in spite of paying for my psychoanalysis I had a most educative, enjoyable time. I cannot remember the names of all the friends I made there, but I am grateful to them.

The teaching of medicine in Vienna was second rate. It was almost entirely by lectures and extremely dogmatic. Patients were sometimes demonstrated at lectures, but students were not allowed to touch them. Only in the psychiatric wards was I allowed to talk to patients. I suppose I learnt a certain amount. In comparison with other branches of medicine psychoanalysis seemed to have a slight advantage: the analysts at least had ideas, even if these lacked proof.

My own analysis went on slowly. I imagine Dr Reik

explored, in his intuitional way, various hypotheses about my troubles: the early death of my father and subsequent deaths of my brothers, and a rather late circumcision. But nothing seemed to fit in. I played the game of free association as fairly as I could. I also had the opportunity of sitting in at one of Freud's seminars. It was disappointing. He was dogmatic and did not encourage discussion.

During this period the fears of a fascist invasion of Austria increased. Refugees poured into Vienna. My group of friends was strongly anti-fascist and there began to be trouble in the streets. My political education made rapid strides, but I was not surprised or sorry when Dr Reik decided on another move – this time to Holland. Though lonely in the Hague at first, I quickly settled down. I was accepted by Leiden as a medical student and started working in a surgical hospital in the Hague, while studying Dutch on the side. I met other students and soon had a satisfactory social life. The only trouble was the lack of progress in my analysis. My symptoms persisted unchanged and I was becoming restless. It was some relief when Dr Reik suggested that I should return to London to complete my medical training. He did, however, suggest that I should return for further analysis if I decided to become a psychoanalyst. I told him I was still undecided.

When I looked back on those years they did seem to have been wasted. My dreams of a good scientific career in medicine had gone, and my symptoms were still there. On the other hand, I argued that I had behaved logically in trying to get the best possible treatment. The steps I took would have been widely accepted at that time, and this was confirmed by my own rather juvenile reading on the subject. The fact that I had been unsuccessful was not really my fault. Dr Reik might have argued that my deep distrust of his "intuition" reduced transference, but he agreed that I had stuck to him through some strange times for about two and a half years.

Additionally I could argue that I had explored the psycho-analytic field both theoretically and practically. I had found it fascinating as regards new hypotheses but lacking in experi-mental proof. I also found that its attempt to found its proof on clinical effectiveness was doubtful. This was not based only on my own experience but on that of many people under analysis I had met. I formed the provisional hypothesis that analysis could treat hysteria, a disappearing disease, but little else.

There were various other aspects of any cost–benefit analysis. I had had a thorough European cultural and political education, which I had much enjoyed. I spoke almost perfect German and fairly good Dutch; and I had learnt to live with my disabilities, which of course most people do without the benefit of psychoanalysis. What I did not appreciate for several decades was that this European excursion may have saved my life. Only many years later did I discover that my sexual difficulties had their origin in an inherited disease from the Cochrane side of the family. The family tree shows its devastating effect. My great-grandfather Cochrane had five healthy sons, but when I die there will be no Cochrane-named descendant. If in the early 1930s I had discovered the hopelessness of the situation, and there had been no European journey, I might well have become suicidal.

On my return to London I found a flat, with the help of my friend George Rink; and fortunately chose University College Hospital as my medical school. One could hardly have hoped for such a wonderful collection of teachers as I found there: Sir Thomas Lewis, George Pickering, Wilfred Trotter, Philip D'Arcy Hart, Sir Charles Harington, and Ros Pitt Rivers. There were also some bright students whose company I enjoyed. The only real irritation was that, although physiology and biochemistry were certainly beginning to enter more and more into medicine, the teaching about diagnosis, and particularly treatment, was extremely dogmatic, although far less so than in Vienna. It was depressing. A few of us used to plague the clinicians by asking them about the evidence in support of the treatment they were giving. Usually we were fobbed off with "In my clinical experience. . . ." When two physicians defended two different and seemingly opposing treatments for the same condition we inevitably became cynical.

My other dominating interest at this time was politics. I had returned from Europe with distinct anti-fascist feelings, for obvious reasons. I feared that fascism would spread to the UK and France. The great problem was what kind of political stance to adopt – whether to join the Labour party or the Communist party. I knew many members of both. In particular there were two friends whom I admired greatly, who both tried hard to persuade me to join the Communist party. But I resisted. (Much later they both left the party.) They attributed my resistance to my upper middle class background; but I believe there were other factors such as the unsatisfactory resistance mounted by the communists to fascism in Germany and Austria, as well as the point that Marxism was unsatisfactory as a scientific hypothesis. (If I had been able to read Karl Popper at that time I would have been a far happier man politically and psychoanalytically.) I joined neither the Communist nor the Labour party; but by 1936 I was beginning to tire of talking about fascism and doing nothing.

SPAIN, 1936–37

London in the thirties was very political, and though I was working hard, realising that I would be a late qualifier, I became involved. I had come back from Europe strongly anti-fascist but critical of the communists, who had not done enough to support the socialists in Germany and Austria against the fascists. The communist idea that fascism was the last stage of capitalism and would soon disappear seemed too facile. I saw fascism as a true menace to western civilisation.

It was the time of the Hunger March, Mosley's Blackshirts, and a round of anti-fascist meetings. Then came the Popular Fronts in France and Spain, and a stream of refugees. Finally, in the summer of 1936, Franco and his Moors invaded Spain[3] and the pot boiled over. My friends and I feared that if Spain went fascist and joined with Hitler and Mussolini, France and the UK were doomed; but we were admittedly ignorant of the complexities of Spanish politics. We were incensed by the UK's commitment to a non-intervention pact,[4] especially

18

when it became clear that Germany, Italy, and Portugal were openly flouting such a policy.

Behind the scenes in the UK an important Spanish Medical Aid Committee was set up. The president was Dr Christopher Addison MP,[5] and the main committee contained a galaxy of important names, with peers, MPs, professors, and leading communists appearing united. There was also a working committee, which I gather was left wing. Ostensibly, the intention was to organise and fund a field ambulance unit to serve the Spanish Republican cause. When an advertisement appeared asking for "offers" from doctors and medical students who were prepared to serve in Spain I began to think of joining them.

I thought I knew more about fascism and its probable effect on Western European civilisation than most other British medical students. I was unmarried and had no one dependent on me. My friends and family would miss me if I were killed, but they would believe that I had died in a worthwhile cause. Those were my conscious thoughts, but I suspect there were other factors. I do not remember how conscious they were underneath my political excitement, but there were the elements of a real depression. I still sincerely wanted to do some worthwhile medical research, but the prospects seemed to get worse and worse. I had developed grave doubts about psychoanalysis and also knew that I was no good at laboratory research. On top of this, I now realised that I would never be a first rate clinician, which would bar my way to clinical research and any chance of following in the footsteps of the likes of Sir Thomas Lewis. All roads seemed barred. I think I discussed the idea of volunteering for the Spanish Medical Aid Ambulance Unit with Philip D'Arcy Hart and George (later Sir George) Pickering, and I think both of these tutors approved. There was, however, one unexpected difficulty. My great friend George Rink had been seriously ill, and although he was now off the danger list I still felt that the shock of telling him of my decision to go to Spain might cause a setback. Therefore I left a note with Dick Cohen's wife, Margaret, asking her to break the news when the time seemed right. She had become very fond of George during his illness and I knew that she would choose the right moment. It was also at this time that I told my sister of my decision. Although she seemed to think little of the idea I still went ahead and volunteered, and dropped out of medical training for the second time. It was a very serious drop out, which indefinitely postponed my date of qualifying. I also ran the risk of being seriously wounded or even killed; but as an enthusiastic anti-fascist I volunteered.

Before recounting my subsequent experiences it seems only fair to admit how little I knew about the Spanish Civil War until I read Hugh Thomas's excellent book[6] many years afterwards. For a year, however, I did experience sectors of this war very clearly.

Although I have little recollection of the occasion, I understand that the small medical aid ambulance unit I joined attracted large crowds and tumultuous applause when it set out from London's New Oxford Street on its journey to Spain.[7] Those travelling by train were conveyed to the station in Daimlers supplied by the London Cooperative Society Funeral Department. The ambulances, trucks, and those travelling by road were led down to the ferry by my Triumph Gloria, with Lord Peter Churchill the front seat passenger. It was all well organised, but I hated such occasions and, being tired, slept throughout the ferry crossing. This meant that my meeting with other members of the party was delayed. Our arrival in Paris was marked by a tumultuous reception organised by Leon Jouhard, Secretary General of the Trade Union Federation, CGT. There were other receptions too. At one I was told that I had shaken hands with Tito, who then had a quite different name. I do not suppose it was true. With all this entertaining and sleeping late to recover from driving so far I still had little chance to get to know the other members of the unit well, although I did obtain insight into one member's mentality very clearly during a big political rally in Paris's Stade Bufalo, where the overwhelming cry was for more planes for Spain. He made a stupid speech and spoke for far too long. On the way down to Port Bou the next day I asked Churchill who the speaker was and discovered that he was the unit's chief political administrator. I was horrified and dubbed him my much-to-be-avoided political commissar of the future.

We probably attempted to complete the next stretch of the journey too quickly, hoping to catch up with those travelling by train. As a result we experienced our first casualty when one of the drivers crashed during a night-time leg of the operation and had to return to the UK injured. Another rapturous welcome awaited us in Port Bou, but I had already had enough of such demonstrations. My main objective was to avoid drink and get as much sleep as possible, ready for the journey to Barcelona; but one still had to make concessions to the public relations demands of the venture. After another massive reception in Barcelona I finally got to bed and had a long sleep.

I awoke to a very unexpected world: a city relaxing after a "great victory." The explanation was that the anarchist dominated public militias in Barcelona had in a few days dealt with the rebellious regular army units there and then used this success as a platform from which to launch an anarchistic class war over the whole of Catalonia, in which they seemed to have been completely successful. This presented the leaders of the field ambulance unit with something of a problem. I had already diagnosed several of the leading lights as secret party members who clearly wanted to link up with the International Brigade[8] in the Madrid area. Now they found themselves in a city dominated by the anarchists (FAI),[9] who wanted us to help on the northern Catalan front[10] to support, *inter alia*, the siege of Huesca.[11] I kept quiet, sunbathed, tried to learn Spanish and Catalan, and observe an anarchist city. I was young and immature and the idea of anarchism was mainly, for me, associated with Tolstoy. On the whole the city seemed to be doing rather well. It was clear that a revolution had taken place. Industry seemed to be run by workers, the clergy had more or less disappeared, and there was no tipping; but life seemed to continue with a few shortages and a general feeling of good will. The only freedom that had been lost was religious freedom. Here, I also learnt something about the Trotskyites (POUM).[12] In England "Trotskyite" was a term of abuse – usually applied to me. In

Barcelona they seemed an organised, serious political party which I ought to respect, not least because they had run the PSUC,[13] a combination of socialists and communists, into third place in the political power structure. Our unit was clearly going to be associated with the weakest political party. I had, at one time, an awful picture of myself helping to run a communist-dominated, front-line hospital in an anarchist revolution in Spain.

If there was further cause for disquiet it came from getting to know more about the team I had joined. I remember making a miserable, exaggerated summary of their credentials to myself after a few days in their company. There were two homosexuals, one alcoholic, one schizophrenic, eight open party members and about 10 secret party members.[14] Time showed that I was wrong, but not by much. (I was assisted in my diagnosis of secret party members by experience recently gained in London. There I knew two secret party members very well and had the chance to discern various characteristic phrases they used in discussing politics. Such conversational clues proved a great help in spotting other secret party members. My greatest triumph was to introduce two secret party members to each other, saying I was sure they would find they had a lot in common. Later they were both very angry.)

On the other hand I found several members of the team I liked and admired.

Everyone liked and admired Aileen Palmer, an Australian, for her friendliness, devotion, and hard work. Everyone trusted her, although she was a self-confessed party member. Another self-confessed party member was Thora Silverthorne, a highly skilled surgical theatre sister. Despite a hard streak, she was friendly and amusing. I also liked Ruth Prothero, a charming, migrant doctor from Vienna. I talked fluent German and she introduced me to some of her Swiss and German friends. Margot Miller, another Australian, was a journalist and party member. She was a robust, efficient hard worker and later became a well known writer of detective stories. I enjoyed her company. A fifth female member of the original party I never did get to know. She was a complete loner and soon separated from us.

The males were worse than the females. Lord Peter was a good public relations figure, a fair administrator, and a friendly person; but I was worried that his fairly obvious homosexuality or bisexuality might run the unit into legal trouble, although I knew little of the laws in Spain. Kenneth Sinclair-Loutit, the official leader of the unit, was a likeable medical student and an obvious secret party member, but I did not think that he would be a good leader. He had a weak streak. O'Donnell, the chief administrator, who had made the bad speech in Paris, was even worse when I met him. I thought him stupid, conceited, and erratic. I certainly did not like the idea of his being in charge. The quartermaster, Emmanuel Julius, also seemed second rate and rather schizoid. The only surgeon, A Khan, who was studying in the UK for the FRCS, was reserved, non-political, and rather worried. Of the other two male doctors, one was an American, Sollenberger, and the other, Martin, a former member of the Royal Army Medical Corps. I took a poor view of them both. In addition there were two other medical students.

I did not have very close contact with the drivers. Harry Forster, a cheerful London taxi driver, proved a great success as an electrician on one occasion, but he moved on all too quickly. Alec Wainman, a Quaker photographer, was a charming, if neurotic, character, whom I liked but never got to know. Leslie Preger, an open communist, was rather a shocker. He admitted that he had only got into the unit because he had claimed that he spoke Spanish and knew about first aid. Both claims were false, but no one seems to have checked. The remaining drivers were the two Charlies, Hunt and Hurling. They were two young, extrovert, working class volunteers who wanted adventure and women. I enjoyed their presence at first, but they quite definitely disliked me, particularly my Cambridge accent. Fortunately they were not permanent. They motored backwards and forwards between London and Spain, so that I saw them only infrequently.

Inevitably some of these views are influenced by what happened later, but I have tried hard to recount my first impressions. Even if I have been only modestly accurate it is easy to understand how depressed I became in Barcelona in those early days. I found the anarchistic political picture confusing. I thought the Spanish Medical Aid Committee should have briefed us better, and I considered the choice of people it had made for the team unsatisfactory and possibly dangerous. I had expected at least one experienced casualty surgeon, one or two experienced male nurses, and some ambulance drivers who had military experience. It was difficult to believe, when I recalled the enthusiasm I had experienced in London, that there were not enough volunteers of the right kind. On the other hand, there was a suspicion that some undesirables got the job "on the nod" if they had a party card, in order to ensure communist control of the unit. (Much later I tried to solve the problem by tracing the committee papers of the Spanish Medical Aid Committee. I was surprised that this was not possible. I was told that all the papers had been bombed. As both committees had large memberships and all must have received papers, the bombing must have been very accurate and selective!) I wondered what to do and came to the conclusion that as I had volunteered I must stay on and see if something anti-fascist could emerge from the mess.

Another issue added to my early unhappiness in Spain. When it became clear that we had little alternative than to establish a field hospital in support of republican forces besieging Huesca, Peter Churchill, using a Michelin map, suggested Grañén as a suitable place because of its rail and road communications. It turned out to be a good choice geographically. He and Sinclair-Loutit asked me to lend them my car to go ahead and locate a suitable building. Most people would have asked me to drive them up, but I suppose they wanted to talk politics and I was not a party member. The result was unfortunate. They allowed the anarchists to steal the car. It was rumoured that it was due to Sinclair-Loutit's carelessness. I was fond of this, my first car, which had already proved useful to the unit, and I was angry despite deciding not to make a fuss.[15] It was an incident that certainly increased my depression.

Our move to the windswept anarchist village of Grañén was on 3 September. The house of a fascist doctor who had fled the district was chosen as the best available for a field hospital. It was well situated as regards Huesca, where the main fighting was, and reasonably near the railway line. We worked hard at converting the house into a hospital, with two operating theatres, wards, and rooms for staff. The fighting at Huesca was always spasmodic, with increasingly long intervals between offensives. One such outburst of activity occurred shortly after we were ready and we coped surprisingly well. We had established a first aid post, with an ambulance, as close as possible to Huesca. There we came upon the Thaelman battalion of German volunteers,[16] who were pleased to hear of the existence of the hospital and with whom I communicated regularly as my German was better than anyone else's in the unit. They were stationed in a series of shallow trenches in front of Huesca; a remarkable group of men and one woman which included Hans Beimler,[17] former communist deputy to the Reichstag, and Ludwig Renn, author of the pacifist novel *Der Krieg*. I got to know them well. They were highly critical of the anarchists, who had run out of steam after Catalonia had been liberated. The Germans believed that with reasonable anarchistic support they could have taken Huesca and Zaragoza and linked up with the Basques to consolidate the northern front. Now they wanted to move to the Madrid front, where they thought the most important fighting would be.

A good deal of my time needed to be spent at the first aid post, giving me the opportunity to spend much of it with the Thaelmans. This was preferable to confining myself to the post and the companionship of Preger, with whom I often shared duties there. Even at the hospital life was dreary, although the regular staff seemed to be doing a good job with the walking wounded, giving anti-tetanus injections, cleaning and dressing wounds, feeding the hungry, and setting them on trains for Barcelona. I saw far less of how the more serious cases fared, although I did transport many of them to the hospital from the field, including some with serious head wounds. It was in this first period that the unit experienced the loss of one of its own members. Our quartermaster, who had already appeared erratic, disappeared and was later reported killed at the front some distance away. We gave him a full, rather embarrassing, military funeral. He was the one I thought to be schizoid.

Then came a lull. This provided an opportunity for us all to meet and a flood of complaints to be vented. The main one was about food, which consisted of hard meat, beans, olive oil, and garlic, resulting in a painful type of diarrhoea we dubbed the "Grañén gripes." There was little we could do about it, except write to the committee in London. Similar action was taken as regards our lack of news. We felt cut off. We even lost our radio. I cannot remember whether it was broken, stolen, or confiscated, but its loss increased our sense of isolation. The most political subject discussed was the problem of secret communist meetings and separate reports to the committee and the British Communist party. I was by this time on friendly terms with Sinclair-Loutit, Thora Silverthorne, and Aileen Palmer, and I think I raised the subject with them, pointing out that although we accepted that the communists and secret communists made up most of the unit, we did not think it reasonable for them to hold secret meetings. These were undoubtedly disruptive. I pointed out that three people had already left the unit, possibly because of this. For a time a compromise was reached, in which I was allowed a seat on their committees. I was able to speak but not to vote. Later O'Donnell came up and denounced this, but I think finally the secret meetings were given up. There was also a lot of criticism of Dr Sollenberger as a disruptive element, but he did not leave until much later.

The periods of activity became shorter and the lulls longer, until there was nothing but lull towards the end of October 1936. The weather became worse. It was often very cold. The food was no better. The food sent from England got held up, first in Port Bou, then in Barcelona. In a recent book I am credited with its recovery.[18] I hope it was true. I cannot remember. More volunteers arrived; some also left. Morale slowly fell. It was to be expected. We were divided by age, sex, class, intelligence, political allegiance, and mental stability – and had not enough to do.

A few events are worth recording. Margot Miller was wounded and had to return to the UK. She was a loss as she was one of the more sensible communists. Amongst the newcomers Dr Reggie Saxton[19] proved most useful. He began a general practitioner service for the village of Grañén and later helped to start blood transfusion on the Madrid front. Another valuable acquisition was the RAMC orderly Keith Anderson, who impressed us all by his dependability and skill. He was immensely likeable. There were also several good nurses, although they were not really needed in this period of inactivity. There were two incidents which I shall mention. The first I considered horrific. During a sunny afternoon I came out of the building to find a heated discussion going on on the back door steps of the hospital. I quickly realised that our Indian surgeon was under attack. A patient had died. I cannot remember whether he had or had not operated to remove a bullet which had lodged near an important artery or nerve. The whole scene of harsh judgment seemed incredible. No one had the knowledge or experience to criticise a surgical decision. I believe and hope that I defended the surgeon. I suspected the communists of organising the attack. The result was disastrous. Our one surgeon, furious at unwarranted criticism, left and returned to the UK. I was glad to discover later that he had got his FRCS.

The next incident was different. It originated in the failure of Churchill and Sinclair-Loutit to consult the Mayor of Grañén at the outset and persuade him to accept a predominantly communist hospital in his anarchist village. The Mayor and leading anarchist, who was actually called Pancho Villa, clearly found this irritating and in November took his revenge by cutting off food and petrol supplies. Fortunately the food from the UK had recently arrived and there was little need for petrol as the front was now dead. In fact the situation quickly resolved itself, due to an accident to Pancho Villa, who tended to smoke while allocating petrol rations. He was admitted to our hospital with semi-serious burns and we were able to put on a rather good act. I think we turned one operating theatre into his private room, where English nurses in starched uniforms waited on him and gave him English food. He also had a good deal of skilled medical attention from our new and excellent surgeon Dr Aquilo, who had arrived to replace Khan. Pancho Villa's wounds healed quickly and as a reward he gave us a feast. A special pan was made and into it, according to rumour, were put a sheep and a goat, chickens and masses of rice, tomatoes, and pimentos. We were truly well fed for once. The scene itself was memorable, lit by an enormous fire. Goya would have relished it. In fact the whole party, with its remarkable paella and what Villa described as "the biggest frying pan in the world," has been well described in *The Distant Drum*.[20]

Our troubles – lack of work, political and other quarrels, a sense of isolation and low morale – were becoming well known and various people were sent up to sort us out. There were four or five of them. I shall comment only on the worst and the best of a bad lot. The worst was a communist English novelist domiciled in Barcelona, who had been a good friend to the unit by giving a home in Barcelona to a number of our convalescent cases. His lecture was a flop. Assuming that a good deal of the discord and unhappiness within the unit must result from sexual frustrations, he took the line that for the duration of the war we should all give up sex. He ended the lecture by saying that until the end of the war he and his wife were going to share something of the deprivation by sleeping in different rooms. We were not impressed, especially when we heard that he was sleeping with his secretary. Also, without outside advice, we had already managed to organise, on a very sensible basis, "married quarters" for those wanting to sleep together. It is an interesting fact that most of the couples for whom we supplied these quarters later married.

The most sensible visitor was Tom Wintringham,[21] a communist then, who took the hard line. The hospital, he pointed out, had great propaganda value in the UK, which enabled the committee to collect a lot of money. He agreed that we might do better on the Madrid front, but explained the political difficulties of transferring from an anarchistic front to a PSUC front. So, we had to put up with it. (Tom was later taken ill – I think it was typhoid – and I visited him in hospital in Valencia. I met both his claimant wives, one communist, one non-communist. I understood why he resigned from the Communist party and was later a great success as a journalist on *Picture Post*.)

The debate as to what to do continued inside the unit. I became, inevitably, the main speaker for the non-communists. The line I developed was that by staying in Grañén, eating Spanish food, using Spanish petrol and electricity, and doing nothing to help we represented little more than an economic burden. (I like to think that this foreshadows some of the "cost effective" arguments I produced later in my career.) I argued that we should either go home or be moved to the Madrid front. Against me the communists argued the established propaganda benefits of the hospital at Grañén, as well as the uncertainties of military control if we did join up with the International Brigade (IBM) on the Madrid front.

The committee in London was almost certainly having similar discussions and Sinclair-Loutit was recalled to report. It was just a little while later that I was sent to meet André Marty, the leader of the International Brigade.[22] I was, however, under no illusion that I was going to conduct important negotiations. I was almost sure everything had been arranged by the Communist party in the UK and that I, a non-communist, had been chosen to put a Popular Front flavour on the deal.

I was glad to leave Grañén. I had never been happy there and looked forward to the trip, although I was rather worried when I got my travel document from O'Donnell. With his usual inefficiency it was undated, did not say where I was going, and merely stated that I could negotiate on behalf of the Spanish Medical Aid Committee. This was the one thing I was sure I was not entitled to do. In the event the trip to Albacete went off smoothly. I had one interesting meeting in a bar in Barcelona with a tall Englishman with big feet, who had been fighting with the POUM militia. In the course of the conversation I criticised the anarchist and POUM militia for not capturing Huesca and Zaragoza and linking up with the Basques. He argued fiercely that the anarchists and the POUM had been perfectly correct to consolidate their revolution before thinking of assistance for the communists in Madrid. I later asked him why he had joined the POUM. As far as I remember he admitted it was by chance. They were the first people he met and he liked them. He said his name was Blair.[23] I often wonder what would have happened to his literary output if he had joined the International Brigade. I later enjoyed his books more than I had that conversation.

The train journey to Valencia was uneventful, but it was interesting how the atmosphere changed from one of happy victory to that of a depressing war zone. I think I briefly met Peter Churchill and Lady Hastings (a real charmer) in Valencia before moving on in some haste to Albacete, where I was apparently expected. After being allocated board and lodging I received the news that I could see Marty that evening. I was nervous. He was already well known as an intolerant leader who was prepared to shoot those he did not like. My only hope seemed my flourishing red beard, although I did take care to prepare a short, cautiously worded speech in French. The meeting went off well. Someone introduced me, while I had a look at Marty. He was an impressive figure – tall, with a bushy beard and small dark hard eyes. I then made my speech offering the services of the Spanish Medical Aid Committee field hospital unit. He replied briefly in French, thanked me, and embraced me. We then sat down and had a drink and I was introduced to the chief medical officer of the International Brigade, a Dr Neumann, who was Austrian, and to Dr Dubois of the XIV Brigade, to which it was thought our mobile unit would be attached. We talked in French and German for a time and then, with a broad grin, Marty turned and asked, "Do tell me, what are you, an English gentleman, doing in Spain?" I replied that I was a Scots anti-fascist who had experienced fascism in Germany and Austria and feared its spread. I also made it clear that I was not a member of the Communist party, but that I was a strong supporter of the Popular Front. He laughed, embraced me for a second time, and handed me over to Dr Neumann and Dr Dubois. The latter, a dashing Pole educated in France, although a communist was much more interested in practical than doctrinal matters. The former, a charming, intelligent Viennese doctor, seemed pleased to have the opportunity to tell me, in German, about the difficulties of building up a medical service for the brigades.

As I left the meeting I suspected that I had been part of a prearranged scenario in which the communists had arranged that a non-communist should hand over a field ambulance, financed in the UK by a supposedly humanitarian committee, to an organisation which was becoming increasingly accepted as communist controlled. By then I did not care. I had decided that despite evils on both sides, the republican side was the lesser evil, and I believed the ambulance unit would be more effective in its support on the Madrid front – and so it worked out.

Here I would like to interpolate a short note on a return visit to Grañén in 1978.[24] I had decided not to return until the doctors eventually allowed Franco to die, although at one time I thought he was going to outlive me. Eventually I did return, through the kindness and arrangements of Dr Xavier Bosch, a young Spanish epidemiologist I met on a visit to the USA in the 1970s. My great embarrassment on arriving in Grañén was that I could not recognise the house of the fascist doctor where we had based our hospital. I later discovered that this was not surprising as it had been bombed and rebuilt as a cafe and cinema, but enough remained to bring back a flood of memories. Grañén is really rather a distinguished place. It is the site of the first international hospital in the Spanish Civil War in 1936. Tito of Yugoslavia lived there in 1937, as did General Walter, later Polish Minister of Defence in 1938. Orwell certainly visited in 1937, and John Cornford probably wrote his well known poem "The Last Mile to Huesca" there.

When the mobile team finally arrived in Albacete only four of its original members remained – Kenneth (Sinclair-Loutit), Thora (Silverthorne), Aileen (Palmer), and myself – a situation which I feel reflected the inadequacy of the original selection process. There were, of course, others from subsequent waves of volunteers. I was glad that Reggie Saxton and Keith Anderson were there. Recent arrivals included Dr Tudor Hart,[25] who had some surgical experience, Joan Purser, a nurse, and Max Colin,[26] a mechanic. Reorganisation and membership changes led to a new leadership contest. To non-communists this proved an amusing open battle for power between two communists. Usually they settled things in secret. Tudor Hart won and Kenneth became his chief administrator.

The unit soon left for the Madrid front to support the XIV Brigade.[27] We had some difficulty in discovering the position of the brigade and even more in locating Sol-y-Cine, a hotel near the Corunna road where we were to establish our field hospital. We lost our way and arrived, inconveniently, after dark. It was on this journey that I first met Joseph Edenhoffer, a Czech driver and mechanic. In those days he spoke only Czech and German and as I was the sole German speaker we saw a lot of each other and got on well.

Even when we reached the hotel there was further trouble. Three Poles appeared from Dubois's staff intending to take charge of the unit. This was strongly resisted and eventually a truce was agreed until after the battle. We then set out, after midnight, to make the hotel's unsuitable accommodation into a functional field hospital. We even got some sleep before the first wounded arrived at around 9.00 am.

My job was to do the triage, as the brigade had its own first aid post. This consisted initially of dividing the wounded, on arrival, into three categories: those with superficial injuries who could be quickly assisted, those more seriously wounded but eminently treatable, and the hopeless. The first decision was whether they were well enough to be evacuated after their wounds had been cleaned and dressed and they had been given anti-tetanus injections (if available). We had to evacuate these people quickly as triage space was limited. The remainder were classified as "flesh," "orthopaedic," "abdominal," and "other," and I added a severity scale. There were inevitably some who were beyond our help. I hated playing God, but I had to. I sought medical advice as far as it was available, but the doctors were far too busy. Therefore it largely fell to me to get on as best I could, preparing the wounded for the theatre and making the dying as comfortable as possible. I do not remember having any morphine. Then came the problem of priority for operation. At first Hart came out and chose his cases, but he soon got tired. Reggie Saxton took the flesh wounds, using local anaesthetic, and Kenneth Sinclair-Loutit gave anaesthetics for Hart. With some cases I noticed that Hart took a long time. A nurse told me, as he did later, that he was not a very experienced abdominal surgeon. I then decided to give priority on his lists to orthopaedic cases and accept that some abdominal cases would consequently die. I think I was right.

Fortunately the attack did not last long, but we were all

desperately tired. Opinion, thank God, thought that I had run triage rather well. I was pleased that I had discovered an activity in which I appeared to be effective and which also offered some intriguing problems as to how to save the most lives, given a certain mixture of wounded and limited resources with which to treat them. I was also fortunate to have been spared the most harrowing experience of the triage process. That came later.

After the attack Dubois gave us light jobs. I think Kenneth went as medical officer to the brigade to cover for Dubois, whose duties had expanded. The rest of us were sent to organise a medical hospital and a surgical hospital at El Goloso. It was light work for a short time, but the comfortable relief was soon shattered by Dubois's promotion of one of the Poles he had attached to the unit. The rather insignificant looking Dr Boulka, who spoke good English, became the unit's political commissar. He claimed to have a medical qualification from Edinburgh and to be the Scottish representative of Communist International. The medics disputed the first claim and the communists the second. He was conceited, stupid, and loved interfering – a general nuisance – and his compulsory educational lectures were puerile.

It was during this brief break, in January 1937, that I managed to visit Madrid, just a month or so after the battle of Madrid.[28] There were still many stories of the hand-to-hand fighting in the University City and occasional outbursts of shelling and bombing to reinforce continuing fears for Madrid. On the social side of this visit to the capital I met Ernest Hemingway, who seemed an alcoholic bore, and J B S Haldane, who had failed to teach me chemistry at Cambridge. I spoke at length with Haldane and somehow we got on to the subject of what motivated people to come to Spain. He was almost childlike in his belief that most of them came for purely political reasons. I argued that motivation was a far more complicated issue and that I should arrange a football match between escapists and masochists. He was shocked!

The short break did not last long. We were soon called upon to set up a field hospital at Villarecho,[29] near to where fascist troops were attempting to cross the Jarama River to cut

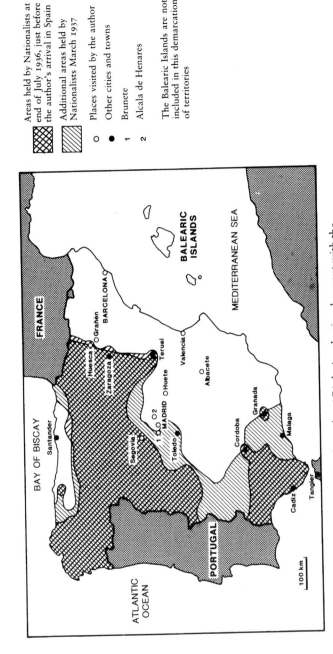

Areas held by Nationalists at end of July 1936, just before the author's arrival in Spain

Additional areas held by Nationalists March 1937

O   Places visited by the author

●   Other cities and towns

1   Brunete

2   Alcala de Henares

The Balearic Islands are not included in this demarcation of territories

Figure 1   Places visited by the author (O) during the time he spent with the Spanish Medical Aid Committee's field ambulance unit, August 1936– August 1937.

34

the Madrid–Valencia highroad (see figure 2).[30] I believe Hart chose the house, a beautiful old hotel. It was an easy choice. It was the biggest building available and the only one with running water, although sanitary facilities were primitive. It was of course no longer a British hospital but an international one, although the hard core was still there: Hart, surgeon; Kenneth, anaesthetist; Thora, chief operating sister; Aileen, principal secretary; and myself, still running triage.

We started with only one surgeon and too few nurses, but additional staff were quickly drafted in to increase our potential once the scale of the offensive had registered. With more surgeons, more nurses, and more drivers we achieved a reasonably efficient hospital. It was also a reasonably happy one. I do not remember many quarrels. Certainly this situation was helped by Boulka keeping a low profile in the early days. There was also the fact that no one worked too long at a stretch, though we did work long hours. My own work benefited greatly from the collaborative spirit of the new surgeons, who liked my way of organising triage and helped me to improve it through various useful discussions. Both new surgeons were Spanish, and one of them, Broggi,[31] was of high calibre. Another improvement in circumstances was the provision of a separate area for the dying, removing them from the tensions of triage space and reducing some of the stress of overcrowding there. I also found myself with helpers to assist with the cleaning of patients awaiting surgery. Perhaps the most significant advance, however, was the arrival of blood for transfusion from the transfusion service Dr Norman Bethune had established in Madrid. Bethune brought supplies of stored blood and a refrigerator from the capital to inaugurate this facility, which was steadily expanded by Reggie Saxton, who soon had local donors involved. Although blood transfusion initially generated some disagreement as to who should receive blood – the most critical or those for whom there was greater hope – such questions were amicably resolved and there were far more benefits than difficulties.

It was at Villarecho that I started making "aeroplane splints" for upper arm and shoulder injuries, devices so named because of the way in which they elevated the arm up and out

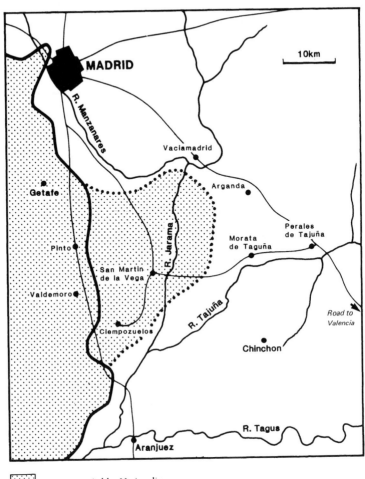

Figure 2 The Battle of Jarama, February 1937. Nationalist troops advance over the Jarama River in an attempt to cut the Madrid–Valencia highroad.

from the shoulder, rather like a wing.[32] It was fascinating to find how, by working at various opportune moments to maintain a ready supply, I managed to reduce throughput problems in the operating theatre. For the first time I was also called upon to give some anaesthetics (God forgive me!). In addition I did a vast amount of dirty work, as orderly, nurse, and grave digger. I certainly worked hard and became exhausted as well as deeply shocked by the carnage.[33] My only comfort was the thought that I was being of use.

In addition to enormous casualties – many on both sides – the most difficult aspect of the battle of Jarama was its duration. It lasted far longer than anything we had previously experienced, taking up most of February 1937, a month which at times seemed as though it would never end.

When I revisited Spain in 1978 I went to Villarecho and parked in the village square for Xavier to make inquiries. To my embarrassment the parking officer claimed that he recognised me as the doctor who, by surgery, had saved his life in 1937. I did not believe it, but if it was true it was my only surgical success in a long medical life, with the possible exception of a child at Wittenberg-am-Elbe much later (see page 103). We discovered that the house in which we had based the hospital had at one time belonged to Don Juan of Austria, who had saved western civilisation from Islam centuries before. I wondered which side he would have been on in this later conflict of values. Sadly, I concluded that he would have supported Franco, as the defender of the Faith.

I shall always remember the Jarama valley by McDade's sad dirge:[34]

> There's a valley in Spain called Jarama.
> It's a place that we all know too well,
> For 'tis there that we wasted our manhood.
> And most of our old age as well.

After Villarecho the 35th Division we had been supporting was rested at Alcala de Henares, and we went with it. For me, however, the rest ended all too prematurely. First Boulka took me with him on a fool's errand, trying to trace the whereabouts of a Canadian driver who had disappeared from the unit. He even insisted that I should be the one to accompany him on a visit to the Canadian Consulate in Valencia. I think he chose me because of my being non-communist and my Cambridge accent. (I am reminded now of how some committee makers search for black lesbians. Although they dislike both characteristics, they think they will look well on a committee.) Then came orders for me to organise a convalescence hospital at Valdegrango, which I did fairly successfully. It was not a difficult assignment. I was pleased to find two of the patients arriving there comfortable in the aeroplane splints I had made. My next assignment was a much bigger job – the conversion of a lovely old nunnery at Huete into a base hospital. I started out with only a German sergeant to help, but I soon devised a plan and recruited others locally, including an exceptional find – an English plumber. Certainly considerable enterprise was involved in preparations for an efficient hospital centre there and I surprised myself by my own courage in undertaking such a task.

I did not, however, have time to carry all my plans through to completion, although the hospital had started to function. Dubois arrived in a car chauffeured by Joseph Edenhoffer to take me on a tour of convalescent camps on the south coast to attempt to locate volunteers lost but not accounted for. He had already made arrangements for my replacement at Huete. The tour proved interesting and an enjoyable break. Dubois was in jubilant mood because of the war news. The Italian fascists who had attacked at Quadalajara had been satisfactorily repulsed by the Italian International Brigade. We visited several pleasant convalescent homes, including one at Benicasim, named after the young English communist poet, Ralph Fox, who was killed on the Andújar front. We received only minor complaints, but the main subject of discussion inevitably became the seriously wounded who could not fight again. Dubois had considerable power and I think it was during this tour that he set in progress arrangements for many of the badly disabled to go home, if their return home was possible. Repatriation to France, Belgium, and the UK was not too difficult. Getting people back to the USA was more of a problem. And of course there was no chance of returning volunteers to Germany and Italy. For such unfortunates

Dubois thought Mexico might be the solution, and so it proved for some cases.

I returned to Huete and was warned on arrival to expect a difficult situation. It was thought that I would object to finding myself with little authority in a hospital I had brought into commission, and especially to the appointment of Mildred,[35] an American, to my former position of hospital administrator. They little knew that I had come to the conclusion that there was no point in a non-communist wanting a senior post. There would always be a communist plot to get rid of him or her. It was not difficult, therefore, to take a back seat. I also retired to bed with dysentery, an indisposition made memorable only by an unlikely visitor, Harry Pollitt, the leading communist in the UK, who was spending a day at the hospital. He had a perfect bedside manner and would have made an excellent general practitioner. On my recovery I took satisfaction from discovering how well the hospital was functioning on the lines that I had planned.

Towards the end of May 1937 an attack was to be launched towards Segovia, and a team of staff from Huete, which included a number of us from the old group, was summoned to man a new front line[36] hospital at Club Alpino, a skiing resort on the road from Madrid to Segovia. (It is generally recognised that this was the site of the attack round which Hemingway built his novel *For Whom the Bell Tolls*.) The site chosen for the hospital seemed good, with adequate space for triage. I can remember taking a good supply of aeroplane splints with me. Again, Reggie Saxton was there with blood supplies and I think we had two or three good surgeons on the team.

The Republican offensive – one of two mounted in the last week of May 1937 to draw the Nationalist fire from the heavily pressurised Basque front around Bilbao – began on the morning of 31 May.[37] It was heralded by some spasmodic shelling and then we heard the sound of Republican aeroplanes attacking. The casualties arriving at the hospital were high for two days and then fell on the third, when it became clear that the attack had failed. Sadly, in the closing hours of the action a bomb fell close to the hospital and killed a delightful young Canadian driver, Issie Kupchick, and wounded another colleague. Soon afterwards a retreat was ordered and the hospital staff were despatched in various directions to work in base hospitals at Huete, El Goloso, and Alcala de Henares.

There was about a month between the Club Alpino attack and the next offensive. I think I spent this period at Huete, although I find I have only vague recollections of the place. What I do remember clearly is that it was a depressing time. There were rumours of disagreements in the Madrid government; there were rumours about the suppression of the POUM in Barcelona; there were rumours of volunteers from the UK being discouraged from joining the International Brigade by our representatives in Barcelona and Valencia. In addition, the problem of whether or not the communists should hold their secret meetings surfaced again. It had been simmering since Grañén. But there were also newcomers to cheer us up. I remember Julian Bell,[38] Sir Richard Rees, John Boulting, Chris Thorneycroft, Portia Holman, and Larry Collier. I was particularly glad to meet Julian Bell, who had been a good friend of mine at King's College, Cambridge, in what seemed another world. Julian was a striking, almost old world figure in his topee, but everyone soon recognised his courageous driving.

The lull was eventually jolted by growing rumours of plans for a massive Republican attack to relieve the pressure on the west of Madrid. We could only wait, but morale rose. I think I slightly increased my rate of splint making. The call soon came to go to El Escorial, 30–40 kilometres north-west of Madrid and some 10 kilometres north of the battle lines,[39] to set up a large, front line hospital. I was involved only in the organisation of triage. The building chosen was a modern monastery, down the hill from El Escorial. It was large enough and gave good facilities for the arrival of ambulances and enough space for triage, but the stairs up to the wards were steep and difficult for stretcher bearers. The wards themselves were reasonable, although water supplies were inadequate and the sanitation deplorable. However, we made vast advances in triage. As we had three theatres to serve I was given

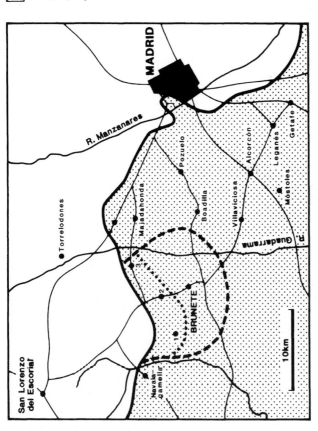

Areas occupied by Nationalists
(but note the changing battle lines)

— Battle line on 6 June 1937

– – – Battle line on 12 June 1937

······· Battle line on 26 June 1937

1 Quijorna
2 Villanueva de la Cañada
3 Villanueva del Pardillo

Figure 3 The Battle of Brunete, June 1937. A massive Republican offensive intended to end the encirclement of Madrid. Early successes were soon reversed and the Spanish Medical Aid Committee's field ambulance unit found itself under intense pressure in the second half of June.

41

a nurse and an orderly to help me; Reggie Saxton was there with his blood transfusion service and there was even a small *x* ray unit, which did occasionally locate odd bullets.

There were three chief surgeons, Jolly, Broggi, and Hart. I had worked for Broggi and Hart before, but not Jolly, who turned out to be a man of the highest competence for whom I developed a great admiration. He was a New Zealander and was, in my opinion, the most important volunteer to Spain from the British Commonwealth. (Much later when I read his obituary I could not understand how he never got his FRCS.) The hospital was well prepared when the attack started. We hoped the attack was equally well prepared.

The battle of Brunete was quite different from that of Jarama. Jarama had been essentially a defensive measure. Brunete started with the great hope that it was going to end the encirclement of Madrid. The plan was to advance on the small village of Brunete and break through enemy lines to cut off troops besieging Madrid from their supplies and reinforcements from the west. At first all went well. There was a rapid advance and casualties were slight, with the hospital functioning well and within its capacity. But soon the atmosphere changed. The casualties mounted rapidly and we were all put under real strain. What I particularly remember of this exhausting period are the valiant efforts of the ambulance drivers, who were always under pressure and often under fire. I also think that we in triage coped rather well and that Jolly ran a remarkably efficient ward for abdominal cases. There was so much activity that inevitably much of it is hazy in retrospect. Towards the end of the battle[40] there was a small incident which upset me, possibly unreasonably, but I was tired and emotionally overexcited after two or more weeks of triage. An ambulance arrived. The stretchers were brought in and I hurried to classify the wounded. The first case was lying on his right side with his face partially hidden. His left thorax was completely shattered. I could see a heart faintly beating. I signalled to the nurse, by dropping my thumb, that the case was hopeless (language was dangerous). I moved left to see the next case and, by chance, glanced back. To my horror I recognised the face of Julian Bell. (I suppose one must accept the probability of putting a good friend amongst the hopeless category. I have never met anyone who had run a triage in any war, but I am sure the effect is always devastating. A still small voice from your unconscious mutters, "You have condemned your friend to death!") I rushed off, telling my nurse to carry on, to find a surgeon or physician to confirm or refute my diagnosis. Fortunately I found Philip D'Arcy Hart, who was visiting the unit. I showed him the wound. He agreed with my opinion. I did not know whether to be pleased or sorry. We moved Julian to a ward, where he died some time afterwards,[41] and I went back to triage, a changed man.

The battle ended towards the end of July. There had been little to lighten my depression. Julian had died. Another colleague was missing and others, including Dubois,[42] were wounded. I was further depressed by the poor results of the Spanish Republic's efforts to build an army. The pathetic young Spaniards whom I tried to comfort in triage were not trained soldiers. I began to doubt that the Republic could win. But I kept this doubt to myself.

Back at Alcala de Henares, to where many of us were returned, there were dramatic changes. Nearly all the old gang of British volunteers had been given leave in the UK. Rather more surprisingly, all medical students were ordered to return home to qualify. This was just what my unconscious wanted, but my conscious, as a volunteer, had been too proud to suggest it. I was delighted.

On my flight back to the UK I tried to sum things up. I was glad I had gone to Spain; glad that I had not given up in despair at Grañén. Given my limited abilities, I had made a reasonable contribution to the anti-fascist cause, rather than merely talking about it. I had also learned a lot. Although I had come to hate war, I now knew that fascism would have to be fought and that pacifism was impossible. I had, too, become increasingly suspicious of the communists. There had been valuable opportunities to discuss political theories with knowledgeable people of different persuasions – anarchists and Trotskyites; Russian, German, French, and American communists; British socialists and communists; and a few British liberals. I realised that no one knew how to run a

43

country or a revolution. There were also a number of friend-ships I valued, some of which were to endure. As I write, I am still in touch with Joseph Edenhoffer, who was treated abominably when he returned to Czechoslovakia in 1946. Overall I had a general feeling of satisfaction that I had risked my life for a cause I believed in; but I was relieved that I had not lost it in the process.

HOME AGAIN, THE ARMY, AND CRETE

I was not sure how University College Hospital would receive me after my year's absence. I decided to put it to the test by going on a clinical round with a man whom I thought to be the most right wing physician on the staff. I was very bronzed and had a striking red Van Dyck beard, and had been absent for a year. The University College Hospital establishment rose to the occasion. The physician spotted me and said, "Ah, there you are, Cochrane. How nice to see you. Had an interesting weekend?" I think he won, but I knew I was safe.

The next years until 1941 were full of intense political interest, some amusement, and hard medical work. (I was already qualifying very late.) I still lived a rather upper middle class life, with a comfortable flat in London. I went skiing at Christmas; and I went to parties, left and right wing. On the other hand, I took an increasing interest in Jewish refugees, and my flat finally became a sort of transit camp in London for recently arrived refugees.

I have two contrasting memories of my social life after the return from Spain. The first was a lunch party given by Clive Bell, where I was subjected to questions about Julian's death. I do not remember the details, except that it was a disaster. Virginia Woolf behaved particularly badly, although it was a considerable time since Julian had died. It was difficult to get Clive Bell and his other guests to see the situation as Julian would have wished – in its political and social context. They were still bitter about a personal loss. Although I played no part in persuading Julian to go to Spain (he was in China when I went there),[43] they seemed to blame me for his death, to such an extent that I came away angry but nevertheless with a feeling of guilt. Perhaps as a result I have never had a high opinion of the Bloomsbury set. I admired Keynes, of course, and thought Duncan Grant a good second rank painter, but on the whole they seemed overinterested in the small stream of feelings engendered by their unhappy lives and curiously uninterested in the way Earth's foundations were shaking around them. Recently I tried to make amends by rereading Virginia Woolf's novels. I found *Mrs Dalloway* a superficial figure, got stuck in *The Waves*, and gave up.

The other memory is entirely different, a weekend at Mr C's (Dick Cohen's father) country house in Surrey. Mr C was a lovable old eccentric and a kind host. He always referred to me as "The Madcap Fellow", not perhaps because of stories of my exploits in Spain but because of the way I drove my car. Dick and his wife Margaret were there, together with Patrick Wilkinson, Christopher Morris,[44] and his wife Helen. The talk was good, as was the weather and the food. I was happy; after Spain it was "paradise regained."

Medically I became more and more influenced by Sir Thomas Lewis and Dr George Pickering. I began to see that science could influence medicine, and Dr Philip D'Arcy Hart was telling me of the miners in South Wales and their troubles. (He had recently joined the Medical Research Council.) I qualified in 1938, fairly easily, and then got a house job at the West London Hospital with Dr Konstam. (University College Hospital had, I thought, taken a rather cheap revenge on me by arguing that I had not been a full-time student, so I could not have a house job there.) I thoroughly enjoyed life as a house physician and learnt a limited amount. Then came a research appointment at the University College Hospital Professorial Medical Unit, through the kindness of Professor Harold Himsworth.[45]

I had always considered that fascism had to be fought and that war was therefore inevitable. But I hated the idea of being involved in war again, knowing what it was like. I remember the critical point being the summer of 1939, when I motored with John Stokes to France. We managed first to get Joseph, the Czech, out of his terrible camp in the Pyrenees for Spanish war refugees and back to England. We then went to Switzerland, where we heard the news over the wireless – oddly enough while visiting Sheila Grant Duff – that Germany had signed a treaty with the Soviet Union. I realised at once that a dreadful war was inevitable. We rapidly returned to London, where I soon found myself helping to turn University College Hospital into a casualty clearing station. I believe I was of some help as I was perhaps the only person with any experience of war. Then there was that curious interlude of the "pseudo-war." I recall it chiefly because of a memorable meeting with Ros Pitt-Rivers (later FRS) and Gordon Butler (later a distinguished Canadian atomic energy scientist). I also at that time had an interesting short friendship with Sheila Grant Duff. I am grateful to all three of them.

Finally, I joined the Army; did my basic training; and was appointed to a field ambulance unit. I did not think highly of my fellow officers; but we were in Dorset, which is a lovely county, and there I watched the Battle of Britain. I am ashamed to say that on several occasions I watched it while playing tennis. On the other hand I can claim to have captured a number of German pilots who had been shot down during my daily round. I hope I impressed them with my line that so many were being shot down that we had organised a special service of German-speaking medical officers to look after them.

Then came the threat of invasion. I was on duty that night and heard the code word (I think it was "Cromwell"), but nothing happened. I became bored and volunteered for service overseas. I was accepted and soon began a course at the London School of Hygiene and Tropical Medicine (which I was to know well for the rest of my life) on diseases in other parts of the world. Thus I was able to return to my flat, which was a great joy. Towards the end of the course I decided to give a party, which I knew might be the last I would give there. There was a good turnout, with representatives from King's, University College Hospital, the Spanish war – and others. Point was given to it by the fact that it coincided with the first bombing of London. It was frightening indeed, but no one at the party was hurt. I had to leave the next day for my unit. I took with me Dr Bill Foreman, a New Zealander, who had been on the course, and at the party. I was to see a great deal of him for much of my life.

Soon I was ordered abroad and sailed from Glasgow. (Possibly the most interesting thing about the voyage was that another doctor on board was Richard (later Sir Richard) Doll.)[46] I spent most of my time trying to guess what language I ought to be learning. I settled on Arabic, which in the end was useless. Richard, on the other hand, excelled at arranging concert parties. I still remember his organisation of the singing of "You'll get no promotion this side of the ocean."

On arrival in Egypt I became a medical officer in a general hospital set up somewhere between Cairo and the Canal. I saw the condition of the poor in Egypt, and was horrified. I was then posted, under rather odd circumstances,[47] to become medical officer to D Battalion Layforce.

Layforce had been formed from the original Middle East commandos and a new commando regiment which had recently arrived from the UK. There were four battalions in Layforce. D Battalion differed from the other three in having about 70 Spaniards. Their story was a strange one. Many Republican soldiers retreated into France at the end of the Spanish civil war. They were put into camps under foul conditions. (It was from one of these camps that I rescued Joseph the Czeck.) Some Spaniards joined the French foreign service battalions in Syria. Syria became Vichy France, so they next sought refuge in Palestine, then a British Mandated Territory. There they asked to be given British officers and to serve as British troops for the duration of the war.

The transition from serving in a general hospital to becoming a commando was traumatic – chiefly from a physical point of view. I was fit enough when I arrived, but the commandos had been in training for some months. I remember a particularly arduous long desert march, with limited water supplies. Colonel Young, for whom I developed a great respect, advised me to march just behind him and not to worry if I hallucinated. I was treated well by everyone, though I developed few friendships. With the help of the sergeant major I learnt how to run the sick parades, and soon settled

47

down. The main medical problems were venereal disease, desert sores, and, of course, blisters. I felt contented, chiefly because I became so fit.

The one military action in which I was involved ended disastrously – the landing on Crete.[48] I had just taken a few days' leave in Cairo, staying at the Mena House Hotel, where I knew my father had stayed shortly before his death in 1917. The order arrived and I returned to camp at Sidi Bish, near Alexandria, to prepare to embark. Our first effort to do so ended in the train at Sidi Bish where, after waiting around for over an hour, we were returned to camp. I was not sorry as my batman had disappeared, reportedly "dead drunk," and it seemed he had put my equipment together during an attack of delirium tremens.

The next alarm came within 24 hours and was heralded by a very senior officer on the medical side. He told me, in a rather apologetic way, that casualties were going to be high and that as it was quite likely that I would be killed he was taking the unusual step of sending a second medical officer with the battalion. The medical officer himself arrived shortly afterwards, appearing at odd intervals during the rest of my free days with Layforce, like Banquo's ghost, to destroy my peace.

We were sent on destroyers, sailing under a bright May sun for Crete. Evelyn Waugh, the brigade intelligence officer, told me he knew about the plan of attack. His account was so vague and the plan so fantastic that I could not take it seriously. It was, roughly, to land on the south of the island, do a night march over the hills to the north, contact some unknown troops, and then retake an aerodrome at Maleme not marked on any of our maps.[49] As far as I remember I laughed in disbelief and went back to my sunbathing. The sun was hot, the sea blue, the speed of the destroyer terrific; and I lay and thought of anything but impending catastrophe. Then, quite suddenly, "the sun grew dark and ugly grew the sea." The destroyer started dancing as only destroyers can. Many were vomiting within 10 minutes, and I was soon longing to join their ranks. Unfortunately I had to spend two unhappy hours qualifying for the experience. It was during this period that the powers that be decided it was impossible to land and we found ourselves on our way back to Alexandria, where we trans-shipped to the mine-laying cruiser *Abdiel*.

The next day was different. It was cold and dull, the sea was choppy, and there was a feeling of gloom. I learnt to my horror that the officer commanding Crete[50] was a VC. It had always been one of my pet theories that the psychology of VC winning was incompatible with that of efficient command of a large number of troops in modern warfare. My gloom deepened. The Royal Navy, too, contrary to its traditional hospitality, refused us all alcoholic refreshment. They needed it, they said, for their return journey. Considering the relative risks of a commando raid and their return journey to Alexandria, they were, I think, a little mean.

This time we went round the east of the island and then along its north coast to Suda Bay, arriving there an hour or so before midnight. We could see a few fires in the distance; but all seemed oddly quiet and deserted. We were even more aware that all was not well when there were no immediate signs of landing craft to take us off. It was close to an hour before we saw the first lighters; and their cargoes of wounded did little to ease the gloom. While awaiting the completion of the landing exercise the ridiculousness of our situation became clear when I overheard a conversation between my colonel and the general officer commanding. It appeared that the decision to evacuate Crete had been taken many hours before, that our arrival had been unexpected, and that it was uncertain what should be done with us. I had lurid impressions of what had gone on at the evacuation of Dunkirk and Greece and I secretly prayed that we would be sent back to Alexandria. It was not to be so.[51]

The decision reached was that we, in association with Royal Marines under the command of General Weston, were to fight a series of rearguard actions across the island, from north to south, to cover the withdrawal to Sphakia of various British and Greek units, as well as a brigade of New Zealanders[52] and one of Australians. From any military point of view it was an odd decision as we were only armed with hand-to-hand weapons suitable for a raid. We had, for example, no mortars. But there was nothing we could do about it. Psychologically it was devastating. There is a vast difference between screwing up your courage for the kind of in-and-out raid we had expected and facing up to a long and drawn-out series of rearguard actions.

There followed a long, weary night's march up a winding hill road, where cart, car, horse, and truck competed with peasant and soldier for space on the narrow track. We went on until dawn when we had to consider the possibility of air raids and seek shelter. The countryside offered only olive trees, thin and uninviting as protection, as we took up our positions on both sides of the road, near Stilos. I added to my cover by constructing a low arc of stones under a tree, where I rested, although rest was not easy in the circumstances. The scene on the road soon became fascinating. We had come straight from the ordinary, strenuous life of Sidi Bish camp, and our first view in daylight in Crete seemed to be the decline and fall of the British Army. It came in small groups, some with arms, some without, some with kit, some without, from various units and usually without NCOs or officers, fighting to get into any transport available. All were struggling south to safety in what appeared to be a general *sauve qui peut*. It was unpleasant to see so clearly exposed exactly whom one was fighting a rearguard action to save. It was probably not as bad as it looked. Many of the troops had been evacuated from Greece – without arms or kit or units – and ordered to find their own way to the south; but we did not know that then.

Then came the planes. The scene on the road took on an almost ludicrous aspect, as the disorderly rabble bobbed in and out of the ditches as the planes came and went. I watched fascinated until it became too dangerous to put my head outside my little Stonehenge. I could just see a small vista of glorious Mediterranean landscape through the chinks in the stones; the blue sky and contrasting sombre and luxuriant greens of olive and of vine, in a rather barren countryside, dotted with deserted-looking white houses. I thought of El Greco (a print of one of his paintings was on the wall of my little flat in London) and of Spain and the Spanish war. The planes were temporarily forgotten in a long, dreamy comparison of that war and this. There were times in the Spanish war when for the only time in my adult life everything seemed either black or white, either right or wrong. Though only a small part of my experience there, they were invaluable and happy times. But on Crete, perhaps because I was older, doubts were in much greyer shades and far greater, even though the enemy was the same. In many ways it was the same war, but the feelings were different. I remembered Chamberlain and what he stood for and the difficulty I had had in raising enthusiasm for a war in which he was in charge. The coalition government under Churchill had pleased me more. I had decided that at any rate it was much better than the Hitler gang, and I had started on the journey that had led me to Crete. The Russian–German alliance had upset my scheme of political values. It seemed to be the Russian policy to let Britain and Germany fight themselves stupid and then walk in and pick up the pieces. The idea may have looked attractive to Stalin, but it seemed too inhuman a theory and it did not seem to have worked out in practice. From my viewpoint, in Crete, Germany looked anything but silly. I thought of my communist friends and their violent anti-war propaganda, I thought of Russia supplying goods to assist the German war effort, and nothing seemed particularly black and white. Everything looked grey. I felt a fool to be where I was and I went back in my mind along the chain of chance and decision which connected Crete with University College Hospital. Suddenly I was asking myself whether, if I had to die a pseudo-soldier's death, would it not have been better to have died in Spain when it was all black or white. I was brought back to reality by a bomb landing very near. Then the bombardment grew worse and worse and the olive tree above me was swept by machine-gun fire. It was difficult to decide whether the enemy had spotted the battalion. They would leave us for a while to bomb a neighbouring village, but they always came back. There was nothing we could do. I could not even search for the wounded. Any movement would have given away our position. I eventually decided to try and turn my incoherent thoughts into verse. I am no poet, but I thought the difficulty of the undertaking might make me concentrate, and for the next few hours I managed to achieve relative peace.

COMPARISON

The branch seemed needle fine
Between me and doom
Of air born death;
But sun on terrassed vine
and white, still, broken home
Drew sharp my breath.

I'd been there long before,
When hope was still white bright
For life in Spain.
I'd worked there long before
When heart and mind said "Fight"
"And die for Spain."

The issue there was clear;
No shades – only black or white,
Not grey as here.
We knew the fearful stakes,
but doubt was lost in fight,
while here it aches.

Sent by the very shame
Of our own county's name –
"A Chambermaid,"[53]
We fought – to win or lose;
But now we have to choose
The lighter shade.

So now if have I must
A pseudo-soldier's cross
– a total loss.
Oh! may the day be cursed
That chose this end in grey
To blaze of day.

So friend, remember if you pass this way
To pause and say:
"There is a corner of a Cretan Lane
for ever Spain."[54]

Somehow the day passed and we moved off in the twilight to take up the rearguard position for the next day, leaving one company to hold the hill position. It was the Spanish company and I felt worried about them after the day's gruelling experience. I hoped they would do well. Ridiculously, I felt responsible for them.

It was bitterly cold that night and I could not sleep in the few hours' rest we had before dawn, but the colonel was generous to me in allocating an excellent first aid post where I remained throughout the day, more or less submerged and more or less safe. It was my first and only experience of a rearguard action, and in some ways it was fascinating. First came the stragglers through our lines; then rumours that the Spanish company had broken; then a period of silence and loneliness, shattered suddenly when the battle started. The fight seemed unequal. They brought up mortars almost at once, to which we had no effective answer. The position continued to deteriorate; we thought they would outflank us. Suddenly there were some strange noises behind us, and a British tank appeared as if from nowhere. We had been told that all our tanks were out of action, but this one had risen from the dead, at an opportune moment, for almost an hour of glorious life. When it finally died the situation was again under control, but by then the first aid post was beginning to fill and there was no discernible means of evacuating the wounded. "Banquo," who had gone off to Brigade Headquarters, had promised to organise evacuation, but he had no doubt found it difficult. A little temporary assistance came with the arrival of a colonel with a Lagonda. He transported two or three of the worst cases. He also told us that we would probably have to fight rearguard actions for three more days.[55]

When darkness came the Germans seemed to have had enough and we were able to get ourselves together and march off without difficulty. It was eerie to be at the end of the retreat column. You felt that there might be a German on a bicycle, with a tommy gun, close behind you. But in Crete, at any rate, the Germans seemed only to sleep at night.

The march proved horrific. We were carrying the battalion's remaining wounded and the men bearing the stretchers were already exhausted, for they had fought all day. I had done comparatively little, yet I felt worn out with the strain of it.

The journey seemed to go on and on, becoming more and more of an effort. First we lost our way, and then we had to go off course to get water supplies. Eventually an ambulance arrived to take away the wounded. Crete seemed to have been designed on the worst possible lines, at least from our point of view. It slopes uphill all the way from north to south and then drops almost precipitously to the coast. We travelled uphill all the way that night. Early in the morning we based our rearguard post close to Imvros in the hills above the port of Sphakia, where, after modest reorganisation in our ranks, most people fell asleep, including me. When I woke I was told that the wounded were to be evacuated that night, so I collected together all those who qualified and helped them down the gorge to the embarkation area. The journey was far from easy; it would have been difficult even for a fitter group. My reward was a further period of rest on my return to the battalion, before we moved to a new position above the Sphakia gorge. What I remember most clearly about that day was a chance meeting with a party of Layforce Spaniards on my journey with the wounded and being given two or three spoonfuls of a stew they had prepared.

We had had little to eat since Suda. We had lived on excitement. Suddenly, when we had a period of inactivity we felt desperately hungry. Alas, there was little food left in Sphakia. Our only hope lay in the daily list of units to be evacuated that night, but each day an officer arrived to cut short our hopes. All we could do was wait in local caves and fill our stomachs with water to prevent hunger pangs.

On what was to prove the second last night a seaplane arrived to take off the generals. We raised an ironical cheer. It was the first British plane we had seen on Crete. Someone remarked in loud tones: "It's wonderful what service you can get, paying ten bob in the pound income tax."

The next night, very late, we were ordered to march down to the jetty. It became a desperate contest about a mile from the beach and then ended in a thick, solid queue of humanity crowding the narrow way to the jetty. Another seaplane removed the brigadier. This time there were no cheers. We could hear the embarking craft shuttling backwards and forwards across the water and then there was a long silence when it slowly dawned on us that we were going to be prisoners. It was extraordinary how few of us had thought of that possibility.

I remember hearing Colonel Young reading out the reasons for the surrender. As a fluent German speaker I offered to go with him to translate. He accepted. I slept badly that night. I was too hungry. I have been told that an Australian officer accompanied us to the German lines. I have no memory of this, but I do recall the unpleasantness of the journey: we were fired on from the air, mortared, and consistently harassed by snipers. I suspect that there were also some shots from our own Army. I recall spending some of the time waving a white flag with one hand while trying to progress on two legs and one arm. Our first contact was with a young Austrian lieutenant, who took the surrender of eight thousand men with superb aplomb and treated us with politeness. Colonel Young was later led away to meet senior German officers, while I was asked to remain with the Austrian lieutenant to go between the two armies to try to prevent unnecessary loss of life.[56] Our efforts had some effect; but lack of communication between German ground and air forces was in part to blame for a further air attack on surrendered British and allied troops. I remember one incident particularly clearly. As we got close to the British Army a German soldier exclaimed: "Mein Gott, sie sehen ganz wie uns aus" ["My God, they look just like us"]. If after only two years of propaganda young Germans expected us to look like apes, what would they think in 10 years' time? Nothing has depressed me as much since. The Soviet Union was allied with Germany; the USA had not entered the war. I assumed I would be a prisoner for 10 years at least. I thought I was unlikely to see home again.

PS. *It has been said of D Battalion Layforce, not without justice, that seldom in the history of human endeavour have so few been so messed about, so completely, by so many.*

NOTES

1 Dr T S P Strangeways had introduced tissue culture to Cambridge. Neville Willmer subsequently had a pioneering role in establishing interest in cell growth, while Dr Honor Fell concentrated attention on the other fundamental field of interest, cell differentiation. Dr Willmer remembers A L Cochrane's research interest in tissue culture arising from a reading party weekend in Wales, which he hosted at his father's cottage just a short time before ALC took his tripos.

2 Theodor Reik: an early follower of Freud and leading non-medical member of the Vienna Psychoanalytic Society in post first world war years. As a non-medical practitioner he experienced a lifetime of hostility from the medical lobby within psychoanalysis, a situation assisted by the prominence he gained and the controversy his work generated. It is now known that Freud wrote *The Question of Lay Analysis* (1926) to defend Reik against a charge of malpractice. Reik's most famous book, *Listening with the Third Ear* (1948), proved widely popular and influential in introducing psychoanalysis to the general public.

3 Between 29 July and 5 August 1936 German and Italian planes conveyed the first airborne contingent of Franco's Moorish troops from Morocco to Seville, where Franco arrived on 6 August. The first major military airlift in history had begun. When the operation ended in September 1936, a total of 12 000 men of the Army of Africa had been transported to the mainland.

4 In August 1936 a number of European powers, including France, Britain, Germany, Russia, and Italy, agreed upon a policy of non-intervention in the affairs of Spain.

5 Later Viscount Addison.

6 Thomas H. *The Spanish Civil War.* 3rd ed. London, 1977. See also Firth D. *The Signal was Spain.* London, 1976. It includes reference to the Medical Aid Committee's field ambulance unit.

7 The Spanish Medical Aid Committee's field ambulance unit set out for Spain on 23 August 1936.

8 The author is here anticipating interests which were to develop in later months. The International Brigades were not inaugurated until 12 October 1936, the result of an international collaboration of Communist parties. The brigades have been described as "legions of anti-fascist volunteers," many of them exiles from fascist or other extreme right wing regimes.

9 FAI: Federación Anarquista Ibérica.

10 More commonly referred to as the Aragon front.

11 Huesca: the only remaining point of hostilities on an otherwise quiet Aragon front.

12 POUM: Partido Obrero de Unificación Marxista.

13 PSUC: Partido Socialista Unificado de Cataluña.

14 Of a party of 28.

15 The Spanish Medical Aid Committee in London duly reimbursed the author for this loss.
16 The Thaelman Centuria: named after Ernst Thaelman, German communist leader in the late 1920s, who at this time was held in a concentration camp.
17 Beimler had also been imprisoned in Germany but had made a remarkable escape from Dachau.
18 Cochrane's recovery of the food supplies is also acknowledged in a report from the unit's quartermaster to Spanish Medical Aid Committee headquarters, 15 November 1936.
19 Reginald Somes Saxton.
20 Toynbee P, ed. *The distant drum*. London, 1976.
21 Tom Wintringham, an editor of the *Left Review* and a military correspondent of the *Daily Worker*, commanded the British Battalion of the 15th International Brigade at the battle of Jarama, February 1937.
22 André Marty: French communist leader.
23 Eric Arthur Blair: George Orwell.
24 See Cochrane A L. Forty years back, a retrospective survey. *Br Med J* 1979; ii: 1662–3.
25 Alexander Ethan Tudor Hart.
26 Then Max Cohen.
27 At the battle for Las Rosas.
28 November 1936.
29 Villarejo de Salvanes.
30 The attack in the Jarama Valley, which took Republican forces by surprise, began on 6 February 1937. On 11 February fascist troops crossed the Jarama River (see fig 2).
31 Dr Broggi-Valles.
32 Injuries to the upper arm, including the shoulder, often required the elevation of the upper arm to a right angle with the trunk. Light metal splints could be bent to the appropriate angle, with one arm of the splint bound to the trunk and the other to the damaged limb. Dr Tudor Hart had learnt this method in Vienna and introduced its extensive use in Spain. Held by such a splint, the arm gives the impression of imitating an aeroplane; hence the name "aeroplane splint."
33 On the Republican side there were more than 10 000 casualties, including around 1000 deaths. On the other side the Nationalists suffered over 6000 casualties.
34 A McDade, to the tune of "Red River Valley."
35 Mildred Rackley.
36 The Segovia front.
37 Three Republican divisions broke through opposition lines at San Ildefonso.
38 Julian Heward Bell (1908–37): son of Clive and Vanessa Bell, grandson of Leslie Stephen, nephew of Virginia Woolf, and first cousin once removed of H A L Fisher.

39 See figure 3.

40 18 July 1937.

41 Julian Bell was struck by a fragment of bomb while sheltering beside or under his ambulance at the battle of Brunete. He was brought into the 35th Division hospital. Dr R S Saxton has pointed out that he did receive greater attention than the author suggests. Despite the hopelessness of his condition, Bell received a blood transfusion and careful dressing of his chest wound.

42 The author's friend Noel Carritt was later found to have died in this battle. The battle of Brunete also claimed the life of Dr Sollenberger.

43 Professor of English at the Chinese University of Hankow.

44 Christopher Morris: Fellow of King's and distinguished historian and author.

45 Later Sir Harold Himsworth and Secretary of the Medical Research Council.

46 Later Regius Professor of Medicine, Oxford, and first Warden of Green College, Oxford.

47 The author has said that as the only medical officer in the Middle East who spoke Spanish he was ordered to volunteer for this posting because of the Spanish interests of D Battalion Layforce.

48 See Stewart I M G. *The struggle for Crete*. London, 1966; also Waugh E. *The diaries of Evelyn Waugh*. Davie M, ed. London, 1976, 490–509. (When Italy attacked Greece in October 1940 the British occupied Crete as an island invaluable to the defence of the Mediterranean, especially Egypt. Subsequent failure to garrison the island adequately left it vulnerable to invasion as the Germans overran Greece in the early months of 1941. On 20 May they attacked Crete with parachute forces, achieving swift successes, including capture of the aerodrome at Maleme.

49 See Waugh E. *The diaries of Evelyn Waugh*. Davie M, ed. London, 1976, 498. Waugh's notes indicate that the main objective at this time was to provide reinforcement for the forces holding Maleme aerodrome. The news that the aerodrome had already fallen to the Germans had not reached Layforce at this time.

50 General Freyberg, Commander in Chief, Crete.

51 Eight hundred men of Layforce were landed on Crete (Battalions A and D).

52 Recently in action at Maleme aerodrome.

53 Chamberlain.

54 The last two verses of this poem were written some days later in Athens.

55 Colonel Bob Laycock, accompanied by Evelyn Waugh. See Waugh E. *The diaries of Evelyn Waugh*. Davie M, ed. London, 1976, 505.

56 The surrender took place on 1 June 1941.

3 The forties

AFTERMATH AND ATHENS

The first job after the surrender was to help to manhandle the wounded up the steep gorge leading down to Sphakia and then get them to the north coast, whence they were to be flown on to Athens to hospital. The German front line troops were very correct and even friendly, but they had no food to give us, and we were hungry. I was finally flown to Athens with some of the wounded, but was separated from my patients there and left by the side of the airfield. I sat there hungry and disconsolate until a friendly Greek gave me a drink of ouzo. I nearly passed out, but I felt much better. I later talked to some German soldiers who had fought on Crete. They seemed generally agreed that if we had not retreated they would have evacuated. This was hardly cheering. We were then put in trucks and taken to a Greek barracks, where we were clearly not expected. It was already overfilled with Greek and Cretan soldiers and civilians. The place was filthy. There were only two lavatories, which had overflowed so long ago that the whole adjacent area had become acceptable for defaecation. There was one water tap for several hundred people. There was no food.

As the only German-speaking officer I had to head the delegation of complainants – a task I could not avoid and one which was to become a critical aspect of my life for the next four years. I got into trouble with both sides. The Germans assumed that I was an activist and disliked and punished me accordingly. The prisoners of war, on the other hand, because I rarely brought back good news, thought that I had not argued well enough or (rarely) that I was in league with the

Germans. I sometimes became very unpopular. But over the four years I have no doubt that my fluent German was of advantage to the prisoners and, occasionally, to myself. The German sergeant, to whom I spoke in Athens, was exceedingly rude and with him I achieved nothing.

There were three other British medical officers in that camp, and the day after our arrival we cleaned up the lavatories, with the help of some heroic Royal Army Medical Corps orderlies. There were other problems too. We had now some seriously sick people. My German this time achieved an ambulance and, even more surprisingly, got me a place on it with the patients. At the hospital for prisoners of war in Athens I contacted a British officer and asked him if he could give hospitality to several prisoner patients, medical officers, and orderlies in his hospital. He said he would be only too happy to do it if the Germans agreed. Off I went to the German administrator. He rang up a senior British officer at the camp, in my presence, and then told me that the senior British officer did not want us. I do not know if there was faulty interpretation, but I had to accept the answer and the German officer's icy remark "You see what your colleagues think of you." It was hard to take. It was an unfortunate fact that many of our troubles were caused by friction between subgroups of prisoners.

The next day was extraordinary. I imagine the Germans wanted to stage a sort of Roman holiday in the streets of Athens. They collected about 40 rather scruffy British officers, including myself, put us on lorries and motored us round the streets of Athens. I do not know what effect they expected, but the prisoners loved it. The Greeks showered food and cigarettes on us – though they were short of both – and cheered us on our way. One incident I remember clearly. I was sitting on the edge of the lorry with my legs hanging over. Suddenly we were held up in the traffic, and I looked up and saw the Parthenon. I had always wanted to see it but never imagined it would be like this. At that moment a small Greek boot boy ran forward and started to clean my boots. I can still remember the tears welling up in my eyes.

The rest of the time in Athens was grim, but it did not last long. I made no friends; there was nothing medical to do; food was scarce. I retired into a corner and rewrote the verse I had begun on Crete and started a new one. I think it saved my sanity. We were delighted when we were told that we were to go to Salonica. It could not, we thought, be worse than Athens. We little knew. Part of the journey was by rail; but the line had been blown up in a number of places, so we were forced to walk a lot of the way on empty stomachs.

SALONICA

The old cavalry barracks were in an appalling state of repair and grossly overcrowded with about 10 000 prisoners,[1] including Jugoslavs, Greeks, Cretans, Cypriots, Palestinians, Arabs, Indians, Australians, New Zealanders, English, Scots, Irish, and Welsh, and of course the Spaniards from Layforce. My first impressions were lack of food and lack of sleep. The diet consisted of one cupful of unsweetened coffee for breakfast, one plate of vegetable soup with a vestige of meat at midday, and two slices of bread (or a large biscuit) at night. Sleep was wrecked in two ways: by bed bugs, and by having, at first, to sleep on long sheets of wire netting, stretched in three tiers over wooden struts. There was an unmusical twang when anyone moved, and in the night there was a hideous cacophony.

There was a large hospital with about 200 beds. Surgeon Lieutenant Singer, a charming doctor from New Zealand, was in charge. He appeared to be doing a good job under difficult conditions. I joined the hospital to help out, and quite soon, to my surprise and embarrassment, was appointed chief doctor by the Germans as Singer had had an inevitable row with them. He was, fortunately, very good about it and my knowledge of German helped communications, not only with our hosts but also with the Jugoslavs. I soon realised what a thankless job I had.

The one great asset I had were the orderlies, a mixture partly from a section of the Friends Ambulance Unit (Quakers) and others from Australia, New Zealand, the UK, and Jugoslavia.

They were all devoted workers but chief praise must go to the Quakers, who were magnificent. Amongst them was Bill Miall, who later worked with me in Cardiff, became director of the MRC Epidemiological Unit in Jamaica, and is now at the MRC unit at Northwick Park. Another was Duncan Catterall, now director of the Venereology Unit at the Middlesex Hospital.

Life at the beginning of July was just tolerable. A typical day was as follows: reveille 5.30 am; parade 6 am (this often lasted an hour, for the Germans seemed incapable of counting correctly); then there was time for the "acorn" coffee and any bread one had managed not to eat the night before; then sick parade for other ranks (there were often 200, of which I did half); then another sick parade for the officers (we were lucky to finish by 10.30 am); then a ward round (I often had 100 medical cases); then I did a short sanitary round to try and keep the latrines working. At midday we had our soup, which did not take long to swallow. I rested until 1 pm when I either went to make complaints to the Germans – a rather profitless task as they always claimed that Salonica was a transit camp and that all prisoners of war would soon be sent to Germany (it is true that all officers, except two or three medical officers, were soon despatched to Germany, to be followed later by the Jugoslavs) or tried some crude psychotherapy on those suffering from severe battle neuroses. I saw them in my room alone and encouraged them to tell me about their experiences and fears. They soon started crying, which I encouraged. The sessions often lasted some time and the men often fell asleep afterwards. It seemed effective in most cases. At 4.30 pm we ran a skin sepsis clinic. After that I did another medical round, then got my two slices of bread and went on parade at 7 pm. Next followed an "outpatients" for those who had been working in the town. Then there was curfew, after which it was dangerous to go out. You could get shot. In the evenings I was tired but had difficulty in sleeping because of the bed bugs. I sometimes talked to the Jugoslavs, but more often to the Quakers. Sometimes to comfort myself I wrote verse.[2] There is one poem I still like. It combines my generation's guilt at not preventing the war and my personal guilt I felt when travelling to Edinburgh too late to see my mother before she died in 1937.

SIMILARITY

The track was hard as fate,
The train was singing:
"She must not die"
(I'd loved but not enough)
The wheels were ringing
"She cannot die"
(I'd tried but not enough)
and then I came too late.

Now prisoner, down in Greece,
The news is stinging.
We're down and out
(I'd loved but not enough)
The "goons" are grinning[3]
of Russian rout.[4]
(I'd tried but not enough)
and there is no more peace.

There were some other curious incidents in those early days. The first was my only success. I still felt responsible for the Spaniards who had been in Layforce and were worried about what would happen to them when they had to register as prisoners of war and give personal details. I promised to be there with them and argue that they were in the British Army and must be treated as British prisoners of war. As we began to march up to get registered I was suddenly inspired. I decided that all the Spaniards had been born in Gibraltar! I held a hurried discussion with them and the whole registration went off without the Germans raising one eyebrow. The Spaniards were delighted and I felt a mild glow, but I had another problem on my hands – a really unpleasant one – a traitor. He was an English regular sergeant major, about twice my size and very muscular. He had a German wife, and on capture expressed his willingness to join the German Army. He lived with the Germans but moved freely in the camp and had a devastating effect on morale. It fell to my lot to see him, read a quote from King's Regulations, and promise that I would try and see that he was court martialled after the war. He roared with laughter throughout and I felt rather foolish. I checked up after the war. He was killed on the Eastern Front.

Another incident showed the effect of chronic hunger. During my sanitary round I found a padre, whom I had met earlier in Alexandria, taking food out of clothes stupidly left in the barracks while the owner was out working in Salonica. I went up to him and said, "You must not do this. It's stealing." He answered without any show of embarrassment, "Why? I'm hungry." I know no better example of the awful effect of hunger. There was another level at which hunger showed its ill effects – the language and dreams of the British Army. The language of the British Army must have bored others as well as myself by its compulsive sex orientation. This disappeared completely in three weeks on the German diet of 600 calories per day.[5] The talk was only of beef steak and milk chocolate. I remember a tough sergeant major telling me all about a dream he had had about a Cadbury's bar.

After this early period (I remember saying I could only last out four weeks) the situation deteriorated in two different ways – disease and shooting. Both climaxed at about the same time. I know how near to breakdown I was driven.

Dealing with the shooting first. There had always been some intermittent shooting at night, but it slowly increased. Whenever I complained the Germans said that if no one left the barracks at night there would be no shooting. I wanted permission for prisoners to go to the outside latrines when necessary as the inside ones were often insufficient, with results that can only be imagined. They refused.

In August the bad month when everything happened, night shooting increased and then day shooting started, and for some reason it was concentrated on the hospital. The first shot put a bullet into the roof of the dental clinic and brought down plaster on the head of the New Zealand dentist when he was extracting a tooth. A few days later a bullet whizzed through my hair when I was doing my inpatient round. I remember that my right hand had just felt the outline of the spleen in a case of malaria. I have never felt the same about spleens since! On each occasion, of course, I made my routine complaints. The Germans apologised and said it was all a mistake and that it would not happen again, but of course it did.

Then came a day I shall never forget. It was in August. I had nearly finished my inpatient round when a terrified orderly told me that another orderly, a New Zealander, had been shot in the arm at the door of the hospital. I rushed to the Germans to organise his transport to the local hospital for surgical emergencies. The wounded orderly later lost his arm. I was on my way back when news came that two more orderlies had been shot, a Yugoslav and another New Zealander. They both had serious abdominal wounds. Again I was successful in arranging ambulance transport, but the German doctors refused to speak to me. I was in a rage. The Germans refused to see me at 1.30 pm, the usual time, so I had a while to cool down a little. I could not understand why they were shooting at us.

Still worse was to come. One of the orderlies died – though the other made a more or less complete recovery. That night there was a lot of noise. A German sentry called me out and led me to a lavatory in one of the barracks. There I saw blood, faeces, and naked human flesh, illuminated by flash light. I vomited. I remember hearing the German sentry telling his sergeant that he had thrown a hand grenade into the latrine because of *verdächtiges Lachen* (suspicious laughter). I collected some devoted orderlies and together we treated the wounded and cleaned up the mess. Fortunately the wounds were not serious, but I spent a sleepless night. The final insult came the next morning when I was ordered to attend a German parade during which the *Kommandant* congratulated the sentries on their vigilance. I took the rest of the morning off.

Surprisingly, at 1.30 pm I received an order to appear before the Germans. Usually it was hard work persuading them to see me. It was curious that both the *Kommandant* and his deputy were present. I also sensed some disagreement between them, for I noticed that they were sitting fairly far apart. They asked me if I had anything to say. I had recovered from my wild rage and decided to try another line. I said in fluent German – and in German I have rather an upper class accent – how much I had admired German culture in the past. I mentioned the usual names – Goethe, Heine, Beethoven, and Mozart – and how much had been contributed to medicine through Robert Koch and, more recently, the discovery of the sulphonamides. How shocked I was therefore to find Germans, in breach of the Geneva Convention, trying to starve prisoners of war to death, murdering medical orderlies, and attempting to shoot dentists and doctors. There was a short silence, after which the *Kommandant* said the past might have been unpleasant though necessary, but the future would be much better. And this time he was right.

The medical troubles started slowly, with skin sepsis, dysentery, and sandfly fever. The Germans gave us an old pink solution for skin sepsis and some curious pills for dysentery; both medications were ineffective. They gave us aspirin for sandfly fever, which is, fortunately, a self-limiting disease. There was a little malaria for which we got a small quantity of quinine. I thought we could survive, but then came the deluge: epidemics of diphtheria, typhoid and hepatitis. I was not too bad at diagnosing the cases. To my credit I diagnosed the early diphtheria cases and even got the first typhoid case right. The "rose" spots were unmistakable. But what could I do about them? The Germans would give me no help, either in treatment or prevention. I had to watch the epidemics go through the camp. I was terrified and sleepless night after night; but in the event very little happened. Those with diphtheria developed frightening neurological complications but no one died. The only intervention I could think of was the forceful removal of the membranes twice a day to be sure no one suffocated. I told those with typoid to lie still on their own faeces and I would see they were well hydrated and given as much glucose as I could get out of the Germans, and in fact only one died. Hepatitis was a different story. Everyone wanted it because it stopped hunger although it made one itch. I had it myself and it gave me my first good night's sleep for a long time, but it did not stop me worrying about the long term consequences.

Then came the final blow. Towards the end of July I noticed an increasing number of prisoners complaining of heavily swollen ankles – ankle oedema. This seemed to affect the British most seriously. The few remaining Indians, Jugoslavs, and other non-British prisoners were less affected. I also noticed that cooks were not affected, and assumed, I hope reasonably, that the cause was nutritional. I diagnosed hypoproteinaemic oedema (famine oedema) and asked the Germans to measure the protein level of the blood. They refused, saying it was all due to the sun. I asked for senior physicians, who had been captured and whom I knew were in Athens, to be brought in to advise me. I was conscious of my own ignorance. They refused, saying *"Ärzte sind überflüssig"* ("doctors are superfluous"). In retrospect, I think they were probably right, but it made me angry at the time and I was driven to write some verse:

SUPERFLUOUS DOCTORS

"Superfluous doctors" – what a phrase to rouse
Dulled prison fires to flicker with the muse
And build a brave new world. There, there would be
No famines, wars, or other acts of God
To break the Peace on Earth. No! Man would turn
From wanton killing of his cousin's kin
To face his very foes, and Science and Art,
With Labour an ally, would fight and kill
Want and its very fears, disease, its very roots,
Squalor and filth and loneliness and pain,
And then let doctors quit the centre stage
To usher in the prophylactic age.
But death was near and hunger, and prisoners'
Dreams were rare.
The doctor in Salonica sat down and tore his hair.

We were soon seeing more than 20 new cases of severe oedema every day, and the figures were rising. As soon as the pressures of the diphtheria outbreak had subsided we had established a simple procedure for assessing disease incidence levels. This was based upon the efforts of a disabled Quaker colleague (he had been at King's College Cambridge), who sat through all sick parades and to whom doctors reported their findings. In the case of all the main diseases diagnostic checks were then carried out in the hospital and incidence levels calculated. This we did using the prisoner of war population figures supplied to the cookhouse by the Germans.

It was through this crude epidemiological procedure that my fears and problems grew rapidly. In fact, the rate of incidence rose so dramatically that I felt obliged to change the diagnostic criteria to disguise the fact. To qualify for inclusion in the incidence figures oedema now had to be "pitting" oedema above the knee. Many people saw the figures and I did not want a panic to add to the troubles we already had. Even then the number kept rising, and I became desperate. I knew I must do something, despite the Germans' lack of concern, and I examined the problem from a number of directions. Then I remembered having read somewhere of "wet beriberi," caused by vitamin B deficiency, which resulted in severe oedema. For a time I must have convinced myself that I was witnessing an epidemic of "wet beriberi," for I decided to do an experiment modelled on that of James Lind, one of my medical heroes.[6] I chose 20 men, all in their early twenties, all emaciated and with oedema above the knee. I put 10 in each of two small wards. They all received the standard rations, but those in one ward were given a supplement of yeast three times a day (I had to use my own reserve of Greek money to get it on the black market). In the other ward they got one vitamin C tablet each day (I had kept a small reserve for an emergency). I had meant to measure the volume of urine passed, but that proved impossible. I could obtain no buckets, so I had to fall back on "frequency" measurements. Each man counted the number of times he passed water in 24 hours. I kept the whole thing secret. I expected, and feared, failure. I noted the numbers each morning. There was no difference between rooms for the first two days; on the third day there was a slight difference; and on the fourth it was definite. In addition, eight out of the ten men in the "yeast room" felt better, while no one felt better in the "vitamin C room." I wrote it up carefully and took it to the Germans at 1.30 pm. I must have presented an odd figure, in tattered khaki shirt and shorts. My face was emaciated and deeply jaundiced, but it was surrounded by a mass of red hair and an impressive red beard. The oedema round my knees was all too obvious.

I told them what had been done and what the results were. I claimed that it was proof of a serious deficiency disease, "wet beriberi," in the camp. I suggested some of the dire consequences that would result if nothing was done and became very emotional. I suddenly realised that I had truly shaken the Germans. One reason for this was the fact that the younger German doctor had heard of the trial of lemon juice in the discovery of the cure of scurvy. He even asked what I wanted in a very civilised way. I said, "A lot of yeast at once, an increased diet as soon as possible, and the rapid evacuation of the camp." And the Germans promised to do their best. I felt elated as I left them, but I was as depressed as ever by the time I reached the hospital. I did not think the promises would be kept. I did not really believe in "wet beriberi" and was horrified that I had, for a time, deceived myself and the Germans. I was, deep down, sure it was famine oedema. I was also aware that it was a pretty awful trial, so I did not talk about it further. I merely closed it down by giving all those in the "vitamin C room" a good helping of yeast. Afterwards I returned to my room and wept. The outlook seemed hopeless.

But the miracle happened. The next morning a large amount of yeast arrived; in a few days the rations were increased to provide about 800 calories a day; and the evacuation of the camp was speeded up. The results of my trial were even more miraculous. They are shown in figure 4, which illustrates something of the speed with which the incidence of famine oedema declined after supplies of yeast arrived, an improvement which preceded the slight upgrading of the diet. Unfortunately I cannot pinpoint the date from which yeast was added to the diet. My notes were taken away from me when I left Salonica – but not the original graph, from which figure 4 has been prepared. Nevertheless, it is possible for me to be accurate to within a day or so, because the climax of the shootings, which I can date, coincided with the trial period. On this basis I have placed the arrival of yeast supplies three to four days before the main peak (point B) in the oedema curve.[7]

In retrospect it is impossible not to accept a causal relationship between, on the one hand, the rapid fall in incidence and rapid clinical improvement of the cases and, on the other, the

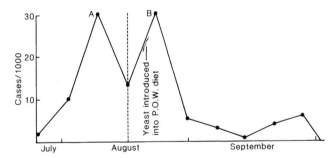

Figure 4 The weekly incidence of sickness figures for hypoproteinaemic oedema in the Salonica prisoner of war camp, July–October 1941. The broken line indicates the point from which the author adopted a change in classification procedure to produce, as he explains in the text, the artificial low shown for mid-August.

consumption of yeast and the slight improvement in diet. Although I am almost certain now that the condition was hypoproteinaemic oedema and not "wet beriberi," the mystery still remains as to why it appeared and disappeared so quickly. The simplest explanation is that it was the protein in the yeast that did the trick, but there could well have been something else.

As regards the trial, I have always felt rather emotional about it and ashamed of it. I have seldom referred to it since. It was a poor attempt. I was testing the wrong hypothesis, the numbers were too small, and they were not randomised. The outcome measure was pitiful and the trial did not go on long enough. On the other hand, it could be described as my first, worst, and most successful trial.

Whatever the cause, a vast change came over the camp in September and October. The shooting stopped; the oedema disappeared; we were less hungry; and the evacuation of the camp started. (The Germans did not tell me that the delay in evacuation was due to the Germans' rapid advance into the Soviet Union.) We all began to relax a little. I started playing bridge and even once played for bread – winner takes all. I have never played so well.

After a time we were even able to discuss the "bad old

days." One subject which always came up was which nationality had behaved best during the bad period? There was a curious unanimity that the New Zealanders were the best and the Australians the worst.

The next big event was the evacuation to Salonica of the prisoner of war hospital in Athens. The doctors, orderlies, and patients arrived, in the charge of Lieutenant Colonel Le Soeuf, an Australian surgeon whom I liked and respected. With him was my old friend, Bill Foreman, who I was to see so much of in the future. I have never handed over responsibility more willingly.

The camp was not completely evacuated until 30 November, but I had a much happier life. I was able to write a letter home, and to add a PS, "Love to Sonia. ALC" (an anagram of Salonica), which amused my sister. Later we even got British Red Cross parcels, and the effect was amazing. A lot of people seemed to be drunk on tea, while wondering what to eat first. We felt, for the first time, that we were not altogether forgotten. There was a charming Scots doctor called Johnny (I have forgotten his other name), who improved my bridge enormously. I noticed that I had had no attacks of migraine since arriving in Salonica, but if this was a cure I preferred the disease.

August in Salonica was perhaps the grimmest month in my life – so bad that I almost gave up. I managed to survive, chiefly, I think, because I had responsibility and was able to write (bad) verse. The following poem, "Duet for Two Voices," was written in the depths of despair.

My Body

A My eyes and ears, back, arms and leaden feet
    send to the brain their neutral neural waves;
    They cross the synapse, surge and meet
    To etch in blood, and weariness and graves,
    A martial chaos, gluttonous in defeat.

B Oh, Christ, make memory blank.
    Give cloud in clear!
    What fool or blackguard gave me eyes to see
    Or ears to hear.

My Heart

A   My heart is tired of war and all its
     Lonely boredom under redcapped fools,
     Comma'ed by steel of blitz,
     With pity for the men, the patient tools,
     And fear for them – for me – in sudden fits.

B   And yet this heart would gladly die for England.
     Oh, Christ, you fool, you're still that fat and filthy fag,
     On the touch line
     Shouting "Up, up School."

My Mind

A   My mind can pierce the cause of war today
     And see the moneyed marrow of its ills,
     The way the Marxists say – can see much good can grind from
         martial mills,
     And can approve the end, but not the way.

B   And so the intellectual picks his doubts,
     But never clean.
     Oh, Christ! Decide! Come left or right!
     There's no room in between.

The "I"

A   And then the "I" – the body, heart and mind.
     What can it do to make a perfect whole
     Of doubt, divided, blind.
     How can it ease the tumult of a soul
     By treating sick? By trying to be kind?

B   "Christ that my love were in my arms
     and I in my bed again!"

HILDBURGHAUSEN AND ELSTERHORST

It was a long, slow journey from Salonica to Germany, but we
learnt on the way that the USA was in the war and I had, for
the first time, real hope of getting home again. I had to leave
the train and many friends at Hildburghausen, a small
German country town. The set up there was that two
"houses" in a large psychiatric rural set up had been given
over to the prisoners of war, one for surgical cases and one for

medical cases. An interesting result of this organisation was that on many occasions one found oneself "inside the wire" while the German schizophrenics were wandering free in the park outside.

I was assigned to the medical section where there were two other British doctors, who had been captured at Dunkirk. My first reaction was to the food situation. German rations at about 1500 calories a day and regular Red Cross parcels, which took us over the 2000 calorie mark, were heaven on earth. This transformed me. I lost my oedema and jaundice, put on weight, and became, I hope, a more useful doctor and more reasonable human being.

I slowly assessed the situation and decided on the jobs I could most usefully do. I knew a certain amount about tuberculosis and offered to take over that section of the work, which was not popular with others. With my knowledge of German I tried to arrange facilities with the local clinic for screening and x raying patients. In this I was successful, and the local doctor, who was a lady, was cooperative. (This early specialisation in patients with tuberculosis had one unfortunate consequence. When the International Red Cross visited us they asked to see the cemetery, and one of them inquired who had looked after the patients who had been buried there. I had to admit that all of them were mine. The fact that tuberculosis was the sole cause of death amongst prisoners did not salvage my reputation. There was a tendency afterwards to refer to the cemetery as Cochrane's Corner. This tuberculosis work took up only a small part of my time. I realised that the rest of my efforts must be devoted to "care," as the chance of a cure among the other cases was minimal. I also realised that "care" in a prisoner of war hospital was far more than the "tender, loving care" in a London teaching hospital. It involved looking after the total morale of a lot of very worried human beings. In particular, there were the Yugoslavs in the hospitals. They needed total care more than the British as they knew no English and none of the doctors knew Yugoslav; they also got no food parcels.

I tried to cope with these problems and had some success, but I did not solve them. As a start I made a determined effort to learn Yugoslav – although there were no grammar books. The patients were peasants and knew no other language. It was uphill work until, later, a young Yugoslav cadet officer was admitted who spoke German; then progress became faster. I discovered, to my embarrassment, that I had been muddling up two words of great medical importance and quite different meaning, *Bolye* meaning "better" and *Boli* meaning "pain" (no one had died as a result!).

I discussed the food parcel problem with the British colonel in charge of the two British hospitals for prisoners of war. He was sympathetic and helped me greatly in channelling British food to the Yugoslavs. The individual British prisoners were kind enough. They gave a lot to the Yugoslavs but they did so as an obvious charity or in return for services, and this did not improve international relations. With the help of the young cadet officer I was able to conduct a survey of Yugoslavs as they left the hospitals to find out whether they thought more or less of the British after meeting them for the first time. The results were depressing (see figure 5).

I had some unusual experiences while at Hildburghausen – one purely medical and the others medicosocial. The first was the admission of a young British soldier in mild coma, whom I diagnosed, on smell alone, as diabetic. The German doctor informed me that insulin was in short supply in Germany and that none was available for prisoners. I was shaken. I believed that I would eventually get the insulin through the Red Cross. But how could I keep him alive until then? I had heard that in pre-insulin days patients were starved of carbohydrates, but the boy was going into coma and I had heard at University College Hospital that the best thing to do was to give carbohydrates to control the ketosis. I decided to take the risk. The Germans gave me some glucose to get him out of coma, and then we gave him a high potato diet. He was bad tempered and passed water frequently, but he survived until the insulin arrived, much later.

The second was on Christmas Eve 1941. The German *Unteroffizier* asked me if, in return for listening to the English news and a bottle of Bols, I would do something medical for him. All prisoners usually agreed to such offers, and I went out

74

with him and found myself helping a Polish-Jewish girl to have a baby in a stable, with an animal in the next stall. The birth was normal. There were no immediate complications. I have kept my promise of secrecy until now, but I would like to know what happened to that baby.

The third experience was with "Bill," a Polish pilot who had been shot down. He had no visible wounds, but his sexual, urinary, and rectal functions were paralysed. He was a cultured, athletic young man, whom I learned to like very much. I had to explain to him the seriousness of his condition. He was greatly upset. Twice Bill asked me for the means of committing suicide. I refused. I thought he must have a good neurological opinion in the UK. He was of considerable help to me when the Katyn affair was widely publicised by the Germans.[8] Some of Bill's relations were listed on the German propaganda sheets. We discussed the problem at length. We both thought the Russians had done it, but decided that until the end of the war we must pretend that the Germans were responsible. (He was repatriated early and unfortunately no one saw any point in surgery. I visited him often in the hospital for incurables in North Wales after the war. After his death I received a letter from him asking why I had not let him commit suicide in Hildburghausen.)

I was never quite clear as to why I was ordered to leave Hildburghausen so abruptly and go to Oflag IX A. I think it resulted from my accidental diagnosis of the first case of typhus in that area. I had considerable experience of typhoid in Salonica, and when I examined the critical case I made a confident diagnosis of typhoid on the basis of a typical history and "rose" spots, but as there were rumours of typhus in Germany, and as I believed the two diseases were similar, I asked for a Weil–Felix[9] reaction as well, and it was strongly positive. There was a lot of fuss. The German consultant who came down and saw my notes thought I had done a wonderful job in asking for the Weil–Felix reaction, but someone had to be blamed for the epidemic and they chose me.

I was only in the officers' prisoner of war camp at Oflag IX A for a few weeks, but realised how lucky I was to be medically qualified. Although many activities were ingeniously organised, the unemployed officers had a much less satisfactory life than I had had at Hildburghausen and even at Salonica. The food was good, the company fair, but active medical work was much more satisfying.

I was relieved when I was ordered to Elsterhorst, which had become known as the prisoner of war tuberculosis centre in Germany. It was a large hutted camp with an operating theatre, whither all prisoners of whatever nationality were sent if they were diagnosed as tuberculous. In charge of it was my old friend, Colonel Le Soeuf from Salonica, ably assisted by Major Wallis, and, from the Quakers' Field Ambulance, Duncan Catterall. They welcomed me, and put me in charge of a ward of patients with tuberculosis. The other doctors there were from Australia, New Zealand, Poland, France, and the UK. The patients were Russian, Polish, Yugoslav, French, Indian, and British, with the odd Spaniard, South African, and Norwegian.

Colonel Le Soeuf had done a good job on the food side. The hospital was well supplied with Red Cross food parcels, and every one of them went to the central kitchen, so all patients, of whatever nationality, got the same diet. I later repeated my questionnaire about Yugoslavs' opinions here, with quite different results, as shown in figure 5.

The situation about the treatment of tuberculosis at that time was that one could give bed rest, pneumothorax, pneumoperitoneum, or thoracoplasty. I also knew, from some cynical conversations at University College Hospital, that there was no real evidence apart from opinion that any treatment worked. We could "screen" our patients (without protective gloves or apron) but it was difficult to get x ray films. We had facilities for examining sputa. The problem was when to intervene. I learnt the hard way. Starting very conservatively, I found how difficult it was not to intervene when patients deteriorated. I learnt how much it improved my patients' and my own morale if I did intervene but how disastrous the results could be. I learnt slowly, as I had begun to learn in Hildburghausen, that my main job was caring for people until the end of the war, or death.

Much effort was put into providing this care. Two compli-

76

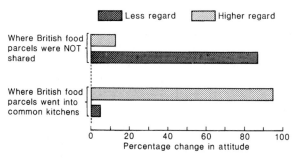

Figure 5 The changing attitude of Eastern European prisoners of war (Germany, 1941–42) towards the British after meeting them in hospital, according to the sharing or non-sharing of British food parcels.

About 100 consecutive Yugoslav prisoners of war were asked on leaving the two hospitals, at Hildburghausen and Elsterhorst, whether they thought better or worse of the British after meeting them for the first time in hospital. At Hildburghausen only the British received food parcels while at Elsterhorst everything was shared.

cated stage productions of *Macbeth* and *Journey's End* were put on, with the dialogue translated into all the relevant languages. We ran an excellent news service. It was based on secret radios transmitting from different countries, and bulletins were issued in the wards almost every day. Nearly every evening most doctors, including myself, lectured in the wards on any subject they knew something about. Boredom was endemic in the hospital, and it had to be fought. Then I found that by provoking a row with the German doctor during a ward round I was able to raise morale. The German doctor was not particularly bright (I was aware that a country would not order its best doctors to look after prisoners of war). I did not enjoy starting these arguments but morale was the overwhelming priority, so I did it.

There were, too, the so-called minor activities: painting (I still have a portrait of myself painted by a Spanish prisoner of war)[10] for which the paints were provided by the Red Cross, and regular competitions for players of draughts, chess, and bridge (I have vague memories of winning a bridge tournament, playing for Scotland against Poland, in which I won for

Scotland by a brilliant "psychic" bid). We helped our patients to write letters and, rarely, arranged divorces.

The "alcohol" industry was initiated by the Soviet prisoners, who knew the technique of turning bad potatoes into vodka. It was taken up in a big way by the prisoner of war staff and we were soon redistilling the primary product to get rid of the methyl alcohol. This was done in the tuberculosis sputum laboratory. The Germans were terrified of tuberculosis and never visited the room. I remember a ward Christmas party in 1943 at which we were able to give every patient a glass of red wine if he wished it. There was a good staff party, too, at which even the Poles embraced the Russians – a rare event indeed.

The black market worked well. Backed by cigarettes and chocolate from our food parcels, this market grew and grew as shortages increased in Germany. Through it we were able to buy such things as x ray films, white bread, and pigs. I was at first embarrassed by the idea of bribery, but it was so easy and so acceptable to the Germans that I regularly engaged in it. Another job I did was to run the officers' mess, and, with an excellent French cook, I think I did it fairly well. I introduced stuffed marrow to make the meat ration seem more. It was a great success, but I ran into trouble when the French cook's relatives were killed in a British bombing raid, and the standard of food in the mess fell rapidly.

The problem of death, which occurred frequently and inevitably, was a serious one. The Germans had a good rule that the doctor in charge of the patient was responsible for the funeral. It was a good idea in that it brought home to physicians their case fatality rate. On the other hand, it meant a lot of hard work. We had, at times, a resident padre, but we had to organise many of the funerals ourselves. There was a lot to learn – Church of England, Catholic, Non-conformist, Greek Orthodox, Hindu, Moslem and Soviet funerals – and the funerals were important from the point of view of national morale. I did my best. I was even congratulated on my Greek Orthodox service; but it was difficult and emotional work.

All this gives the impression that the doctors were always too busy to have time for introspection and depression, but unfortunately there was still far too much time for both. The doctors and their staff quarrelled intermittently over trifles. One Englishman on the staff did not speak to me for a year. I have no idea why. Nights were often sleepless, and to our credit we were often desperately worried about our ill patients. I remember trying to give some psychotherapy to a shotdown rear gunner with tuberculosis. I often wondered if he was more neurotic than I was.

I still possess a diary of the latter days of Elsterhorst. On 9 September 1944 I wrote: "I feel depressed about the future, both for the world and myself. Churchill's strategy has won the war, but it shows no sign of winning the future for humanity." We knew the war was nearly over, but the bombing worried us a lot. We knew the Russians were advancing fast and there was endless debate as to how far they would get. The majority were convinced that Poland and Germany would go communist, and that France would waver. (I was fascinated by the idea of my old friend Marty becoming President of France!) I should make it clear that no one in the camp – British, French, or Polish – wanted to go communist. Everyone thought it would happen through force of arms. Even the Russians admitted privately that they would prefer to be liberated by the British. We blamed our troubles – possibly unfairly – on the delay in building up the second front.

One other aspect of this period is worth mentioning. In addition to trying to learn Russian and Yugoslav I read a great deal of German poetry, which I think the German Quakers made available to us. My diary at that time is full of quotes. At first I revelled in relearning the poems I had learned in my youth, such as "Wer reitet so spät durch Nacht und Wind" (*Erlkönig* – Goethe), "Ich weiss nicht was soll es bedeuten" (*Lorelei* – Heine), and many others. I found a great deal of pleasure in reciting them to myself, but my true search was for something that expressed my own feelings then and there. Goethe went a certain way towards it in

Nur wer die Sehnsucht kennt weiss was ich leide,
Allein und abgetrennt von aller Freude.
[Only someone who knows longing can understand my suffering,
Alone and separated from all happiness.]

But my real discovery was in Rilke (to whose other poems I am not very sympathetic):

DER PANTHER

Sein Blick ist vom Vorübergehn der Stäbe
so müd geworden, dass er nichts mehr hält,
Ihm ist, als ob es tausend Stäbe gäbe
und hinter tausend Stäben keine Welt.

I translated this as

His eyes are tired of moving round the cage
so tired they lack both image and recall,
Endless cages loom outside his own cage
and behind those cages, no world at all.

(I still think it is rather good.)

After Salonica this was a time of mild turbulence after a hurricane, and I found little need to write verse. I was only roused to it by the increased bombing. One raid came very near to our camp, arousing powerful unpleasant, ambivalent feelings. The aeroplanes appeared so beautiful as they flashed from sunlight into cloud, looking like black and white birds; but they caused such terrible damage. The poem runs

AMBIVALENCE

Oh! home birds, our own birds,
Singing above,
You bring to each prisoner
Something of love.

Oh, bright birds, oh brave birds,
Flying on high,
You touch every heart with
Hope's bitter lie.

Oh black birds, oh bold birds,
Drumming with hate,
High heralds of slaughter,
Hangmen of fate.

We greet you, we need you,
Links with our loves;
You maim, us, you shame us,
Eagles and doves.

We fête you, we hate you,
Vultures of lead!
We long to forget you,
You and your dead.

Oh love birds, oh hate birds,
Silver and black!
What shall we think of you
When we look back,

When we see how we fought
To defend
What we thought was an end in itself
was an end.

(As verse it is second rate, but writing it relieved my intolerable feelings of ambivalence.)

There was another curious incident in the camp. The Germans announced the visit of an important Indian visitor who was to be given VIP treatment. As I was in charge of all Indians with tuberculosis I was on duty. The Germans introduced me rather curtly and then, fortunately, left. I took him round the ward and introduced him to all the Indians socially. The Indians had been well treated by the Red Cross, with special food parcels. I had taken a particular interest in them. It became a friendly round. I then took him into my room and, with histories and chest x rays, showed him how ill the Indian patients were. He listened attentively and when I was finished he was silent for a while and then said something like this: "I must admit that I came here to recruit Indians to fight against you in India. I agree that none of these Indians are suitable recruits. I also admit that you have looked after them well and been kind to them. I can't leave here for another two hours and I rather like you. Could we have a talk?" It emerged that we had both been to Cambridge. He made all the points about British misrule in India that I knew so well. I agreed with nearly all he said, but argued a few points. He then told me that in desperation he had tried to make an alliance with Hitler (I think he said he went by submarine). He then admitted how disillusioned he had been by the Nazi regime. He really thought the British might be a lesser evil. He wanted some assurance from me that India would be free if we won the war. I did my best, but it did not altogether satisfy him, though we remained good friends. (I fulfilled my promise, as far as I could, by voting Labour in the 1945 election.) He did not tell me his name but I am almost sure he was Dr Subhas Chandra Bose, who was said to have been killed later in an air crash in China. He was a most intelligent, likeable young man.

Another event at Elsterhorst had a marked effect on me. The Germans dumped a young Soviet prisoner in my ward late one night. The ward was full, so I put him in my room as he was moribund and screaming and I did not want to wake the ward. I examined him. He had obvious gross bilateral cavitation and a severe pleural rub. I thought the latter was the cause of the pain and the screaming. I had no morphia, just aspirin, which had no effect. I felt desperate. I knew very little Russian then and there was no one in the ward who did. I finally instinctively sat down on the bed and took him in my arms, and the screaming stopped almost at once. He died peacefully in my arms a few hours later. It was not the pleurisy that caused the screaming but loneliness. It was a wonderful education about the care of the dying. I was ashamed of my misdiagnosis and kept the story secret.

The next happening after Christmas 1944 was the visit of the Red Cross to decide who should be repatriated. The problem was how much to cheat. I had many cases about which there was no doubt. I decided to cheat in one case only. It concerned a young Norwegian who was still politically at risk. He had tried to escape to the UK and was captured in the sea. He claimed that he was captured from a sunk British naval vessel by whom he had been accepted as serving in the Royal Navy. The Germans argued that he was captured before he got to the British ship. I had argued his case several times while he was in the hospital, and always got away with it, chiefly because I pointed out that he was suffering from tuberculosis. I knew, however, that the repatriation officers would not be so easily fobbed off by a healed looking focus at the right apex of the lung. With great difficulty I managed to insert into his notes evidence of a positive sputum for tuberculosis, carried out in a German laboratory. It worked and he was repatriated. (I persuaded a Norwegian to visit him long after the war. He was asked how he thought he had survived imprisonment. He answered that it was all due to the "Grace of God"!) I got all my cases through, as did most of the other doctors. Indications for repatriation, inevitably, vary with the state of the war, and the next big problem was the growth of the hospital as we became one of the main repatriation centres. This involved a great deal of "processing" while we were heavily involved in keeping our own cases alive until they reached the UK.

The hospital bulged like a pregnant woman, and, corresponding to the birth, the transport arrived and the repatriation started. Unfortunately the Germans ran out of suitable transport and on one awful day (24 January 1945) I saw them loading my precious patients (two with double pneumothoraces) on to an open truck, with little protection, while snow was falling. I had looked after these patients for a long time and had done my best. I loved them dearly. I thought this was murder. I lost my temper and jumped on the wagon and made a loud speech to the Germans. There were several of them about as it was an important occasion. I do not remember exactly what I said, but it ended with the phrase "Das ist doch ein Skandal im Lande von Robert Koch" ["This is scandalous in the land of Robert Koch"]. It had an immediate effect. I got an ambulance, but the Germans did not forgive me and I was dismissed in disgrace within a few weeks.

In spite of all my troubles there I had learnt a lot about myself. I was satisfied that I had really cared for my patients as well as I could have in the circumstances. I had found it emotionally satisfying and distressing at the same time. I knew my patients so well that I was miserable when they died. I also found "caring" intellectually unsatisfactory. What I decided I could not continue doing was making decisions about intervening (for example, pneumothorax and thorocoplasty)[11] when I had no idea whether I was doing more harm than good. I remember reading a pamphlet (I think from the BMA) extolling the advantages of the freedom of British doctors to do whatever they thought best for their patients. I found it ridiculous. I would willingly have sacrificed all my medical freedom for some hard evidence telling me when to do a pneumothorax. I feared I had shortened some lives by doing it on the wrong cases. (This was certainly the birth of an idea which culminated in *Effectiveness and Efficiency*.[12])

I was sent off to an unknown destination, but allowed to take my books and papers with me. I had not enjoyed myself at Elsterhorst, but I was a wiser man.

WITTENBERG-AM-ELBE

I arrived at Wittenberg-am-Elbe on 6 February 1945. Although I knew the war was nearly over, I was worried about survival. The nearer the end, the greater my fear became, and I realised that this move reduced my chances of survival. I also felt lonely, and I expected that life in the future would be less comfortable, and I was right. I was to be the one doctor in charge of a kind of first aid post (*Revier*) with some beds, serving a large number of prisoner of war working *Kommandos* (camps), making up a *Straf* (punishment) area.

The building itself was a ramshackle wooden affair. It could previously have been a pub or a brothel. The only water available came from a pump, which was often out of order. The electricity worked intermittently. Cooking was done on a coal stove and there was little coal. There was no bathroom and only very primitive latrines.

Medically there were about 20 or more primitive beds, a few drugs, and a curious mixture of nationalities – Russian, French, Italian, Dutch, South African, and British – in a staff of nine. One trouble was that they could not all speak to each other. I was warned by the South African doctor, L, whom I was replacing, that I could not expect help from the local medical people, either in arranging hospital admissions or in *x* raying those suspected of suffering from tuberculosis.

Of the staff there were four whom I got to know well – the Dutch secretary and the three Russians. The Dutch secretary (unfortunately I have forgotten his name) was first class. He was a good linguist, well read, and excellent company. He had taken over nearly all the administrative work from the German sergeant (*Feldwebel*). This gave us access to the German's files, and his radio. I missed the Dutch secretary badly when he left. Then there were the Russian orderlies, Ivan, Megved, and "Don Juan." I first got to know them because I thought they would be useful if we were liberated by the Russians, and also to improve my Russian. I ended up a very close friend of Ivan and Megved. Then there was "St Boswells," so called because he came from a small town of that name near Galashiels. He was suffering from a chronic skin complaint – which we managed not to cure – and he really became part of the staff. He was always cheerful, always willing, and made a great difference to my morale. He was the only one who stayed with me to the very end. F was a rather difficult South African orderly.

My daily work started at about 7.30 am with a vast sick parade from all the neighbouring *Kommandos*. It sometimes lasted until about 1.30 pm. Those who attended were mostly healthy, tired, miserable people who wanted, and needed, a rest. Then, there were the less serious illnesses – backache, minor burns, and skin infections – and the seriously ill – fractures, influenza, famine oedema, and just occasionally pneumonia and tuberculosis. As usual my pharmaceutical resources consisted mainly of aspirin and so-called antiseptic skin lotion. The parade was watched by an armed German sergeant who checked all I did, but he was at first fairly benign. I did what I could in getting people off work for as much time as I dared, taking as many into my wretched hospital as I could, and persuading the *Feldwebel* to arrange for the admission of others to better equipped hospitals.

After a frugal meal I did a quick ward round and then had a variety of duties. One was giving TAB (anti-typhoid) injections to all prisoners of war in the area. This was tiring and, I thought, ineffective as most of them had had these injections fairly recently, but it gave me an opportunity to talk to the people in the various working groups and hear of their problems, and to talk to German civilians when the *Feldwebel* and I travelled by train. Another afternoon occupation was to visit the same working parties to see those who were really ill and could not come to sick parade. Alternatively, I walked to the military authorities in Wittenberg to make a series of complaints. Then came another round in the hospital; another meal of a kind; and a discussion with my staff about our increasing problems. Finally I went to my room, but sleep was difficult as I slowly realised my present and future difficulties. Sleep was also made more and more difficult by increasing air raids, but, as my diary shows, I solved the problem by reading and writing verse. I was lucky in having, with the help of my Dutch secretary, a fair selection of books in English, German, French, and Russian. But I felt the tension rising.

I first concentrated on the problem of food. I was determined not to have a rerun of Salonica. It was not hard to discover through the German sergeant in charge roughly how much we were supposed to have. With the help of my secretary we checked what we got. My diary is full of jottings like this:

Diet received per person per day	Estimate of calories	Later checked in the UK
100 g potatoes	85	80
200 g bread	414	466
12.5 g butter	91	92.5
200 g spinach	50	60
200 g cabbage	58	30
25 g margarine	72	30.7
25 g sugar	100	98.5
5 g cheese	5	20.3
20 g meat	35	42.8
	910	920.8

We were due about 1100 calories a day and whenever it fell below 1000 I complained like hell. On the whole the officer responsible was reasonable and my complaints had an effect.

It is only fair to say that German civilians who were not engaged in hard labour were not getting much more.

An associated problem was the distribution of British, American, and Canadian food parcels, of which we had a small reserve supply. I first discussed the problem with the few British patients and staff (there were no Americans or Canadians in the hospital then). We all agreed we had to share with others. I should stress that sharing meant quite a lot at that moment. A Red Cross parcel per week, which was the standard ration, added about 1500 calories a day to your diet. I then discussed the problem with the Dutch, French, and Russian staff, and finalised a plan that was fair, but left me in charge of an "iron" reserve for emergencies.

My next problem was the sick parades. Here I produced one or two ideas. Most of the people were technically malingering in the sense that they were merely very tired and needed a rest, which they certainly deserved. To enable me to get them off work when I was being watched by the *Feldwebel* and occasionally by "Otto" the chief doctor in the area they must be taught to malinger better. To this end I started a sort of school for malingering. Those who came into the hospital for a short stay were trained in ways of simulating backache and migraine. I chose the diseases for their lack of physical signs. When the prisoners went back to their *Kommandos* they were instructed to have one person (or more if it was a large *Kommando*) using these techniques every day. On the whole it worked well. The French and Russians were best at it.

My other idea was prompted by chance. A prisoner was admitted suffering from mumps, and an orderly discovered that by blowing hard with nose and mouth closed he could blow up his salivary glands to look like mumps. Soon I had arranged a small epidemic of mumps amongst patients about to be discharged from hospital. I knew I was safe. "Otto," the German doctor, had a horror of touching an infectious case. We spread the word to the *Kommandos* and soon there was a mild epidemic of "mumps." (Fortunately not too many people can use this technique.) By these means we slowly got more and more people off work.

My biggest problem was policy in the long term. The Soviet

troops were approaching from one side and the Americans from the other. I thought that the River Elbe might be a meeting place and we were on the Russian side. As I saw it I had two duties (1) to the patients and staff in my comic hospital, and (2) to the many thousands of prisoners of war in that area, where I was the only allied officer they knew. They were all very worried indeed as to what to do when, as everyone expected, chaos started. I got to know these people fairly well, by visits and on sick parades, and they began to trust me – chiefly because I spoke French and German and a fair amount of Russian and Yugoslav. I became slowly aware that they needed a focal point to go to in a crisis. I discussed this problem with my staff, who were not helpful, and I finally decided that it was my duty to stay in Wittenberg; but as a corollary I decided to get all seriously ill cases to the other side of the Elbe before the crisis. As things turned out it was probably a wrong decision. Only a few hundred prisoners used the hospital as a focal point, but on the other hand, given the notice I had, it would have been practically impossible to get them all across the Elbe before the bridge was blown.

From here on I think my diary speaks more honestly and more clearly than anything I could write now. I have altered it very little – a few times to avoid unfairness and to avoid repetition, and on some occasions to add details that I was afraid the Germans, or later the Russians, might see.

It starts on 15 February, when I had had time to review the problems of the various working *Kommandos* I was serving.

15 *February 1945*

I have already screened some cases for tuberculosis and established good relations with the German doctor at the clinic. He is willing to screen 10 cases a week with me. I can work the numbers up later. I can apparently send the Russian TB cases to a special hospital, but God knows what to do about the others.

The various nations all present different problems.

SLOVAKS Completely demoralised, dirty, lousy, and with a

88

high percentage of TB and starvation oedema. All I can hope to do is to avoid typhus by delousing.

POLES (from Warsaw)   Their morale is good, but they are difficult in the *Revier* as they fight with the Russians.

DANES   They are all policemen who have only just arrived in Germany. Their physique looks good, though some have oedema. They are just incredibly neurotic, but rather likeable.

INDIANS   The language question is serious here. Their food has just been cut and they are miserable. They all ask to be sent to the Indian POW headquarters at Annaberg. It's usually the only word I understand. I have demanded an interpreter.

RUSSIANS   They are in a bad way, but are fairly cheerful. The TB and oedema rates are high. I have started shaking hands with them all on the sick parades as I did at the outpatients at Elsterhorst and it is going down well. Relations are good, so far.

AMERICANS   They are very new POWs, captured in Rundstedt's offensive. Their "acute geganenitis" (POW neurosis) is the worst I've seen – presumably because their standard of living was the highest before being taken prisoner.

ITALIANS   Few now as the majority have been "liberated."

DUTCH   Only a few; cheerful and cooperative.

JUGOSLAVS   Not many – chiefly workers on farms. They get American parcels once a month; very friendly.

FRENCH   Have all the best jobs in the town, but are beginning to feel the pinch now as there are no parcels. They are the most impressive malingerers.

BRITISH   Few and healthy. The only trouble is the number of NCOs who have volunteered to work. It's all "for love" but it must stop.

In the *Revier* I'm seeing a lot of the Russians and they are slowly getting less suspicious.

The general prognosis is fearful: hunger, loneliness, bombs, artillery – and then freedom.

I've had some interesting talks this week: (1) the Danish Red Cross – they actually told me how angry they were that Danish POWs were treated like other POWs! (2) an officer of Vlassov's[13] army – very pleased with himself and confident;

(3) with L about South Africa and the difficulties of socialism there and how difficult it is for any white man in South Africa to give up his high standard of living. He told me about it: it is high. Shortly afterwards I was talking to Ivan. He still believes that my standard of living must be higher than L's because I live in London and L lives in an exploited colony!

I did a routine examination of the nine staff. I found one bilateral optic atrophy (partial blindness), one TB (?), and two illiterates (one Italian and one Russian). The optic atrophy is presumably due to "hooch" (POW alcohol made from potatoes).

I have started doing the routine anti-typhoid injections on the working parties round about here. It is interesting, but tiring, as trains are now infrequent. It took 11 hours to inject 240 men!

Air raids are frequent at night, but not too near. Our air raid shelter is poor.

My long-term policy must be: (1) to get on good terms with all nationalities, so that they may take my orders in a crisis; (2) to resist schemes of evacuation of the *Revier*; (3) to improve relations amongst the staff. The problems are (1) food; (2) coal; (3) baths; (4) evacuation of TB cases to hospital. I've started the ball rolling for all these, but it is going to be a fearful battle.

19 February 1945
The orderly who had gone to Elsterhorst with L came back with the story that Elsterhorst was about to be evacuated. So far, I'm lucky. "Bim" (Major Wallis) nobly sent some porridge, and some penicillin from the Red Cross. Bless him!

The German food is fearful – 16th, 910 calories; 17th, 1200 calories; 18th 1100 calories – so I have divided out some of the remaining Red Cross food. I gave some to the Russians, French, and Italians. There were no objections from the British, thank God.

With the help of the Dutch secretary I managed to get some interesting statistics out of the German office. It is an interesting area as regards TB, as it was completely mass *x* rayed in 1942, and all "positive" cases were said to have been removed in early 1943. Since then the incidence of new cases has been as follows:

	No parcels Russians per 1000	Some parcels French per 1000	Regular parcels British per 1000
July–December 1943	6	0	0
January–June 1944	14	1	0
July–December 1944	31	1	0

The figures show the incidence of TB amongst the Russians, French, and British since then. You see the effect of food parcels! (It was published in the *British Medical Journal* much later. It was probably my first epidemiological paper.[14])

Another interesting statistic is the percentage of people off work during January 1945, by nation: French, 24%; British, 8%; Russian, 25%; Indian, 11%. The French must be excellent actors! Most of the Russians are genuinely ill.

Several long talks with my Dutch secretary. Nice story as to why "Hallo" was banned in the Netherlands by the Germans. It means "Hang alle Laffe Landveräters op" ["Hang all traitors by the neck"].

My Russian and my relations with the Russians are improving.

20 February 1945

I have been warned by the *Feldwebel* that a most unpleasant secret report has arrived about me and that there would be trouble when "Otto" came – as he did today. My usual technique with new German doctors is to start quietly and try to get all I want as between doctors – it is less tiring and sometimes more effective – but "Otto" didn't give me a chance. He didn't know I spoke German and was very rude about me to the *Feldwebel* in my presence, so I chimed in, in German, and after that the whole round was a pretty fierce verbal battle. I was in a strong position – the place was clean and tidy and there was plenty to criticise on the German side. The ward enjoyed it very much. I finally dragged some promises out of him: (1) we are to have a *Speise Karte* (food ration card) showing how much food we should be getting, and I can check it; (2) hot showers once a week; (3) starvation oedemas can be sent to hospital. I had great fun over the oedemas. He said they were all due to bilateral varicose veins! It was rather awful at the end; he practically broke down when talking of air raids. He must be living under a frightful strain. I suddenly felt sorry for him, but I didn't show it – and he left, hating me. It's great fun putting on these acts, but it's tiring and may be dangerous.

27 February 1945
New orders have just come through about columns of refugees and POWs which are expected to pass through Wittenberg. We are to put them up, feed them, and treat them. Have worked out rough plan.

Some interesting visits. (1) to a *Panzer Faust* (secret anti-tank missile) factory. We went there by mistake to give TAB injections to POWs. It is a vast place, well scattered in a wood and completely wired; (2) to an American working party. Really shocking; they have completely lost their self respect; they are dirty and ill. It meant walking 18 kilometres back – I must stop this – it makes me too hungry.

The food is still bad and the *Speise Karte* hasn't come.

The Russians are burning themselves in the most gruesome way to avoid work. I admire their courage.

Turkey and Egypt declare war on Germany – rather silly!

28 February 1945
Goebbels speaks of "great political reorientations." The Slovaks leave the district – thank God. Air raids bigger and better. Up to the present there has been a lot to do, but now I'm getting lonely and depressed. I like neither the immediate nor the distant prognosis for myself or the world.

2 March 1945
Hot showers cancelled. Damn "Otto!" I shall have a bath in the sink. There are great advantages in being small if you're a POW!

3 March 1945

Big meeting at the *Stadt Küche* (town kitchen) about my complaints. The chief cook there was the local *Fuhrerin* (political leader) and was a tremendous woman – rather like a classic brothel keeper – while her young assistants were just like the "ladies." She stormed, shouted, and threatened and finally promised to improve the food.

Rather worrying – I found an American patient in the *Revier* with lice.

6 March 1945

An Englishman with serious illness has been admitted. He has had diarrhoea and vomiting for some time and is seriously oedematous (swollen). He's a fearfully difficult case to nurse here, but there is nowhere to send him.

8 March 1945

The Englishman is a little better. I saw another "Vlassov officer." He is quite happy, believing he will be captured by the Americans. The chances of getting out of here alive are very thin and if we do get out the future is grim.

10 March 1945

Trip to a factory to do TAB injections; an amazing scene on the train – an SS sergeant on leave said he was willing to die for Germany, but he wasn't going to die of hunger for it. I'm beginning to feel hungry too.

There are rumours that the local military have ordered British POWs to dig trenches, so I must start protesting. Englishman still very ill. I've received warning that my sick parades are going to be "controlled" in future. I can't complain as I've shoved the sickness rate up pretty high. I'll have to be careful for a bit.

12 March 1945

Big tragedy: the water pump is broken – we're sunk. The ill Englishman has been evacuated, thank God.

Hitler – a new line – "Der allmächtige Herr Gott kann

seines Segen nicht versagen" ["God cannot deny us his blessing"].

Finally dealt with the last of the NCOs who had volunteered to work. It was a woman in every case.

15 March 1945

My Dutch secretary has gone. The *Feldwebel* himself is to do the sick parades with me and watch me. He tells me they are trying to get me on a sabotage trial, so I gave myself a special treat with thick pea soup. I'm getting rather food conscious.

16 March 1945

"Otto" came to Wittenberg today, but didn't see me. The food position is finally corrected. I've gained about 150 calories a day for us after a month's battle. I suppose it's worth it. Also, the pump is repaired.

The air raids are averaging three in 24 hours. The evening ones are far too punctual. It's 10 pm every night, so they lose their psychological effect.

The sick parades are much longer now that the *Feldwebel* does them. Today was from 7.45 am till 2 pm and the strain is much greater, as malingering is very much more difficult to arrange. I find working at Russian too much now. I've been reading *Rob Roy* for relief – Dai Vernon is as charming as ever.

19 March 1945

The worst sick parade so far. It has now become a sort of multilateral battle, with the *Feldwebel*, the *Posten* (guards) from the POW's working party, and myself all fighting to decide whether a man can come off work or not, while the German doctor is a sort of court of appeal. The position is that when I say that a POW must not work either the *Feldwebel* or the *Posten* can say that all sick from that particular working party must go to the German doctor. He invariably marks everyone *dienstfähig* (capable of work), so that it now requires a great deal of tact to get anyone off work. And all this in six languages. Very tired, hungry, and lonely.

94

23 March 1945

Life is intolerable – the sick parades continue in the same battle order and I have now a lot of medical secretarial work in German to do which the *Feldwebel* can't do, and if I don't do it I can't "screen" anyone or send them to hospital. The place is just riddled with TB.

The nights are bad now with air raids and rats.

Some talks with the *Feldwebel*, who was a POW in the last war in Serbia. Awful story how he collected hard peas out of faeces when he was hungry. I am now getting really hungry. I have to shut up the rest of the bread when I'm eating, otherwise I just eat it all.

There have already been three warnings tonight, so I think I'll go to bed.

25 March 1945

A quiet Sunday at last. The new food problems are solved. I convinced the *Feldwebel* that we were done out of sugar last month and he has applied for it.

I found a magnificent poem on POW life by Lermontov and showed it to the Russians. They all loved it and wept, and so did I!

I've also read some Valery: "Il incombe au spiritualisme et aux amateurs d'inspiration de nous expliquer pourquoi cet esprit ne souffle pas dans les bêtes et souffle si mal dans les soux", and "Il y a des vers qu'on trouve. Les autres on les fait." Perfect brevity.

News excellent: Mainz and Ludwigshafen.

I am amused at how highly I value my life now.

27 March 1945

A few pleasant things from Yeats:

> But where can we draw water
> said Pearse to Connolly,
> When all the wells are parched away?
> O plain, as plain can be;
> There's nothing but our own red blood
> Can make a right rose tree.

And that magnificent one, ending

> To bundle time away that the night come.

This poetry has been a wonderful relief, though the sick parades are as bad as ever. This is the first time in my life that I've disliked medicine. My appetite horrifies me as I smoke less and have less to eat.

29 March 1945
A wonderful break yesterday. I was called out late at night. We went to the Danish *Kommando*. The case wasn't serious and afterwards they fairly extended themselves to give me a meal. They were all leaving the next day for home. It is the first time I've been really full for quite a bit. The Danes were very charming. I'm amused at the way in which my feelings about the Danes vary with the way they treat my stomach.

Today I'm back on the old rations. Hunger is infuriating, stimulating and weakening, all pervading, killing concentration, and rousing the wolf. Today's tragedy: I opened my last tin of margarine and found it was the "stinking" kind. Krilov, on Germany: "You are already guilty, because I am hungry." I'm feeling very weak, but I think it's mainly psychological.

31 March 1945
A bad night. First an air raid, but this time the *Kontroll Offizier* came and caught everyone in bed. There was the usual shouting. In the afternoon, I was waited on by a deputation of Danes to give us some parcels before they left. One made a charming speech, thanking me for looking after them. I did my best in reply, but it's always embarrassing getting your reward in actual food.

1 April 1945
Easter Sunday. I was rather touched by the presents. The Russian orderlies gave me the traditional bread, salt and sugar; the Russian *Kommando* white bread and sugar; the German *Posten* gave me onions, and the German sergeant cake, and I gave myself and "St Boswells" porridge for breakfast. In the

afternoon I was given a great welcome by the Dutch and Russian *Kommandos*.

Wrote a letter of thanks to the Danish Red Cross.

4 April 1945

A foul day. A long sick parade which continued into a migraine which continued into an air raid. The British Red Cross add their quota of stupidity to this lunatic world – a letter asking if we would like a little more vitamin C so that wounds would heal more quickly. "Dear Madam, I see every morning on my sick parade starvation oedema in seven different nations. Do you think I want vitamin C?" Is England so out of touch? It reminds me of a letter I wrote from Madrid to the Spanish Medical Aid Committee about the difference between running wars and garden parties!

7 April 1945

A long sick parade after a bad night of raids and rats. The Germans have something of that clockwork quality, like people carrying on after a death.

I have read Schiller's *Don Carlos*. It's extraordinary that they knew so little about 1550 in 1850, and the plot is too complex. Still, the Duke of Rosa is a fine hero in a big way. I found Lermontov's cradle song perfect when the Russians sang it for me, but the famous one on Pushkin's death I found more difficult. It reads like a lot of special pleading in a rather doubtful cause.

Later there was a tremendous raid, rows and rows of burning lights and not a sound – oddly impressive, like a good silent film after a talkie.

Pump broken, repaired, and broken again.

10 April 1945

The results of the air raids are getting colossal – some like immense Christmas trees, others like glowing banks of embers, but there is still the ghastly ambivalence of "white birds and black birds." We can now hear the guns in the distance, but no one is quite sure from which side!

I've done reasonably well: I have good contacts in all the

Kommandos and am reasonably well liked. The rough plans are ready. All the serious cases have been evacuated.

I'm getting neurotic. I'm worried about the future. Will Britain, Russia, and America lie down like lambs?

I've arranged a party for the staff with all my remaining food. They've been behaving better recently, but this should bring them closer together.

I've been reading odd things: the history of Serbia (there's little to beat it) and some of Spender.

11 April 1945

Guns getting nearer. The sick parade was better – the *Feldwebel* was away. German propaganda fairly piling on the agony: "German POWs in Russian hands are branded and then sent to Siberia," and "German women in American hands are put into US brothels, and to make matters worse they are put on full rations!" Alerts all day.

The staff meal went off well. The menu was potato and gherkin salad; salmon; meat, onions, and potatoes; pancakes; cake and coffee. It looked good, even if the helpings were minute. Conversation was difficult owing to language difficulties, but in the end they managed in *Stalag Deutsch*! There was a sad touch at the end. The English tried to sing a song as a compliment to the Russians and tried "Volga Boatmen" but the Russians had never heard of it! If it is difficult to have peace between Russia and the rest here, it certainly won't be easy after the war. Still, it emphasises the two main difficulties – economic and communication (language and knowledge of each other).

12 April 1945

I found, to my amusement, that I had spent a whole hour looking out of the window – watching for tanks! The Germans are quiet and polite, but F claims that a German woman in the city spat at him when he looked at her lustfully.

I am in a great state of excitement about the present, with gloom about the future. The arrangements are as complete as I can make them. I have nominal rolls of all British POWs in the area. I can neither work nor read, so I've taken to writing verse.

I found an old photo of myself taken in Alexandria. It's difficult to believe it's the same person. I not only look, but feel, different – there's little sense of continuity, and yet somehow when I get back I've got to pick up the trail somewhere.

13 April 1945

Complete evacuation of POWs from Wittenberg ordered. After some argument the Germans agreed to leave us in the *Revier*, and to concentrate there all POWs unable to march. So far Serbs, Indians, and Russians have come into the "zoo." I've made a fair distribution amongst all nations of all stores and talked endlessly to all of them, otherwise there is a sudden outbreak of local peace. It's a perfect day, with a slight haze and bumble bees, and the noise of distant farm work. We're to have five continuous minutes of the siren as *Panzer Alarm* (tank alarm) instead of Fidelio's trumpets! The present inactivity is intolerable. Our problem is how "to bundle time away that the tanks come." Artillery now, west and north.

14 April 1945

New order to evacuate the *Revier*. I compromise by saying that I'll get some of the worst cases ready for transport tomorrow (I had no serious cases left). Artillery now much nearer – apparently north west – almost certainly American. The waiting is intolerable. Wrote more verse:

THE SINS OF THE FATHERS

From Wittenberg-am-Elbe came
Luther and his creed,
And John Knox came from him to save
Poor Scotsmen in their need.

And planted deep the sense of sin
in every good Scots soul,
With gaol and gallows and hell-fire
he fanned the burning coal.

99

The flames are flickering lower now;
It's dead – the creed he built;
But seeds he sowed are with me still –
A tyrant sense of guilt.

So, Wittenberg, you gave me
The role I had to dree;
It's right that you should save me
By dying to make me free.

(I had been much teased, particularly at Elsterhorst, for being overconscientious.)

15 April 1945
A heavy raid in the direction of Berlin – then artillery, then a raid on Wittenberg station. No news. The Russians are worried at the idea of being liberated by the Anglo-Americans, but I think I've cheered them up. Little artillery fire. Why don't the Americans advance from Dessau and Magdeburg? F was caught visiting his French mistress in the town, but nothing happened.

16 April 1945
Bombing and straffing of Wittenberg this morning. No trains now by day. 3 pm, complete peace. 6.30 pm, big attack on station – one plane down. I wonder if anyone knows where I am?

17 April 1945
A quiet night, followed by a lovely day with battle haze to the south, west, and north. The Germans are now shaking hands with me and being helpful. Long talks with the Russian orderlies. We get on well together, but our countries don't. Two raids at night.

18 April 1945
Some good jokes from the Germans about the *Volksturm* (people's storm – the latest German call up). The first runs: "The storm is over, there's only the wind now" (with lavatory associations). The second concerns a group of the *Volksturm* who were found digging in the cemetery. When asked what

they were doing they replied, "We are looking for spare parts for the *Volksturm*." Spent time organising the air raid shelter.

19 April 1945
Another quiet day. Read some Cowper.

20 April 1945
Plenty of activity. Two machine-gunning raids and three bombing raids. Gave out some parcels. Saw a dropped newspaper but there was no advice for people like me. Americans, 30 km; Russians, 100 km.

21 April 1945
Slept for the first time in my clothes. Yugoslavs coming into my zoo in larger numbers and now a Portuguese! I felt much comforted by one of Pushkin's poems:

> Sing not again fair maiden, the songs of sad Georgia;
> They remind me of another life and a distant shore.

And feel vaguely comforted by Heine:

> Und wie viel ist dir geblieben
> und wie schön ist noch die Welt
> und mein Herz was dir gefällt
> Alles, alles, darfst du lieben.
> [And how much is still left, and how wonderful is
> the world. My heart, you can love everything you want.]

... as long as one can love after all this.

Midnight. Panzer alarm given for first time, but nothing happened. Americans, 30 km; Russians, 3 km.

22 April 1945
New American pilot POW has arrived here. He has no news. (The list of nationals I have cared for as a POW doctor are: English, Scots, Welsh, and Irish; Canadian, Australian, New Zealand, American, South African, Sierre Leone, and Algerian; Channel Islands, Portuguese, Spanish, French, Italian, Maltese, German, Austrian, Greek, Yugoslav, Dutch, Polish,

Danish, Albanian, Montenegro, Cypriot, Cretan, Palestinian, Egyptian, Soviet, Indian, Norwegian, and even Brazilian.) Heavy artillery. A drink with the *Feldwebel*.

23 April 1945

Bad night – artillery and nightmares. More talks with Ivan and Megved. They are exactly like the nineteenth century imperialists with their "My country – right or wrong," except that the most intelligent are the most enthusiastic. Friction between Russians and Indians, Russians and Poles, French and Americans, British and Yugoslavs.

Put up Red Cross flags. Midday. Heavy artillery fire on town from east. Very short of food. 7 pm. Still new complications. The American pilot accuses me of starving American POWs to the advantage of the French and Russians. He had seen a Frenchman eating a lettuce! He was incredibly rude. Now the Russians have passed out with "hooch."

F's mistress now demands protection here – from F? I am fed up with this bloody hospital. "St Boswells" is the only sane one left. 6 pm. Factories in town burning.

24 April 1945

A mortar has started outside my window and murdered sleep. F's mistress is causing a lot of trouble. I want her to go but the Germans say she can stay. Food situation serious – went out and scrounged 30 kilos of potatoes and 40 lettuces, and made an issue. First rumours of armistice. Artillery is now going both ways over our heads. Completed plans for liberation by Red Army. Hope to find British liaison officers. I smoked my last cigarette and enjoyed it.

25 April 1945

Complete peace. This is too much – if this is modern mobile warfare, give me Agincourt! I am the only doctor in this area now, and so I agreed to see some German civilians. The day is lovely. "The naked earth is warm with Spring" – but the rest won't do. I retreated into verse!

WITTENBERG

She'd sold herself to him, so now,
she does as he demands;
Harshly discards her cloistered air,
and builds the barricades;
While boys, playing pirates,
earn the right of death
With a plain arm-band.

The hazy sunshine of the April day
Hides boys and barricades,
And decks the tumult of the mind
of nun turned prostitute;
Excited and afraid
She's waiting, waiting
For what night may bring.

(Wittenberg had always been considered a religious city, but it had not openly opposed Hitler. It had tried to be declared an "open city," but Hitler refused, and ordered all boys to be given armbands and arms. I see the city as a nun who realises she hasn't done too well in the past, wondering what is going to happen.)

The Portuguese demands to go and work on the railway; he once got food when he worked there and wants it again, so off he goes into the barrage! I am getting rather maniacal. Everything seems oddly simple: one personal axiom, "Know yourself"; one social maxim, "Treat others as you would like to be treated yourself"; and one international axiom, "One standard of living, equal opportunity for all, and one language."

4 pm. Heavy artillery again, but some POWs insist on sunbathing.

5 pm. The German civilians brought in a small girl; her arm must be amputated. The operation was done in the cellar under the worst possible conditions. When I had finished I found the German guards gone. I took over the hospital with Ivan as second in command. I am now very tired, and theoretically free.

26 April 1945

1 am. Child has secondary haemorrhage; I opened it up and

tied it off. Slept very little. We sent out some Russians to try and make contact, but they failed. 10 am. Little girl much better. Had a long meeting and arranged routine. More Indo-Russian troubles. 12.10. Saw a soldier coming up on a bicycle, with his rifle slung and no tin hat. He seemed casual in no man's land and he turned out to be a Russian. We were officially liberated!

THE RED ARMY

Our liberator was a private soldier, young and healthy. I talked to him with Ivan. (Later the Soviet soldier, Ivan, and I did a tour of the hospital and during this "medical round" the soldier removed a lot of the watches and rings from the patients. He then departed, but returned fairly soon with an officer, who was not medical but very political, and we did another "medical round." His job was to divide my patients into those good and bad politically. All British, American, and French prisoners of war were good. The trouble came with Yugoslavs and Poles. All Soviet patients were removed without discussion. I put up a spirited case, in Russian, for the Poles and Yugoslavs, but I lost a lot. It was the most dreadful travesty of a clinical round that one could experience. It probably helped towards my final resolve to abandon clinical medicine.

The Russian officer told me that I must move out at once. I was angry and upset about the young girl with the amputation, whom I had to abandon, and left a lot of things behind that I should have taken with me. Then we all trailed off. He was most vague about the way, but we finally came into the Russian front line during an artillery barrage.

The Russians were incredible: no tin hats, no shelter; the company office seemed a shambles and no one had any idea what to do with us. The liberated Russians all joined up at once – the chronic tuberculosis cases and those with optic atrophy. They obviously did not want me to protest. I was sorry to say goodbye to Ivan, Megved, and "Don Juan," and they were sorry too. Ivan saved me from becoming the

Figure 6 My restricted corner of the world, November 1941 to May 1945. After Salonica most of my days as a prisoner of war were spent at Hildburghausen, Elsterhorst, near Elsterwerda (from 1965 known as Nardt), and Wittenberg-am-Elbe.

Russian medical officer by saying I was a tuberculosis specialist. There were lots of promises of food and drink, but none came and we were sent off to see their colonel. I made an embarrassed speech of thanks for liberation, while shells landed all round. The Russians were completely unmoved – even when someone was killed quite near. I started thinking them brave; I soon found them callous. We were then sent off to an unknown town. We did not wait; the barrage was too heavy. The remaining party – Serbs, French, Indians, Americans, and British – took to the road. We soon collected bicycles and trucks, and a holiday spirit prevailed. F's mistress managed to keep with us. She was now terrified of a Russian rape – with reason. I talked to several Russian officers. Some were hostile and suspicious. One asked, "Why should we let you go home if you're going to fight against us?" I decided to go to Zahna where we knew there had been a hospital for prisoners of war which had been liberated some time before. I soon lost my watch and so did my patients. I had asked a Soviet soldier the way and, although he had four watches already, he was very persistent and fingered his tommy gun.

We reached Zahna by nightfall, dead tired, and I fortunately met a Russian orderly whom I had known in imprisonment. He had somehow become a doctor since liberation, but was friendly and gave us some rooms and food. I got a great welcome from my old Russian patients. The Russians refused, at first, to look after the Yugoslavs or French. After some argument I got permission for the French to stay, but the Yugoslavs were not recognised. The oddest thing is the complete lack of mechanisation in the Red Army. We saw no mechanised vehicles all day, except some cars captured from the Germans. I'm very tired; liberation has been a bit of a flop!

27 April 1945
A quiet day. The French, sensing hostility, went off to live off the land, leaving F, a French orderly, and F's mistress. She insists on having F, the French orderly, and myself in this tiny room to protect her. An Englishman has arrived from the POW camp at Luckenwalde. His story is that they were liberated some time ago. The senior British officer ordered all POWs to stay there, but the Russians couldn't give them any food, and this one got fed up and came away. He says there is a lot of friction between allied POWs and the Russians.

Here my chief impression is one of extreme variety – cruelty and kindness, discipline and indiscipline, friendliness and suspicion, efficiency and inefficiency. I have failed to arrange anything as regards food and we can't get a radio. My party is now reduced to 4 Americans, 1 Indian, 2 British, 1 South African, and 2 French.

28 April 1945
Very disturbed night – got up in a foul temper. The sanitation is disgraceful. Spent the whole day talking to the Russians. In general they are charming and ignorant, but I was a bit upset when they had never heard of the International Brigade. All liberated Soviet POWs and civilians are being given three days' training here before going into the Army at the front. Efficient inhumanity! I visited the local *Kommandant*. He knew very little, except that we couldn't have a wireless. I'm getting worried.

29 April 1945
Another bad day and night. The *Kommandant* said we ought to go to Schönewalde, wherever that may be, but agreed it was impossible without food or transport. He also said he couldn't give us any food. He gave me permission to go to Wittenberg, as long as I walked. More talks to Russians – they are incredibly conceited and childish. The local military paper has a terrific attack on our policy in Greece. Is the alliance as thin as all that? The two armies met at Torgau on the 25th. General Nyxob got a big write up for liberating Wittenberg.

Life is pretty intolerable. Thank God "St Boswells" is still here. The Russian sanitation is hopeless.

30 April 1945
Up early and did the long walk to Wittenberg and visited the Russian *Kommandant*. He was a quiet, worried man. He said he couldn't send us to the Americans, but agreed we ought to have food although he wouldn't give me a written order to the *Kommandant* at Zahna about it. I then went back to the old hospital – someone had been through it very thoroughly. I talked to the civilians round about. The stories of sudden death and rape are impressive. I asked about the little girl, and was told she was in a house down the road, so I went down to see her. To my surprise she was very well. (I cleaned her up

and put on a clean dressing, and then a very tough Soviet tankist came in and for the next hour and a half I was very near sudden death. The young Russian said he was going to shoot me for helping the Germans and pointed his gun at me. In absolute despair I asked him about his medals and fortunately it worked. A sudden death for helping fascists, after Spain and POW life, would have been rather hard!) I hurried away – and then back to Zahna. I went to a lecture for liberated Soviet POWs. I couldn't understand very much, but the possibility of future wars was laid on heavily. I talked to the Russian doctor about the lavatory – it was flooded and stinking. He saw no need for action.

1 May 1945
Woke to find someone had made the last lavatory unusable. Went to the *Kommandant* – long talk over Schnapps. Summary: Russia wants peace for 50 years; Poland and Yugoslavia will be communist at once, Italy and France very soon; Great Britain and America will remain capitalist until about AD 2000, when the last war will take place. They are incredibly ignorant about America. They really think *Uncle Tom's Cabin* is the latest book on the subject. They didn't like the idea of a Labour party in power in England. She would be easier to attack in AD 2000 if she remained capitalistic! No progress about transport or food, but I've arranged a little with the Russian doctor. Mussolini hanged. Rumours of peace.

2 May 1945
Life really intolerable. Everything is so difficult – lavatories, washing, food, cooking, even conversation. The usual long talks to Russians about how they won their medals. No news, no transport, no radio. I have finally decided to go back to Wittenberg. We know where to get food there, and there is more hope of contacting the Americans. Final visit to the *Kommandant*; he was completely tight and couldn't even speak.

3 May 1945

A busy day. I first bicycled to Wittenberg and got permission from the *Kommandant* there to bring the rest. I then bicycled back to Zahna and we set off with a cart, which we pulled, with the patients on bicycles. There are only 10 now. The journey back was tiring. The Americans tended to stray, but we finally did it and got the old hospital organised again. I then went down to the town and fortunately met an American officer. He promised to send transport. We have collected three more British from Luckenwalde. The situation there must be tricky.

4 May 1945

Feeling better – managed to loot a lot of food. In Wittenberg I met an American padre. He offered to take me along, and roared with laughter and called me a sucker when I said I had to stay with my patients. The little girl is said to be doing well, but I am too cowardly to visit her. The food position is much better.

5 May 1945

The British from Luckenwalde decide to cross the Elbe and try to contact the Americans. F decided to go too. I don't blame him, but there will be hell to pay with his mistress. Crowds of Americans are coming through on foot from Luckenwalde in spite of their orders. It's amusing to see how the rank slowly rises. A Russian company is now sharing the hospital with us. They are friendly and have given us some food. Their guns are shockingly cared for. Now F's mistress wants to come back with a French orderly into my room to sleep! She says she is in real danger from the Russians. I finally agreed – and then she went out and worked the pump in knickers and brassiere in front of the Russians!

7 May 1945

The waiting is terrible. Verse again:

REBIRTH

The doors are open and the wire is down;
The Germans gone and we are all but free;
Like birds in cage who find an open door,
And frolic in the room until by chance
They reach a window and can see their kin
Free in the open air,
And then their freedom's naught.
So we gaze longingly across the Elbe;
Half dead as prisoners, half alive as men;
Waiting, waiting,
'Til life shall come.

(I don't think this needs any comment.)

FREEDOM

Why do I think of doubt and death
When tomorrow I may be free?
Why do I think of everyone's fate,
save my own – whoever they be?

You can cut the wire and shoot the "Goons,"
Sink the "Lager"[15] under the sea,
Find me, and free me and send me home,
But I know I'll never be free.

I'm my gaoler; the prison's my soul.
Fate fixed what had to be.
I've fought and struggled and sought out help,
But I'll never, never, be free.

(This latter was, I think, written the day before the American ambulance came. It reflects my worry about the possibility of being rehabilitated after POW life, and my long running troubles, which had in fact worried me very little in POW life. It was the last verse I have ever written.)

At 4 pm the American truck arrived and off we went. My goodbye to F's mistress destroyed any pleasure I might have had. The American officer had refused my request to take her with us, and smiled in a knowing way.

FOUR DAYS WITH THE UNITED STATES ARMY

We went first to the prisoner of war camp at Luckenwalde. The situation there seemed tense. The Russians refused to let any prisoners leave, so we went off to an old prisoner of war camp near Magdeburg on the other side of the Elbe. I did not feel really happy until we crossed the Elbe. We got a meal there and then went off to sleep – a long glorious sleep in which I shed all my responsibilities.

8 May 1945
I had left all my books and papers in a wooden box, with my name and rank on it, with the staff sergeant at the company office. I went to see them the next day and found, to my horror, that not only had the box been broken open but the books had been stolen and all my papers torn up. I nearly wept, quite literally. The books didn't matter, but the notes and essays were really all that was left of four years. A lot of diaries from Hildburghausen and Elsterhorst had gone and some of the papers about Salonica, including those concerned with the "case-control" trial. I decided to go for a walk before doing anything. My feelings were a bit too strong. Finally, after an hour's walk I decided to do nothing. The papers were irreplaceable; the books I could easily get again. A row would not help at all. There was enough ill will between the Americans and the British without adding to it. What with Russians and Americans, I shall leave imprisonment as naked as I entered.

The food is good but ill chosen. It is high in protein and vitamins and low in fats and carbohydrates. This stimulates without satisfying. POWs want to feel full. Surely the Americans should know that. The POWs from Luckenwalde are very truck conscious! Once bitten ... They never leave the trucks now except for meals.

9 May 1945
Said to be V day – no sign of it here. Woken at 5 am unnecessarily. There is no organisation here. Americans think that if they give you enough food you'll be happy, so they

don't think of anything else. It's really a gloomy place; conversation is mostly about the "F–ing French" and the "Bloody Russians." Germans now get little mention. I haven't heard the whisper of an intellectual, but they may exist. The mass neurosis of the POWs from Luckenwalde is frightening. Some are going off on foot. A young Canadian got drowned trying to save a German girl who fell into the river.

I spend the time reading and writing, and am not too sanguine for the future. All we know is that we may move tomorrow. All movement of POWs over the Elbe is forbidden by the Russians. Anglo-American feeling is still fair. I met a Lithuanian girl engaged to a Czech boy. What are my problems to theirs? Heard English news for the first time. Rumour that the Russians are holding the POWs until the Polish question is settled.

10 May 1945
Up early – usual shambles of organisation. Someone has stolen my soap and cigarettes. Truck journey to Hildesheim. In general big towns are bombed flat; villages unaffected. Houses suffered more than railways. We finally got out and were marched into a camp, where I became an officer again and was duly installed in a reasonable room. Unfortunately my companions turned out to be Polish officers from Warsaw and I had to listen to the whole Katyn problem over again. When will this Polish problem end? I have been discussing it nearly continuously since the news first broke in Germany in 1941. I am utterly convinced the Soviet were responsible but what can we do about it now?

11 May 1945
Flew to Brussels and reached the quiet friendly efficiency of the British Army at last.

(Salonica and Wittenberg were the two main crises in my prisoner of war life. I think I survived the latter because of a better supply of books to read, but in both a feeling of responsibility and ability to write bad verse helped a great deal.)

HOME

I reached London by train and took a taxi to my old flat in Gloucester Place. I was relieved to see it still standing – though there had been a bomb very near. I got into my flat – I cannot remember how – and, though it was down at heel, it was still my own place, reflecting my own taste, and it warmed my heart that there was this much continuity.

My first need was for human contact and I seized the telephone and my old book of telephone numbers. I must have made about 30 calls that night, without achieving a single contact. I fell asleep feeling lonely. I do not remember clearly what I did the next day. There was some useless telephoning; a visit to the bank where I laboriously had to prove that I was I; and a short visit to University College Hospital where I could not see anybody I knew, and fled. I hated London – the noise, the crowds, and the traffic (prisoner of war life in general had been rural). I decided to leave at once for Scotland where my sister lived, and where I knew I would get a warm welcome. I tried to telephone her and failed again. I caught the night train. It was crowded and I got little sleep. I got out at Galashiels at about 7.30 am and carried my bags to my sister's house. I arrived when my sister and her three children were at breakfast. (Her husband, Donald Stalker, was still in the Army in Italy.) My sister gave me the welcome I needed. The children were less enthusiastic. They had no idea who I was. One – Susan – with a beautiful Scots accent, asked, "Who's you?" I relaxed and felt sure I would recover as time passed, with the help of my sister. I began to realise my problems. The most important was an unconscious, which later became conscious, sense of guilt about having been taken prisoner, and having been out of the war for four years. It was entirely irrational. I never met anyone who despised those who had been taken prisoner – quite the reverse – but it was a widespread feeling amongst repatriated prisoners of war. This caused social difficulties. I hated meeting people – except immediate family – who had not been prisoners of war and I was embarrassed even when going shopping. My sister found some suitable ex-prisoners of war and slowly diluted them with others. I recovered fairly quickly.[16]

Then there was my meanness. I had, it is true, become an expert black marketeer in Germany, but I had not signed a cheque or used money for four years. The result was that I had become mean. Unconsciously I believed I was poor. It took a lot of argument from my sister and lawyer before I realised that I was actually rather wealthy. I was excused income tax because I had been "resident abroad" for four years!

I recovered quickly thanks to that homely, loving environment, and was soon visiting "Bill" (the Pole – chapter 2) in a hospital in Edinburgh. The surgeons had decided that an operation was inadvisable and he had become a difficult patient. I briefly saw the young Norwegian seaman, in whose case I had cheated to get him repatriated. He, although grateful, was beginning to give most of the credit to God. I also visited some of the patients with tuberculosis whom I had treated in Germany and who lived in Scotland. Most of them were ill and I think only one survived to benefit from streptomycin.

I was enormously impressed by my sister. I had remembered her as an upper middle class, happily married woman with three children and two servants, and a lovely house and garden. She had adapted herself to running everything herself without servants, done a great deal of voluntary war work, and remained intelligent, kindly, amusing, and sociable. I could do little then to reward her except give her my excess food and clothing coupons. I possibly went some way in repaying my debt by helping to save her life some years later (see page 227).

One of my sister's kindnesses had been to members of the Polish Army billeted in Galashiels, and I met many of them. The great debate about the Katyn massacres became part of my daily conversation again, and still crops up occasionally 35 years later.

The Army only gave me six weeks' leave after four years as a prisoner of war. I calculated that in all I had had about 20–30 days in those four years during which I had not been active medically or as a German-speaking officer negotiating with the Germans. I was rather bitter about it at the time, but as regards rehabilitation it worked out well. I think I spent about four weeks in Scotland before going back to my flat in London. I was then able to recontact many of my old friends. I remember particularly meeting Joan Stokes, Ros Pitt-Rivers, Philip D'Arcy Hart, and, I think, J B S Haldane before I rejoined the Army. They treated me kindly. After a lot of thought I rather hushed up the poor treatment I had received from the Soviet troops. I thought that it was so important to help the fragile entente between the Soviet and the other allies. At the same time, I made it clear to my left wing political friends that, after learning all I had about the Soviet Union from Soviet citizens, I would never, ever, join the Communist party of the United Kingdom.

Eventually I was sent to a military hospital at St Albans where everyone was kind to me. I am afraid I have forgotten names, but all the officers, nurses, and staff helped to rehabilitate me. I was put in charge of the tuberculosis ward and was, I think, quite a success from the point of view of morale. I wrote two articles, one for the *Lancet*[17] and one for the *British Medical Journal*,[18] which were later published, and made an application for a Rockefeller fellowship in preventive medicine, which involved a preliminary course at the London School of Hygiene and Tropical Medicine, followed by a year's training in the USA. My rehabilitation was complete. I could review my past mistakes without shame, and I could make use of my past experiences. I was determined to find a useful role in preventing a socially important disease in a way that was intellectually stimulating. Fortunately the Rockefeller Foundation accepted me and I had a real chance of doing something. I was also cheered by being awarded an MBE for services in prisoner of war camps.[19]

The Diploma in Public Health course started in 1946 and lasted until June 1947. The great thing about it was that I was taught medical statistics by Dr (later Sir) Austin Bradford Hill and Donald Reid. It was a wonderful piece of luck, but my good fortune almost ran out before I had finished the course, when I went down with a bad attack of pneumonia. Everyone seemed to think it was tuberculosis, but all went well and I managed to get my Diploma in Public Health. Then I went with my sister's family to Bamburgh, one of Northumberland's great coastal treasures, to await a place on a boat for the USA.

THE USA

It was an extraordinary experience for an ex-prisoner of war, after only 18 months in rationed UK, to arrive in New York in 1947. The first impression was of freedom to do anything you liked, as long as you had enough money. There was the size of the beefsteaks in the restaurants; I was incapable of eating a whole steak. Then the lowness of the Rockefeller fellowship salaries paid by the Foundation in those days. I worked out that if you did not smoke or drink, lived quietly in cheap lodgings and did not have your hair cut too often, you would survive. I raised this financial problem with the Foundation's representative in New York. Clearly he was not interested. I then turned to relatives in the USA to get a loan. There was an Archie Cochrane, a second cousin, whom I knew to be a wealthy man, in Chattanooga. I wrote to him and he responded warmly and invited me to visit him. Unfortunately, I wrote the next letter on Henry Phipps Medical Clinic notepaper. He broke off relations at once. He was the leading Christian Scientist in Chattanooga! The other was a fragile old bachelor in Boston, with whom I spent a weekend. He was a dear and rather hard up, but he entertained me well and I could not bring myself to ask him for a loan. I did get some money through a friend who came for a short visit, but the main reason I lived and worked fairly successfully in the USA with a reasonable standard of living was because of the extraordinary generosity of the American people. It was amazing how they supported me.

Chief amongst them was the Bullitt family in Philadelphia, where I worked for more than a year at the Henry Phipps Institute. My family had met the Bullitts on a cruise to Norway in 1926. Our family then consisted of a widow, one daughter, and two sons, and theirs of an Archdeacon, his wife, and two daughters. For various reasons we got on well together. Margaret visited us shortly after the death of my brother and coped well in a difficult situation. The other sister had visited me in Cambridge, when I had not behaved very well. But when they heard I was living in the YMCA in Philadelphia I was immediately removed to a luxurious life out on the "main line." The family at that time consisted of a charming old lady, an unmarried daughter, and a married daughter with a family living nearby. Their kindness was overwhelming and I am still deeply grateful to them. Apart from those in the clinic, others to help me during my stay in the USA were Eddie Cohn, son of Professor Cohn of vitamin B12 fame, in Boston, and Dr Hardy, the berylliosis researcher,[20] also of Boston. They more than made up for the meanness of the Foundation.

The Henry Phipps Clinic was an excellent experience for me. Esmond Long was a wise and kind director and his colleagues Drs Hetherington and Lurie taught me a great deal. With Hetherington's help I made valuable advances in my interpretation of chest films, and Lurie laid the foundations to my interest in BCG immunisation.[21] I also enjoyed some heated arguments with Lurie about the future of Palestine. Then there was Florence Seibert with whose research I became caught up all too briefly. I developed the greatest admiration and affection for her and greatly appreciated the kind references she made to me some 20 years later in her book *Pebbles on the Hill of a Scientist*.[22]

I started at the Phipps by helping with the routine work of the clinic and improving my interpretation of chest films, but was encouraged to take up some research of my own. As a result I did undertake one or two minor projects on my own initiative, including attempting to improve laryngeal swabs by trying to fashion the swab from a highly absorbent seaweed extract, a material that became eminently transparent in water (I can remember discussing its fascinating potential as a fabric for ladies' bathing costumes), and working with Florence Seibert trying to develop the basis of a test for multiple sclerosis. These projects did not lead anywhere, but it was in this period that an interest that was to remain with me for the rest of my life began to emerge, an interest in medical error. I remember being fascinated by a paper published at about that time by C C Birkelo et al, which measured the inter- and intra-differences of radiologists interpreting chest films of different sizes.[23] At that time radiologists classified chest films diagnosed as tuberculous as "active," "quiescent," or "inactive," but it was far from clear whether the classification had any true predictive value. It slowly occurred to me that the vast data bank of the Henry Phipps Clinic offered a means of testing whether the three terms had real prognostic value. The clinic was a particularly good place in which to conduct such an investigation because x rays were always read independently of case histories, and the follow up of all cases was carefully pursued. Therefore I initiated what I saw as a necessary line of inquiry into the relationship between x ray prognosis and actual outcome. This involved me in extracting from the clinic's massive files all the case notes of newly diagnosed cases of tuberculosis in the period 1925–45, which was quite an exercise. It was out of this work that I eventually published a short paper on the value of x ray prognosis in the investigation of tuberculosis, a paper that very nearly escaped the light of day. Initially it was rejected by the *American Review of Tuberculosis*, after which it almost suffered the same fate at the editorial hands of the *American Journal of Roentgenology and Radium Therapy*. Fortunately Esmond Long's powers of persuasion saved the day for me and it did eventually get into print.[24]

In my leisure time in my last few months in the USA I managed to get in some skiing and riding, having succeeded at last in supplementing my meagre funds with a little extra money from home. I remember, too, a wonderful summer holiday by the sea, given to me by the Bullitts. There was also the last of my unfortunate love affairs. All in all, though, it was a valuable time in which I started to catch up with a world I seemed to have been out of for all too long. As I sailed home, after a farewell dinner with Eddie Cohn in New York, I felt rehabilitated, grateful, and determined to have no further love affairs.

EARLY DAYS AT THE PNEUMOCONIOSIS
RESEARCH UNIT, 1948–50

When I returned home I was optimistic about the prospects of a job. I had for some while hoped to work for my old friend Dr Philip D'Arcy Hart, who was now attached to the National Institute for Medical Research at Mill Hill and involved in a major trial of the effectiveness of streptomycin in the treatment of tuberculosis. Unfortunately the chance of an association with this project did not materialise and I was left at square one. I then became enthusiastic about the possibility of investigating the impact of the most up-to-date facilities for tuberculosis prevention on three Scottish border towns, perhaps because the introduction of comprehensive programmes of BCG immunisation and mass x ray surveillance by local public health authorities seemed, in general, to be remarkably slow. Certainly the time seemed right for a demonstration of their effectiveness in terms of the reduction in tuberculosis that could be achieved across whole communities. My plan was to compare the impact of introducing BCG immunisation, mass x raying, and the hospitalisation of all infectious cases differentially into three comparable Scottish towns – Galashiels, Selkirk, and Hawick. Sir Edward Mellanby, secretary of the Medical Research Council, encouraged the idea initially, but then there proved to be difficulties in early liaison between MRC officials in London and administrators in Scotland, which prevented the project from going ahead. My own preliminary investigations also revealed that the three towns were far less comparable in their experience of tuberculosis than they needed to be for such a project. This second line of interest abandoned, I took up an invitation to meet Dr Charles Fletcher,[25] the director of the MRC's recently established Pneumoconiosis Research Unit in Cardiff; a unit set up in 1945 to advance the study of coal workers' pneumoconiosis, which at that time constituted a major problem for the coal industry. We met for lunch in a Greek restaurant somewhere off the Tottenham Court Road, on one of Charles Fletcher's trips up to town, and he supplied the background information I needed on pneumoconiosis and the challenge it represented for his unit.

It had been known at least since the middle ages that men mining in rock often died prematurely of a disease resembling tuberculosis (phthisis) and actually called miners' phthisis. Paracelsus had written of its effects. When in the nineteenth century silica in rock had become implicated as fundamental to its cause, it had become known as silicosis. Unfortunately, when the first compensation concessions were introduced for those afflicted with silicosis, those mining in coal rather than rock were ignored because compensation was firmly tied to exposure to silica. It was only when chest x rays first began to probe the situation that this anomaly began to be recognised. Coal miners with premature breathlessness and suffering from what had long been known as miners' asthma exhibited similar x ray pictures to those of men disabled by silicosis. Even then compensation was extended only to miners who had at some time worked in rock; a case of old attitudes die hard. Then, in the late 1930s, the findings of an MRC chest x ray survey of miners in South Wales, conducted by Drs Philip D'Arcy Hart and E A Aslett, firmly established that miners who had never worked in rock could be similarly affected. This survey also differentiated an earlier stage of the disease and led to a recommendation that miners should be removed from the mines at this stage and awarded compensation. Hart and Aslett also pointed out that the disease was particularly common among the miners of the hard coal mines of West Wales who were working in anthracite. This opened the way to a massive increase in certifications and, by 1945, 5 per cent of the country's coalmining population, and up to 20 per cent of the miners at some collieries, had been certified as having the disease and removed from work. It looked increasingly as though the future of the industry in South and West Wales was endangered, and at the recommendation of the Ministry of Fuel and Power, the MRC had responded, in 1945, by inaugurating a research unit in Cardiff, close to the heart of the problem, to look into all aspects of the disease's development, prevention, and treatment.[26]

Concerning the natural history of the disease, it had long

been accepted that it was progressive in character and stemmed from dust inhalation, but we needed to know a great deal more about its progression and whether factors other than dust were involved in its initiation and development. The x ray and pathological studies had already demonstrated coal workers' pneumoconiosis to be divisible into two clearly distinguishable phases. It began, characteristically, with the development in the lung of collections of small, fibrous, dust-containing nodules – a condition known as simple pneumoconiosis (pnc) – and only became seriously disabling if it progressed to a more complex sequence of secondary developments, known as progressive massive fibrosis (PMF), which, as the name suggests, involved the formation of more expansive fibrous masses (see figure 7). What we did not know was just how the two phases related, although there was no shortage of hypotheses. The simplest held that all steps in the progression of the disease emanated from continuing exposure to dust, while a more strongly held Cardiff viewpoint saw tuberculosis as the initiator of PMF. Jethro Gough, the professor of pathology in Cardiff, and an associate of the Pneumoconiosis Research Unit, maintained that PMF had its origins in an interaction between simple pneumoconiosis and pulmonary tuberculosis. Certainly there was a lot about PMF and pulmonary tuberculosis that looked radiographically similar, and subjects with PMF commonly showed positive reactions to tuberculin.

I was so interested in the appointment Charles Fletcher was about to make, and for which I had already been recommended by Dr Jerry Morris of the MRC,[27] that I arranged to go down to Cardiff almost immediately to see something of the unit at first hand. I had in fact visited it briefly before going to the USA and had not been impressed. I had met the wrong people. This time things were different. I met with Charles Fletcher, John Gilson, and Philip Hugh-Jones, all Cambridge physiologists like myself; Martin Wright, a pathologist and inventor, also from Cambridge; and Peter Oldham, a statistician trained by Bradford Hill, who had originally been at Oxford. I was impressed by all of them. They were deeply committed to the research, very friendly, and the kind of people with whom I would be able to communicate easily. They were looking for someone who could interpret the chest *x* ray films of miners and who was prepared to do this in the field, while making measurements of the incidence of pneumoconiosis in mining populations. I explained to them that I was not a trained radiologist, but that I had considerable experience of interpreting chest films and had proved reasonably "reproducible." I also added that I was interested in measuring the errors and variation involved in *x* ray interpretation. Beyond this, I thought it important to point out the limitations of my rather amateurish experience in trying to examine populations defined by a barbed wire in wartime.

After references were given I was offered the job and did not hesitate long. It was almost hand tailored to my dreams and abilities: an approach to a considerable social problem in which I would have opportunities to apply epidemiological and statistical methods. There was even a chance that tuberculosis, my initial research interest, would feature prominently in our studies, given its possible status in the aetiology of PMF. My one doubt – and in retrospect I find that I was right to have doubts – was about living in Wales. I had two homes, one in Galashiels and one in London, and Wales seemed like outer darkness. Nevertheless, I went ahead, sold my London flat, arranged to store my furniture in Cardiff, and set out for South Wales. I had been fond of my home at 101 Gloucester Place, W1, and felt something of a wrench in parting. The sadness I experienced, however, was more than eclipsed by the realisation that I had another chance to live up to earlier ambitions. I realised too that it would be my last chance and was determined to make a success of it.

The Pneumoconiosis Research Unit I joined had been established just over two years earlier, and I felt fortunate to be joining it rather late. The difficulties of Charles Fletcher's early days in getting arrangements off the ground have been recorded elsewhere,[28] but it is worth stressing the kind of challenge he had taken on. It was not easy for a lone English physiologist, who had seen precious little of coalmines, to walk into a central role in an essentially Welsh mining drama, even with all the support of the MRC. Whatever his abilities, he had to be seen as an outsider inflicted by London, and it is to his great credit that the unit took shape as quickly as it did, although it cannot have been without considerable personal stress. By the time I joined the unit the early problems of staffing and locating the right accommodation had largely been solved. Arrangements for a new building in the grounds of Llandough Hospital, which lay just south of the city, were already well advanced. Among the staff members I was still to meet were three other medically qualified colleagues: Idris Davies, with whom I was to read many thousands of chest films; Karl Mann, who later became a very senior administrator in Israel; and Owen Wade, later professor of pharmaceutical medicine at Birmingham. They were all good company and excellent at their jobs. In fact the medical staff were generally of a higher calibre than their non-medical colleagues, although there were a number of notable exceptions, such as Peter Oldham and Stan Roach, an engineer who joined us a little later, and I must not overlook the immense contribution made to the quality of x ray films by Bill Clarke, the unit's senior radiographer.

Through everyday dialogue with colleagues, rather than any formal briefing, I soon learnt what was expected of me. In addition to devoting a major proportion of my time in early months to the interpretation of chest films, it was also hoped that I would assist work going on in the unit to develop a better radiographic classification of the various stages of pneumoconiosis. This was important. There were too many systems of classification in existence, most of them predating the kinds of radiographic refinements now available; systems that had grown up in different places, at different times, and which varied widely in diagnostic criteria and terminology. Given the importance of the disease and the fact that it could only be diagnosed in the living subject radiographically, the need for a validated and internationally recognised system of radiographic classification was pre-eminent.[29] Until this problem was solved a high degree of confusion would continue to undermine research, nationally and internationally. A second major aspect of my work would be in surveying mining populations to develop a more detailed picture of the incidence of pnc and PMF. For this it was expected that I would soon begin to build up my own survey team, as well as my own survey skills. A further and related expectation was that I would devise a questionnaire by which to take the industrial histories of the miners we needed to research. There was also, in the background, a hope that I would eventually contribute to the planning of future research.

The first colliery x ray surveys in which I was involved resulted from a visit to the unit by the Minister of Fuel and Power, Hugh Gaitskell, who felt that comparative studies of the incidence of pneumoconiosis across a range of different collieries and coalfields might throw light on some of the major questions, such as why some "high dust" pits clearly had low levels of pneumoconiosis. Although not entirely

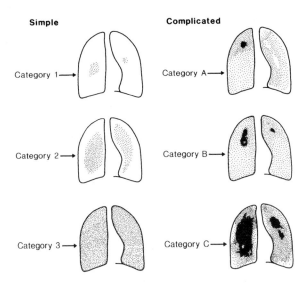

Figure 7 The x ray classification of coalworkers' pneumoconiosis. Radiographic appearances in diagrammatic outline: categories 1, 2, and 3 of simple pneumoconiosis and A, B, and C of progressive massive fibrosis. The MRC Pneumoconiosis Research Unit played a major part in the development and promotion of this radiographic system of categorisation, which in 1958 became the basis of an international radiographic system of classification.

original it was a good idea, and as a result I took part in four comparative colliery surveys in my first two years at the unit. Regrettably they yielded little useful scientific evidence because of the limited thought given to the selection of the collieries we visited, but for me they had other benefits. In addition to wonderful opportunities to improve and sharpen my reading of *x* ray films, I had an invaluable introduction to the cutting end of the industry with which I was now associated.

In the first survey, at the Haig Colliery, Whitehaven, Cumberland, in May 1949, John Gilson was in charge and helped me a great deal. The visit predated the acquisition of our own mobile *x* ray unit, and we made use of equipment available at a nearby clinic belonging to the Millom Haematite and Iron Company, and employed for the *x* ray surveillance of local haematite miners. I remember John Craw, the company's medical officer, attending to our needs very well. It was during this survey that I began to learn something of the caution that needed to be exercised in our relationship with the coal industry, and the narrow path one often had to tread between the interests of the National Coal Board (NCB) on the one hand and the National Union of Mineworkers (NUM) on the other. Two incidents illustrated the sensitivities that prevailed. Firstly, although Charles Fletcher had negotiated the necessary permission we needed for such a survey with the NCB regional headquarters, we were still apprehended by NCB officials, and interviewed by the area manager on the day of our arrival. For some reason information about our work had not filtered down to those in charge locally. Fortunately I found that I knew the area manager. We had been contemporaries at Uppingham School, and he did his best to advise us. So far as I can remember, this was the only advantage I ever received from the famed "old boys" network. The problem rested with the regional manager in Newcastle who we discovered had been unhappy with arrangements from the very beginning. A hastily arranged meeting with him revealed why. His view was that investigations into the state of health and conditions in any colliery could well lead to suspicion on the part of the workforce about management interests and possible redundancies and changes in work practices. Talking with him was difficult, given his stiff and uncompromising attitude, and it was not until Charles Fletcher arrived at the point of calling off the survey that he began to reconsider the stance he had taken. In summing up our position Charles pointed out that the project had NUM support, and that all he required in calling off the survey was an assurance from the regional manager that he would explain to the union and its members why the region objected to relevant medical research.

My initial experience of difficulties between the NCB and NUM was more complex. I have forgotten the details, but during our time at the Haig Colliery we received a request that all the chest films from our survey should be put into a bank, unread, until certain negotiations between the two bodies were completed. Although the miners' union naturally welcomed any initiative intended to assist industrial health interests, it still found it difficult to overcome suspicions about how results might be used. I think we finally got permission to read the films for tuberculosis and cancer at once, but had to agree to the request in all other respects. All in all it was an interesting introduction to such difficulties. Some time later I found myself needing to work out a compromise between an NUM request that I should be available to talk to individual miners about their x ray results and the reasonable alternative demand on the part of the Pneumoconiosis Medical Panel, which awarded compensation, that I refrain from any reference to compensation prospects. As my x ray readings were proving similar to theirs, however, I felt justified in working out a system of merely giving betting odds on the likely results, and conservative ones at that. I did not want anybody disappointed! It was a system that worked remarkably well. All miners understand betting odds.

From the point of view of relations with the NCB and NUM, the next survey, in West Wales, was a remarkably friendly affair. On this occasion our main difficulties were technical, not diplomatic. We got into serious difficulties because of a variable electricity supply, which led to a high recall and retake rate in order to get consistently satisfactory *x* ray films. Clearly we needed an independent and more reliable electricity supply – a requirement soon attended to by John Gilson's technical expertise. The next survey was in Lancashire, at the Bankhall Colliery, and was marked by the arrival of our new *x* ray van (see plate 7), which only just made it, arriving there still in its priming. This mobile unit proved an invaluable acquisition, although while in Lancashire there was one unfortunate incident due to inadequate ventilation in the darkroom. Beyond such advances in our technical resources there was also an improvement in our own performance, bringing higher response rates than we had achieved before. Undoubtedly this was because we were getting to know more about the working miners themselves. It is also true that we were more experienced in our relations with the NCB and NUM, which did a great deal to smooth our path. Of particular interest on this occasion was the low prevalence of pneumoconiosis we recorded, although dust levels were relatively high. Even more puzzling was our finding that where the disease did exist it had a high progression rate. Clearly we needed to know a lot more about dust.

The fourth survey at Wattstown, in mid-Glamorgan, was much the most interesting from my point of view. It was, in the first place, my introduction to the Rhondda Fach, the "Little Rhondda," where I was to spend so much of my working life. I am still working there while drafting this chapter in 1983. It was also my first follow up survey, where my eyes were opened to two important facts. Firstly, I became conscious of the very selected nature of the population of working miners we were examining. All those diagnosed as suffering from PMF, tuberculosis, or cancer at the time of the first survey had left the mine, representing a serious loss of follow-up data. We needed to know how their conditions had progressed just as much as we needed to know about the working miners. It was essential to include ex-miners in all our future reckonings. At Wattstown I also became aware of the possibility of achieving high response rates to follow-up studies and being able to investigate the incidence and attack rates of pnc and PMF with the kind of accuracy often only thought possible in laboratory research.

It was the Wattstown survey that really got me hooked on

the study of pneumoconiosis. It was also the time that I got to know Stan Roach well. It was he who explained to me the various engineering problems of coalmining, not from the sidelines but, characteristically, on the shop floor, underground. We spent many hours with mining teams, watching coal-getting, some on unforgettable night shifts. One of the problems with which we became increasingly preoccupied was that of getting to know more about pit dust and its rates of inhalation by individual miners. It was also in this period that I had the opportunity to get to know some of the miners and to admire their curious combination of earnestness and humour. Pneumoconiosis, which affected so many of their lives, was indeed a problem worth solving.

Technically such surveys led to rapid improvements. We achieved a 100 per cent response rate for the first time. Certainly my reading of so many x rays in such short periods assisted my own expertise. Also, the questionnaire I designed for taking industrial histories proved an unexpected success. It was not necessary to modify it for many years. Even a brief, rather impromptu questionnaire I produced at the time of the Haig colliery survey for recording respiratory symptoms and smoking habits had its importance. Although it demonstrated a large observer error, it could be claimed to be the ancestor of the MRC's well known respiratory questionnaire. It was, I believe, the first time that a well defined population had been asked about its smoking, and as a result we were able to show that there was no association between smoking and simple pneumoconiosis. We also became aware, as a result of these surveys, just how far estimates of the incidence of a medical condition in a community could vary with the percentage of the population examined. I think it was at this point in my research career that I decided always to aim for response rates of at least 90 per cent. I also became convinced in the course of these surveys that x raying pit populations and trying to relate pneumoconiosis incidence to conditions experienced by miners underground was a waste of time until we had the means of collecting data on dust inhalation.

Whatever doubts I held about the value of current surveys, I was completely hooked on pneumoconiosis research and increasingly my mind turned towards future research strategies. In particular I found myself wanting to know more about the cause of PMF, perhaps because I found its results so horrific. If we could show that tuberculosis was the critical causal factor, transforming simple pneumoconiosis into this far more devastating condition, such a finding could have immense implications for prevention, given the increasing availability of BCG immunisation and x ray surveillance. Undoubtedly it was this pressing concern to do something about PMF that led to my formulating a major research proposal within two years of arriving in Cardiff, although I was inevitably assisted by the research climate in the unit, which resulted in day-to-day discussion of ideas and interests in an enthusiastic forum. The research protocol that I finally put forward was called "the two valleys scheme," although it later became much better known as the Rhondda Fach scheme. Its main objective was to test the hypothesis that PMF derived from some interaction between simple pneumoconiosis and tuberculosis. I argued that this could be tested by reducing the level of infectious tuberculosis in one of two comparable mining valleys and then monitoring the subsequent attack rate of PMF in the two communities. If the aetiology of PMF was associated with tuberculous infection then PMF attack rates should decline in the valley in which levels of tuberculosis had been reduced. I proposed a strategy of x raying everyone over the age of 15 in one of the selected valleys. All infectious cases of tuberculosis would be hospitalised; removed from the normal social round. The degree to which we managed to reduce the level of tuberculous infection would be measured by serially Mantoux[30] testing the schoolchildren in both valleys.

In addition to testing the most accepted hypothesis on the cause of PMF, the scheme had the prospect of other benefits. By collecting x ray data on an entire adult population, as I proposed, we would have a wonderful population to follow up in a number of ways. Not only would we have an ideal radiologically charted population in which to investigate the progression of simple pneumoconiosis and the attack rate of PMF, we could also use it to test the validity of our new system of x ray classification, to see whether its different categories did relate to differences in risk and prognosis. There would also be possibilities of testing representative samples of this same population to assess whether or not – or just how far – simple pneumoconiosis affected lung function, which was an important question at that time. We would also be in a position to investigate more thoroughly than ever before the epidemiology of tuberculosis in a defined population.

It was an ambitious scheme and critically dependent on the ability of the survey team to achieve high response rates from much larger populations than we had encountered before. I am deeply grateful to Charles Fletcher for backing the proposal and persuading the various authorities and organisations whose support it needed that it was a worthwhile enterprise. I am also grateful for the support of my colleagues generally, without which progress would have been considerably slower. My original protocol, which has been lost in MRC files, could not have been written much earlier than the autumn of 1949, but we were in a position to begin the survey, in conjunction with the Welsh Regional Miniature Mass Radiography Service as early as September 1950. Dr Francis Jarman, who headed the service, played a considerable part in this and I shall ever be grateful for his efforts, although we did not always see eye to eye and get along easily.

In retrospect the two valley scheme still seems a good idea, but by modern standards an idea that had not been adequately thought through. Shortcomings were soon to reveal themselves. Perhaps I should have given more consideration to a new and important factor on the horizon, which was to change things all too quickly. After all, on my visit to the USA I had heard something of what streptomycin could achieve when applied to tuberculosis. There were also a number of other considerations to which I might have given greater weight before embarking on such a major initiative. It is possible that the impetus of my enthusiasm pushed me on just a little too fast. All in all, though, I still feel that the two valley scheme was not such a bad idea at that time.

So far I have neglected any reference to my domestic life in these early years at the Pneumoconiosis Research Unit. This may well be a better representation of the story than I had intended. Essentially they were years in which I poured myself into the work and paid scant attention to other aspects of life. After arriving in Cardiff I stayed for more than a year at the Windsor Hotel near the docks, where I had lunched with Charles Fletcher and John Gilson when I came down for interview. I had been impressed by its French patron and the quality of his French cuisine. Having rooms at the Windsor proved a convenient arrangement for quite a while. The accommodation was good, service and food were first class, and the proprietor and his wife were friendly and helpful. It was also near to my first work base, before we all moved up to Llandough. It also has to be said that there were a number of disadvantages, not least the fact that the hotel was in the heart of Tiger Bay, a rather notorious area. In addition, despite the "inner cleanliness" of the establishment, it was sometimes daunting to have to enter the premises through a typical dockland drinking bar, where there were often recumbent figures on the floor. As time passed I became dissatisfied, as did two other bachelors on the unit's staff, Martin Wright and Peter Oldham, who had been living in digs locally. The idea was floated that we should buy a large house, find a house-keeper, and settle down to a more domestic existence. Finally, I found Rhoose Farm House, through a tip off from Charles Fletcher's wife Louisa. It was much the best investment I ever made in my life, with the possible exception, from a purely financial point of view, of buying a Ben Nicholson painting for £70. It was, and still is, a large old farm house. It was probably a farm cottage in the seventeenth century, which has been added to continuously ever since. It was exactly the size we needed. The four rooms on the ground floor allowed us a sitting room each and a common dining room, and the four rooms upstairs meant that we had a bedroom available for guests. In addition there was adequate space for a married housekeeper with a child. Martin Wright did not take long to locate the help we needed. He discovered a man in Rhoose who had run an officers' mess during the war, married to an experienced cook, with one child. The Barlows not only seemed made for the job, they had been living in wretched conditions near Rhoose and were only too willing to move in and take it on. We all moved in sometime towards the middle of 1949, after Martin Wright had redesigned the kitchen and the necessary work had been completed. As for furniture, I already had in store in Cardiff various pieces from my London flat, which I supplemented with additional items from Scotland. Martin Wright also had a certain amount, although Peter, I seem to remember, had rather less. Certainly there was enough to get us off to a reasonable start and the situation steadily improved, although the highspot did not arrive until Peter acquired a grand piano.

Rhoose Farm House was a success from the beginning. Our pleasure in sharing this accommodation owed much to the strength of our common research interests and the high degree of personal privacy the arrangements allowed. There was also considerable mutual satisfaction from the mere enterprise of creating a home. I remember that we spent some of our time on trying to increase protein supplies. At various times we kept pigs, geese, ducks, turkeys, and hens. They were not all a great success, but we enjoyed eating the better results. From now on Rhoose Farm House was to figure increasingly in my life. In a way I felt reborn to a new order of things.

If I have overlooked anything in reviewing these important early years at the Pneumoconiosis Research Unit it is the opportunity I had, in 1949, just about the time I was moving into Rhoose Farm House, to revisit Germany on an official visit to the West German mines. This I must mention. As the only fluent German speaker in the unit I was the most obvious person to go, but I found myself more than a little reluctant. There were too many recollections with which I had not come to terms. Finally, however, I recognised that hate was an unproductive emotion and went. I am glad that I did. My new associations with Germany led to many valued friendships with German scientists.

NOTES

1 Possibly an underestimate.
2 For another example of verse written at Salonica see page 67.
3 Goons: Germans.
4 Written after the German invasion of the Soviet Union.
5 Kilocalories. Such a diet supplied only a quarter of the calories generally required.
6 James Lind's mid-eighteenth century investigations of scurvy demonstrated the link between the disease and a deficiency in diet, made good by an intake of citrous fruit, resulting in the subsequent widespread use of fruit supplements to shipboard diets.
7 See also Cochrane A L. Sickness in Salonica, my first, worst and most successful clinical trial. *Br Med J* 1984; 289: 1726–7. The author has also discussed this trial in a video interview recorded for the Royal College of Physicians/Oxford Polytechnic Video-Archive. (Royal College of Physicians Library VTR RCP/OP 12.)
8 The Germans claimed to have found a mass grave of Polish officers, killed, they said, by the Russians. See Zawodny. *Death in the forest: story of the Katyn forest massacre.* Paris, 1981.
9 The Weil–Felix reaction: the then accepted serological test to distinguish between typhus and typhoid in which serum from typhus patients induced a characteristic process of agglutination in a specific bacterial culture (proteus group).
10 This portrait is reproduced as plate 6.
11 Established surgical procedures to induce temporary or permanent collapse (and enforced relaxation) of the lung. These were characteristically employed in the treatment of pulmonary tuberculosis before the introduction of effective chemotherapy.
12 Cochrane A L. *Effectiveness and efficiency: random reflections on health services.* London, 1972.
13 Vlassov: Soviet general who defected to the Germans and raised an army to fight the Soviet.
14 Cochrane A L. Tuberculosis among prisoners of war in Germany. *Br Med J* 1945; ii: 656.
15 Prisoner of war camp.
16 Cochrane wrote: "I was writing this section during the repatriation of the Americans from Iran in 1981 and was inevitably amused by the contrast."
17 Cochrane A L. The medical officer as prisoner in Germany. *Lancet* 1945; ii: 411.
18 Cochrane A L. Tuberculosis among prisoners of war in Germany. *Br Med J* 1945; ii: 656.
19 In 1968 Archie Cochrane was awarded the CBE for services to medicine.
20 Berylliosis: an occupational lung disease emanating from prolonged

exposure to beryllium oxide and resulting in the disruptive development of fibrous tissue within the pulmonary field.

21 Bacille Calmette–Guérin immunisation. Antituberculosis immunisation using the "live vaccine" developed by Calmette and Guérin in Paris in the first quarter of the century and containing the non-pathogenic "bacillus Calmette–Guérin"; hence the term BCG immunisation.

22 Seibert F. *Pebbles on the hill of a scientist.* St Petersberg, Florida, 1968: 128.

23 Birkelo C C, *et al.* The accuracy of roentgen determination of the activity of minimal pulmonary tuberculosis. *JAMA* 1947; **133**: 359.

24 Cochrane A L, Campbell H W, Steen S C. The value of roentgenology in the prognosis of minimal tuberculosis. *American Journal of Roentgenology and Radium Therapy* 1949; **61**: 153–65.

25 Later professor of clinical epidemiology, Royal Postgraduate Medical School, Hammersmith, London, and well known to the British public through his appearances as the first BBC television doctor.

26 For a more detailed historical view see Meiklejohn A. History of lung diseases of coalminers in Great Britain. Parts 1, 2, and 3. *Br J Ind Med* 1951; **8**: 127; 1952; **9**: 93; 1952; **9**: 209.

27 Later professor of community health and director of the Medical Research Council's Social Medicine Unit at the London School of Hygiene and Tropical Medicine.

28 C M Fletcher in a Royal College of Physicians video interview: RCP-OP/VTR3/1985.

29 See Fletcher C M, *et al.* The classification of radiographic appearances in coalminers' pneumoconiosis. *Journal of the Faculty of Radiologists* 1949; **1**: 3–23. See also Fletcher C M, Oldham P D. The problem of consistent radiological diagnosis in coalminers' pneumoconiosis. *Br J Ind Med* 1949; **6**: 168–83.

30 A simple and convenient skin reaction test to tuberculin, indicating the levels to which individuals have experienced tuberculous infection.

4 The fifties

The fifties were the happiest years of my life. If I had been moved to write verse by the best rather than the worst of times, then this is where it would have spilled over. They were years in which I at last found my feet in a field of research where I felt that I belonged and could make a worthwhile contribution. It was also a period of home building in which many valued friendships were formed. I played sport again and went on travels. They were exceptional years in so many ways, and I never worked harder in my life.

DEVELOPMENTS IN RESEARCH

First, a word to non-medical readers about my chosen field of research, epidemiology – although this was not a term commonly used at the Pneumoconiosis Research Unit in the 1950s. My team, I remember, was referred to as being involved in "clinical and environmental studies." Nevertheless, epidemiology is what it all became as this research field evolved with the decades. Originally, as the name suggests, it was a field of study relating exclusively to infectious epidemic diseases, as they traversed populations, but in the 1950s it was steadily becoming associated with much wider intelligence gathering and showing concern for the distribution of all sorts of biological and social variables within populations. Essentially the objective was to chart the patterns of disease in communities and to survey the backgrounds of sufferers and non-sufferers for the kinds of differences in life experience that might relate to causality. Commonly the causal factors initiating disease lie some way upstream of clinical observations, relating to social or environmental influences, and it is the epidemiologist's challenge to conduct surveys sensitive and accurate enough to identify them, inquiries as well planned and statistically relevant as the best political polls. Inevitably such research is fundamental to preventive medicine and health promotion, but the survey methods epidemiologists have developed serve equally well in evaluating how communities or sections of populations benefit from the health services available to them. Back in 1950 my epidemiological interests were firmly in pneumoconiosis and PMF. I badly wanted to do something to help reduce the burden of risk and ill health they constituted for the mining communities with which I now felt associated, and I believed that I could. In particular my sights were set on the aetiology of PMF, which was clearly a source of considerable physical distress for its sufferers. Their all too rapid decline to a breath-gasping existence cried out for attention. This is why I felt so ambitious for the two valleys scheme. It promised a greater understanding of causality, and improved prospects of prevention.

Earlier research had done a lot of useful spadework, but the main questions had still to be answered. It was as though we had only been preparing the way. We had established a reproducible radiographic classification of coal workers' pneumoconiosis, the only reasonable way of diagnosing the disease in the living subject.[1] We had also developed a reproducible way of taking industrial histories. It was also true that we had learnt a lot that was useful from the mistakes and experiences of our earlier surveys. We now knew how important it was to consider whole communities rather than just pit populations. But, if that was the bottom line of the balance sheet for the 1940s, we entered the 1950s with the main questions still against us. We still needed to know how serious a health risk simple pneumoconiosis represented in the various categories to which we assigned it radiographically, and about the factors relating to its progression and transformation into PMF. Despite the strength of the prevailing hypothesis implicating tuberculosis in the aetiology of PMF, we did not know how far tuberculosis had a role. Even our knowledge of the relationship between dust and simple pneumoconiosis was superficial. With challenges remaining on that scale it seemed as though we had hardly begun, and yet I was convinced that the two valleys scheme could supply some of the answers, if only we could achieve the public's fullest cooperation and the response rates we needed. These were my hopes as we entered the 1950s.

In our first valley, the Rhondda Fach, we needed to x ray the chests of as many of the population over the age of 15 as we could draw into the survey. This would provide the data we required on the three diseases we were studying – simple pneumoconiosis, tuberculosis, and PMF – and help to reveal the cases of tuberculosis we needed to isolate from the general community. For this study we had twinned the Rhondda Fach with the nearby Aberdare Valley. They seemed sufficiently alike for the various comparisons we needed to make. In addition to their populations being comparable, each valley had four collieries working the same type of coal and employing approximately the same numbers of miners with similar high certification rates for pneumoconiosis. Similarly, the economic and social conditions corresponded well, although there was some evidence that they were marginally better in the Aberdare Valley.

We began promoting the first survey of the Rhondda Fach in January 1950. Lectures explaining the scheme were given in the numerous social and political clubs characteristic of the Rhondda Fach's eight small towns. The NUM assisted by setting up local support committees to help promote the initiative, and as the survey drew nearer we published a number of posters and leaflets to assist the interest being stimulated. By this time there was also a fair amount of media coverage being generated, locally and nationally, and the BBC gave the initiative considerable publicity throughout.

The survey itself began in the second week of September and continued until the following April.[2] There were two mobile mass radiography teams involved: one from the Welsh Regional Miniature Mass Radiography Service and the other from the Pneumoconiosis Research Unit, which I led. It was a mammoth operation, with my team providing regular x ray sessions at the various pitheads, to suit the times of various shifts, while Francis Jarman's radiography service team worked in the towns, in chapel vestries and other suitable halls. In addition to mass radiography we were soon involved in home visiting as initial response rates declined. In all we made more than 20 000 visits. Some homes needed to be visited as many as six times, but as a result of our efforts we managed to x ray 89 per cent of our target population of 19 218, and as many as 98 per cent of its miners and ex-miners. Such high response rates were all the more remarkable because of the appalling bad luck we had with the very severe winter conditions of 1950–51. We had a great deal of deep snow, while we were working in tents, and yet my team stuck to its task. On one occasion we had even to lower a road by several feet to get our x ray van under a bridge and into the right position at a colliery. Members of the team did this over a weekend to avoid losing time. I cannot praise them too highly.

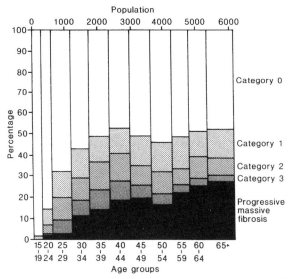

Figure 8 Prevalence of coal workers' pneumoconiosis amongst miners and ex-miners in the Rhondda Fach, 1950–51. In this histogram the area of each column is proportional to the number of individuals in that age group.

To reduce errors in radiological diagnosis all *x* ray films were read by two observers, independently, and all suspected cases of active tuberculosis then had their sputum investigated for infectivity, using a somewhat simplified version of more tedious laboratory procedure. On the basis of *x* ray diagnosis we also mapped the prevalence of simple pneumoconiosis and PMF in the population of the valley (see figure 8). The results were frightening but not as disturbing as those showing the prevalence of pulmonary tuberculosis among the women of the Rhondda Fach (see figure 9).

As the survey unfolded two 27-bed wards in the Tyntyla isolation hospital were made available by the regional hospital board for the cases of infectious pulmonary tuberculosis we were identifying. They were treated semi-conservatively. In addition to the usual emphasis on bed rest and nutrition, they received a course of streptomycin. Most of the cases we identified agreed to hospitalisation, but they could not always be kept under care and surveillance in the wards until their infection had completely disappeared. For some there were domestic pressures to return home, and on occasions others were discharged early due to bed shortages. As a result we needed to make good use of local health visitors. All cases still capable of spreading infection required advice as to how they

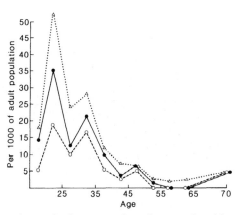

Figure 9 Prevalence of pulmonary tuberculosis in Rhondda Fach females. Active and quiescent (△); active (●); infectious (○).

could minimise the dangers of their own sputum. We were well rewarded. By the time we began to write up the first of our results, early in 1952, we were able to report a 60 per cent reduction in the number of infectious cases of tuberculosis in the Rhondda Fach. At least we seemed to be satisfactorily negotiating the first part of our task. In fact we had achieved three steps forward. In addition to a major reduction of infectious tuberculosis in a defined population, we had conducted a comprehensive survey of simple pneumoconiosis and PMF throughout an entire mining community and obtained an invaluable x ray record of the epidemiological situation at one point in time. Against this record we would now be able to monitor all future developments of the cases of disease we had identified. We had also made the most accurate measurement yet achieved of the amount of tuberculosis in a community.

The next stage of the project was the x ray survey of miners and ex-miners in the Aberdare Valley. As far as I remember we transferred to this right away and achieved response rates just as impressive: 98 per cent of the target population of 2674. Here we needed only to monitor the attack rate and progress of PMF in the pit population as a comparison with what was happening in the Rhondda Fach. If tuberculosis had an aetiological role in PMF then it was reasonable to expect differences in future patterns of incidence in the two communities, given the extent to which we had reduced exogenous tuberculosis in one of them.

I never had any doubts as to whether what we were doing was ethical. Even though the population of the Rhondda Fach had the advantage of exceptional mass radiography services and a considerable diminution of tuberculous infection it would have been impossible to extend such benefits to two communities, and the fact that we could not devote maximal attention to both seemed little justification for withholding it from one. We also knew that health care services in the Aberdare Valley were well in line with provision generally at this time. We were by no means creating an area of special deprivation. In fact Aberdare had a chest service above average for Wales, and the additional benefit of the *x* ray surveillance we were now providing for miners and ex-miners. By far the most important consideration, however, was the prospect that as a result of the two valleys scheme we might soon be in a position dramatically to change health risks not only in both valleys but across the coalfields more widely. We felt that useful evidence relating to the prevention of PMF might be forthcoming within as little as two or three years. Results, however, were to show that we were wrong.

We returned to the Rhondda Fach for the first follow-up survey two and a half years later, in April 1953.[3] We had no wish for another winter under canvas. Pityard blizzards had lost their attraction. This time I was even more enthusiastic than when getting the first survey under way. I was excited by the prospect of knowing more about the origins of PMF and by the fact that this time I would be leading my own team. At the time of the first survey of the Rhondda Fach only a nucleus of this group had existed, and we had needed considerable assistance from Pneumoconiosis Research Unit colleagues prepared to be drafted in to help. Now I had a team of seven: four fieldworkers and three administrative staff. The fieldworkers took accurate nominal censuses of the communities under surveillance, persuaded those on the survey lists to attend for *x* ray, motored in those who needed transport, and helped with the completion of questionnaires and industrial histories. Between surveys they helped to check the voluminous data the surveys produced, which in the early days were all processed by hand. The administrative staff, consisting of a records officer, secretary, and myself, concentrated on coordinating the programme and marshalling incoming data for analysis. A major survey generates masses of information quite rapidly. In addition to being with administrative staff at Pneumoconiosis Research Unit headquarters, I also tried to involve myself in all aspects of the survey so that in emergencies or with changing pressures on the team I had enough experience to be able to lend a hand where it was needed. All this, however, was only half of the story. Again it was the mobile *x* ray units of the Welsh Regional Miniature Mass Radiography Service and Pneumoconiosis Research Unit that bore the weight of the radiography programme. In all there were more than 30 of us involved locally, and various others lent a hand at various times. Vic Springett,[4] a consultant radiologist from Birmingham, played a particularly important part in double checking all our interpretations of chest films.

I well remember the long hours we worked. Although we had learnt a lot from our first survey there seemed to be no less pressure. I did once enumerate what I did in an average day while this 1953 survey was in progress. As far as I remember I interpreted about 100 chest x rays, visited almost a similar number of addresses to persuade people to be x rayed, took approximately 40 industrial histories, and in the evening interviewed between 30 and 40 miners to advise them about their chest x rays. Also I helped as far as I could with other tasks. I even took x rays and worked in the darkroom in emergencies, and everyone was delighted when I produced some double exposures. It took a long while before they let me forget the incident. Finally, quite late each day, my green Jaguar car, which acted as an *oriflamme* for the team, motored a number of colleagues back from the Rhondda to their homes in Cardiff and Barry. I was always the last to turn in after completing this late bus service, with the events of the day buzzing around in my mind. It was a satisfying day's work, and even more satisfying was the response rate we achieved from the population of the Rhondda Fach. Close to 95 per cent attended for x ray. How I enjoyed working among these people.

One problem that arose in the course of this survey was that of overtime remuneration. Administrators at MRC headquarters had never before had to consider the kind of situation that developed, with overtime being amassed on a massive scale by some members of the team. Perhaps this is why my early requests for guidance evoked only scant attention, initially. The MRC was used to professional employees giving whatever time was necessary for research, without question, but I had started to employ ex-miners as fieldworkers, and they had a quite different view of overtime. Two equally unhelpful suggestions eventually filtered down from London. The first was that I should use temporary appoint-

1 Archie with younger brother Robert (*right*) at preparatory school at Rhos-on-Sea in 1920

2 At Cambridge in the
early 1930s

3 In uniform, in Spain in 1937, while serving with the Spanish Medical
Aid Committee's Field Ambulance Unit in support of the International
Brigade

COME·TO·HOLLAND·FOR·A·FREE·HOLIDAY.

PSALMS 146 v 3.
For "PRINCES" read "MINISTERS".
For "THE SON OF MAN" read "CONSULS".

4 "Come to Holland for a free holiday." The Christmas card Archie sent out to commemorate his first experience of prison life. He had been arrested for being in possession of his own car

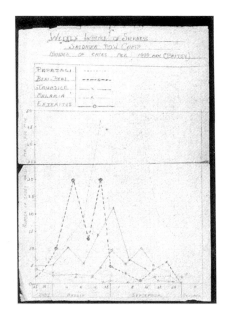

5 Weekly incidence of sickness chart from the prisoner of war camp in Salonica

6 Portrait painted by Spanish prisoner of war "Basilio" at Elsterhorst in 1944

7 The x ray service of the Medical Research Council's Pneumoconiosis Research Unit visiting the Tylorstown pithead in 1950

8 A mass radiography session during the first Rhondda Fach survey

9 Reminders were attached to the lamp brackets of miners who had not yet attended for *x* ray

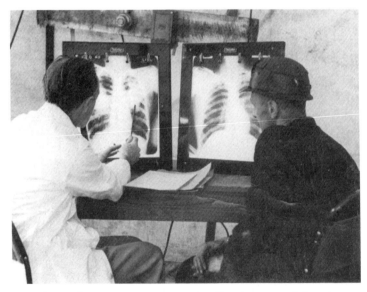

10 Archie explaining progressive massive fibrosis to one of the miners at Ferndale during the first Rhondda Fach survey

11 Part of the massive collection of information on the health of the mining population of the Rhondda Fach, 1950

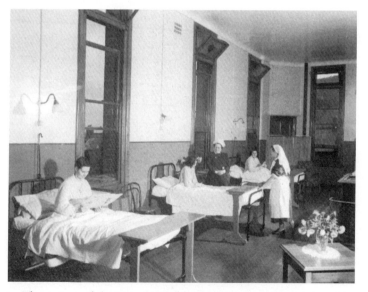

12 The matron of the Tyntyla Hospital chatting to some patients with tuberculosis being cared for under the Rhondda Fach scheme in 1950

13 Archie (*second left*) at York University in 1975 after receiving the honorary degree of doctor of the university

14 Working with Fred Moore, his great companion of many campaigns, during their last project

ments, as and when necessary, to reduce overtime pressures. The second was to allow time off at the end of the survey in compensation for extra hours worked. From where I stood, it did not take long to rule against short-term attachments. They introduced new training and supervision demands, and endangered the confidentiality of the information we were collecting. Time off in compensation also made little sense in a situation where some staff were owed whole months. No one of importance could ever be spared for that long after a survey. Eventually the MRC conceded the necessary overtime payments.

Where we hoped that this survey would tell us more about the aetiology of PMF we were to be disappointed. Even with the sizes of the populations under surveillance, the attack rates of PMF proved too low for us to detect a statistically valid difference between PMF levels in the Rhondda and Aberdare mining communities after two and a half years. In this respect our follow-up investigation had to be a disappointment, even though there was some comfort in that findings at that time looked as though they might be moving in the right direction. They did show a reduction in PMF incidence in the Rhondda Fach, but not by a sufficient statistical margin to implicate tuberculosis in its aetiology. Other influences could have played a part, as there was only a one in five chance that what we were seeing related to our reduction of tuberculous infection there.[5] What we required was the kind of result that left little statistical doubt that tuberculosis was a causal factor. Only then would we be in a position to think preventively in the way I had in mind. On the evidence of the 1953 data we needed to run the project for at least another five years. Although time scales in epidemiology are not quite of the order of those of forestry, it sometimes seems like it. All we could do was to wait, and, while waiting, beaver away at other areas of the jigsaw.

We were better rewarded by the 1953 survey's confirmation that reduced levels of tuberculous infection still held in the Rhondda Fach. Sustained reductions were demonstrated when we Mantoux tested a new cohort of schoolchildren, and also by the results of the mass radiography programme. Our results, too, endorsed a developing view that serious risk of PMF did not arise until miners had moved beyond the first of our radiographic categories of simple pneumoconiosis and were somewhere within category 2 or beyond. This concept of a risk threshold was important. If miners could be prevented from reaching category 2, then even without understanding the aetiology of PMF the great bulk of this disease looked preventable.

Although the two valleys scheme tended to dominate my life in the early 1950s, it never totally eclipsed other essential research concerns. I have already said that we had entered the 1950s confronted by a range of critical questions, not least ones about dust and the validity of our x ray classification of pneumoconiosis. We still needed to know what kinds of exposure to dust were involved in the development of the disease, and whether there was a clear quantitative relationship between dust uptake and risk. The situation regarding different dusts was also interesting. We needed to explain the low disease incidence of some "high dust" pits. The other priority was the validation of our system of classifying chest x ray films. Did the ascending categories we assigned to them really relate to increasing levels of disability and differences in prognosis? In fact, we still lacked evidence that simple pneumoconiosis was disabling, although miners could be laid off work and relegated to living on a disability pension on the basis of chest films showing certain levels of nodulation. Here political expedience had run ahead of research findings. We had no idea exactly what these categories meant in terms of actual disability.

So questions about dust and our categorisation of x rays were never far from our thoughts. We had made scant headway with dust research in the 1940s, and felt a lot of pressure to change the picture. The outlook at the beginning of the 1950s, however, looked decidedly gloomy, as there was still no available instrument capable of measuring the amount of dust a miner took into his lungs from the workplace, and therefore little hope of an early breakthrough in relating pneumoconiosis to dust inhalation. Earlier studies had had to be satisfied with mere estimates of dust concentrations in various parts of the mine, but these hardly began to relate to the experience of the miner. Fortunately, some time towards the end of 1951, Stan Roach and Peter Oldham came up with a revolutionary concept of how to advance the position. Their idea was that despite the lack of an instrument capable of monitoring a miner's dust intake directly it was still possible to achieve relevant quantitative studies of colliers' dust exposure by sampling the atmosphere as close to them as possible throughout the working day with a portable dust meter. Even more important was the way in which they proposed to apply this approach. Because following one miner would be unrepresentative of a whole shift, and following a representative sample would be impossible without serious disruption of normal patterns of activity, they advocated the following of one randomly selected miner each day until a representative picture of the dust exposure of a shift had been achieved. This really was an advance. Before then, the idea of dust dosage (the product of dust concentration and time) was unknown in this field. I can still remember my excitement in discussing with Stan and Peter the opportunities this "random collier" method of sampling opened up for us. It gave us real hope of establishing some quantitative relationship between dust exposure and levels of pneumoconiosis. Then, at last, we would be in a position to recommend appropriate dust suppression strategies or limits to the amount of time miners spent on various coal-getting operations. Of course it would finally be up to the NCB and NUM to decide upon acceptable and workable strategies, but we still needed to give them the best scientific information on which to base their rulings.

After long talks with Stan Roach we were finally ready to mount the kind of investigation we required. We utilised a survey already scheduled for a colliery in Lancashire, which had two coalfaces where conditions had changed very little over the past 10 years and which were different in their levels of dust hazard because of differences in ventilation and shift management. By means of random collier sampling in such a situation could we now relate exposure to levels of pneumoconiosis? As each shift had two main categories of colliers – face workers and their assistants – we used a random collier from each category each day. This meant that for the two faces we had a total of four miners under surveillance on each shift. Our "observers," who followed them throughout their working hours, whatever their duties, employed a standardised pattern of dust monitoring, using the best instrument then available, the thermal precipitator, an instrument developed at Porton Down during the second world war. Essentially this was a piece of apparatus designed to draw a measured flow of air through a tube containing a heated wire and microscope slide. Dust particles were thermally precipitated on to the slide, which could be detached at the end of each sampling period for laboratory examination, when dust counts were made under the microscope. The instrument's main limitation lay in its lack of facility for constant dust monitoring. It could only be used intermittently for short periods, after which it needed a change of slide and readjustment. When it was in use, Stan, who led the team of observers, and his colleagues kept to a strict sampling procedure, holding the precipitator close to the collier, just upwind of him and at head level. When he moved, the observer moved. When he took a break, so did his "shadow." While it was a tough assignment for observers, the miners who became random colliers for a day seemed to value their small departure from routine.[6]

While our new form of investigation was in progress underground, the rest of the team went ahead in the usual way with its survey programme, chest x raying the entire pit population and taking industrial histories. We added to our workload, however, the task of taking more detailed histories of the miners on the two coal faces selected for dust exposure studies. We were particularly interested in men who had worked exclusively on one or other of the two faces and who had no other record of industrial exposure to dust. Fortunately there were enough of these selected colliers for our purposes and we collected invaluable data. Knowing how long they had been on the face and the duration of various kinds of work – as coal getters or assistants – we were able to calculate their approximate levels of dust dosage, based upon the average exposure levels we had calculated for the two faces

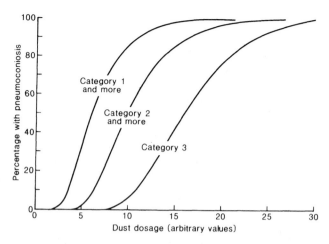

Figure 10 Correlation between dust exposure and radiological appearance of simple pneumoconiosis amongst coalface workers who had only worked "in coal."

and categories of work. In the hands of Peter Oldham such data rapidly transformed into the series of curves shown in figure 10, showing a distinct relationship between dust dosage and category of simple pneumoconiosis. This felt like a massive step forwards, but we were still some way from fulfilling our hopes of quantifying acceptable levels of dust exposure for the mining industry. The figures from one pit could not be related to exposure dangers in others because we knew too little about the effects of different kinds of dusts. We also had to accept that the thermal precipitator had its limitations. Nevertheless, we had established that quantitative relationships did exist between dust and disease levels. We got useful confirmatory evidence of the validity of our general approach when we undertook a second investigation at a Welsh colliery and again showed quantitative differences in risk for different kinds of pit work. The progression rate of simple pneumoconiosis was much greater amongst face workers.

The rapid advances we made in dust research impressed me, and gave me hope that we would soon be in a position to relate quantitatively all the main elements in the pneumo-coniosis story: x ray category, dust exposure, disability, and mortality. This was to take a good deal longer than I imagined, however, especially the work involved in relating x ray category to disability. In fact I was never entirely happy with this aspect of the research, which lay primarily in the hands of the Pneumoconiosis Research Unit's "eagle physi-ologists." The "eagle survey"[7] of pneumoconiosis related disability, which began just before I arrived at the unit, had immense prestige and distinguished personnel, but it looked at research through different spectacles from mine, focusing too deeply on the quality of its physiological techniques and, in my view, far too little on the selection of the subjects to be examined. The groups of miners investigated by the eagle physiologists were not representative of the situation generally. Too many of them were preselected because they had disability, and the kind of investigations that followed were never in a position to determine whether those with disability were disabled by pneumoconiosis or merely more subject to its effects. My way would have been to look at real cross sections of the communities we were already surveying, but there was only one of the physiological tests sufficiently portable at that time to take out into the field. With a little more commitment to this approach the important work of the eagle survey could have been supplemented by the kind of cross sectional data it lacked. This was not to be. High-technology physiology had the prestige to stand its ground and channel the kinds of resources it commanded away from epidemiology. I did not get the portable physiological equip-ment I sought for field tests of lung function, and the eagle physiologists remained in what seemed to me too rarified a laboratory stance.[8] However, my enthusiasm for a somewhat different approach, even a more collaborative one, should not cloud the fact that the work of the eagle survey did make a contribution to the literature and did result in an eminent publication. The MRC published its findings in its Special Reports Series,[9] the highest honour the MRC could give to a research project at that time.

Whatever the differences in approach preventing better

collaboration of my team and the eagle physiologists in looking at disability, we did eventually both emerge from independent studies, largely agreeing that there was little evidence of an association between the primary categories of pneumoconiosis, 1–3, and pulmonary disability, but quite clear that the progression of PMF involved considerable changes in lung function. All the efforts of the eagle survey and the tests we carried out on randomly selected samples of the mining population of the Rhondda Fach showed that PMF in its more severe categories, B and C, was a highly disabling disease, and our follow-up studies of men in these categories indicated that they were associated with a greatly increased mortality. At last, therefore, we had a link between the more advanced stages of our x ray classification, morbidity and mortality. The two valleys scheme also confirmed, as it ran its course, that real risk of PMF related only to miners progressing beyond category 1 of simple pneumoconiosis.[10] Therefore whatever our difficulties in establishing whether or not simple pneumoconiosis was disabling, we still had the means of preventing most of the disability and increased mortality due to PMF. This was clearly possible if we could prevent miners from reaching category 2 of simple pneumoconiosis during their working lives.

While the main emphasis of our work in the 1950s centred on pneumoconiosis this did not prevent our interests from radiating out in a number of directions. Once we had successfully launched the two valleys scheme there were a number of important spin offs, because by then we had a well documented population ideal for other epidemiological studies, as well as an established survey team almost in residence there. Inevitably I became involved in making such facilities available where they might help the study of other diseases, particularly random samples of the Rhondda Fach population. The idea of using randomly selected samples of well researched reference populations as a basis for epidemiological research, in the way that political polls try to focus on unbiased samples of a population as the most logical way to a representative viewpoint, was just becoming popular, and because there were few established reference populations where a good deal of background data had already been collected we naturally attracted interest. Inevitably I found myself a provider of random samples of the population we had under surveillance and collaborating with a range of investigators of varying interests. My research horizons were also regularly extended by the enthusiasms of several colleagues who joined the team in this period. Bill Miall, who had been with me as an orderly in the hell camp of Salonica and who had since qualified as a doctor, introduced important interests in the epidemiology of blood pressure, and Ian Higgins, formerly a pulmonary physiologist, soon had us involved in community studies of chronic bronchitis. It is fair to say that we made a contribution to the epidemiology of several diseases and the surveys of a growing number of associates.

Our first collaborative association was in helping Dr Anthony Caplan to establish that a syndrome he had described in coal workers really existed.[11] This was possibly the first time that a syndrome – a characteristic association of seemingly unrelated pathological conditions or symptoms – had been established scientifically. While serving on the Pneumoconiosis Medical Panel in Cardiff, Dr Caplan had increasingly felt that a certain type of PMF was too often associated with cases of rheumatoid arthritis for the relationship to be purely one of chance. We decided that this was a hypothesis that could be tested on the Rhondda Fach population, and we gave him access to all the x ray films we had read as PMF during the Rhondda Fach survey. He ploughed through them and picked out those cases he thought were likely to be suffering from rheumatoid arthritis, after which we then selected a set of controls, matched by age and x ray category, and had cases and controls visited by young clinicians who were asked to decide whether they thought the people were suffering from rheumatoid arthritis or not. The results were highly significant, totally vindicating Dr Caplan's view. It was interesting that soon after this investigation, during a visit to a medical centre in Germany, I was asked to comment on a number of x ray films of miners, one of which looked typical of Caplan's syndrome. I asked to see the patient and said I thought he would be suffering from rheumatoid arthritis. There was a gasp of disbelief, but when the patient was wheeled in he was such a typical case of rheumatoid arthritis that there was mild applause.

While working on the Caplan syndrome we made contact with my old friend from University College Hospital days, "Yonkie" Kellgren,[12] who was now professor of rheumatology at Manchester and a member of the Empire Rheumatism Council.[13] He helped us with the reading of x ray films relating to the Caplan syndrome, and the association with his team and the work of the Empire Rheumatism Council's research unit led us on to new lines of investigation. The two directors of the research unit with whom we largely worked were Drs John Lawrence and Philip Wood, and we enabled them to study the epidemiology of rheumatoid arthritis and osteoarthritis by adding various bone x ray assignments to our surveys. Regrettably, the results generally were disappointing.

Sometime slightly later we also helped Stewart Kilpatrick of the medical unit of the Welsh National School of Medicine to start a study of the epidemiology of anaemia. Stewart, who had originally been with us at the Pneumoconiosis Research Unit and had at one time lived at Rhoose Farm House, inevitably developed his plans in close association with the team with which he had so recently worked. I shall never forget this particular survey because of a very unusual problem which I had to solve. The anaemia study had been grafted on to another large scale survey which I was in the process of directing, and automatically I received the results of the blood smears. To my horror, when the first inevitable diagnosis of chronic lymphatic leukaemia came through I found I knew the man well. He was a very likeable, cheerful, tough young miner, married with two children, and without symptoms. I found that I could not tell him or his general practitioner without taking further advice. I knew that the usual routine would have led to him starting deep x ray within three weeks, and that he would then have immediately developed symptoms. I also did not believe at that time (1958) that the therapy would do any good. I saw a large number of senior medical people very rapidly. I was finally able to visit the general practitioner involved, tell him the names, in confidence, of the physicians I had consulted and say that, if he agreed it would be ethical, no action need be taken in this case until symptoms developed. The general practitioner agreed and we made arrangements for the man to be seen once a year. He lived happily for another 10 years. He paid off his mortgage and had another child. I felt justified. He died rapidly after developing symptoms.

During this period I also got permission from the MRC to approach Sir Aubrey Lewis, professor of psychiatry at the Maudsley Hospital, about the possibility of adding psychiatric studies to our surveys. I had become convinced, after long and intimate contact with the Rhondda Fach, that much of the unhappiness effecting that community had its basis in psychological and psychiatric causes more than physical diseases such as pneumoconiosis. Lewis was rather suspicious at first, as was justified, and grilled me about my knowledge of psychiatry. He did not know that I had been psychoanalysed, so I came out of it better than he expected. At any rate he agreed to become involved and sent down an excellent team. They were entirely independent, but we supplied them with the facilities they needed. In retrospect, I do not think the venture was entirely successful, but it was well worth trying to relate the distribution of psychiatric distress to other features of life and patterns of disease we were charting in the Rhondda Fach, and the association with the Maudsley certainly had other important benefits.[14] We met a lot of very friendly specialists from another field of medicine who broadened our interests. Among them were Morris Carstairs, later professor of psychiatry in Edinburgh, and still later principal of York University; Ken Rawnsley, later professor of psychiatry in Cardiff, and later still president of the Royal College of Psychiatrists; and Jack Ingham, a very valued friend.

Another important development began to take place as we moved through the 1950s. Increasingly we recognised the limitations of our main survey population of the Rhondda Fach as our interests and horizons advanced beyond mining diseases to incorporate such other important epidemiological issues as the social distribution of ischaemic heart disease; at that time the fastest growing plague. We needed to study other kinds of communities to achieve occupational and environmental contrasts with the highly specialised industrial situations of the Rhondda. We began by looking to the Vale of Glamorgan, an agricultural area just 15 miles away from the Rhondda Fach, where we began a series of surveys, starting with one on ischaemic heart disease in 1957. Here again we achieved an excellent response from the community, which soon provided us with an unexpected secondary interest in simple goitre. During our first chest x ray survey in the Vale we noticed a great number of people with large goitres, and with the help of my old friend Bob Trotter from University College Hospital,[15] a specialist on diseases of the thyroid, we eventually conducted a case-control study. To our surprise the cause seemed entirely independent of the iodine content of the water they had drunk during their lives, but closely related to their consumption of fish. We followed up these cases and controls for many years and it was surprising how little difference these very large goitres made to their lives. On average the cases and controls married at the same age, had the same number of children, and died at the same rate, of roughly the same kinds of disease.[16]

It was in the latter years of the decade that we really began to take special interest in ischaemic heart disease, largely due to Ian Higgins's enthusiasms and some of our early findings relating to ECG diagnosis. It was while we were working on our first surveys in the Rhondda Fach and the Vale of Glamorgan that we investigated the observer error involved in the interpretation of ECGs. We took ECGs of a random sample of males aged 55–64, and Ian Higgins submitted these to four distinguished cardiologists in various parts of the UK. All the ECGs were of high technical quality and our questions were quite simple. We merely asked:

(a) Is the ECG normal?
(b) Does it show coronary heart disease?
(c) Does it show other myocardial damage?
(d) Or does it show other abnormalities?
On the basis of this exercise there were clearly considerable

difficulties in achieving agreement between experts. In fact it appeared that if one had involved a fifth interpreter there might well have been no finding on which all observers would have agreed. It would have been an interesting example of disease elimination by multiple observations! But with our four specialists total agreement was reached at about the 3 per cent level (see figure 11).[17] I think that in a number of ways Ian made valuable contributions to the study of ischaemic heart disease at this time, though they led to an increasing number of connections with the USA and, unfortunately for me, played a part in his eventual decision to move there.

As well as being the happiest this was very likely the most productive period of my life. I think I showed that we could, very nearly, make measurements in communities with roughly the same known error that one can make in laboratories and use them to test hypotheses. I also felt that we had made a large contribution to the epidemiology of coal workers' pneumoconiosis, which might in the future lead to the elimination of disability and excessive mortality from dust

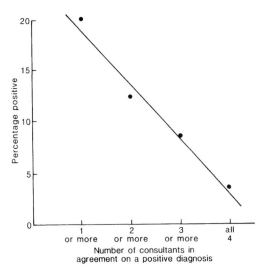

Figure 11 Percentage electrocardiograms read by four readers as compatible with coronary disease.

exposure. We had also demonstrated the value and the ease with which other diseases might be examined by the use of randomly selected samples of populations. For the rest of my life I was to be hooked on making the fullest use of random samples. I liked the search for the truly representative sample and the perspectives it offered the researcher once it had been found. Of course, so much depended upon response rates, and in the early days there were those who argued that we only got the massive support of the mining communities in the Rhondda because of the well known fact that some miners who were investigated would come away with the benefit of a pension. This argument, however, did not survive our experience in the Vale of Glamorgan and a short survey we conducted at Annandale in Dumfriesshire. In these very agricultural areas where we made it clear that all we wanted was scientific information and not to help the community the refusal rates were always about the same – well under 10 per cent. I am convinced that British communities like helping medical research if they are treated properly and things are clearly explained.

The decade ended almost as it had begun, with a survey of the Rhondda Fach and Aberdare Valleys: our second follow-up survey. It was at this point that it became clear that the two valleys scheme would never yield the information we sought on the role of tuberculosis in PMF.[18] With the removal of miners from jobs involving a dust hazard before they could reach categories 2 and 3 of pneumoconiosis the attack rate of PMF had naturally declined, and the introduction of streptomycin into the general treatment of tuberculosis had inevitably eroded the levels and differences in tuberculous infection around which our investigation had originally been based. We did, however, go on to show that the progression of PMF was independent of smoking and further exposure to dust, but very dependent on age. The younger men with category A shadows progressed much faster than the older ones.

So I had had my failures, the greatest of which was the failure of the two valleys scheme to throw light on the aetiology of PMF. In fact I slowly came to think of PMF as a sort of personal enemy. Secondly, we had also failed to convince the establishment, and in particular the NUM, that simple pneumoconiosis, per se, was not a serious disease but simply a radiographical finding. We had also failed to press for the range of "portable" physiological tests we should have had available to complement our field surveys.

Beyond all this, I think that I also failed epidemiology in another way because I did not make enough fuss about a problem I saw looming ahead. It dated back to Nye Bevan's bribe to get consultant physicians and surgeons into the National Health Service. He promised the senior physicians and surgeons that they would get merit awards which would increase their salaries well above that of the average consultant in private practice. The top merit award could double the salary. There were, however, at that time no epidemiologists in Harley Street, so when the scheme was inaugurated, epidemiologists were not included.

The Pneumoconiosis Research Unit had a ward with patients and some of the clinical physiologists were in charge of it. I knew these people would in time get merit awards (the whole system is very secret), while there was no chance of an epidemiologist getting one. I never complained on my own account as I have a private income and I thought the MRC paid me adequately, but I became increasingly worried about recruitment of epidemiologists in the future. There was an increasing interest in epidemiology amongst bright young men and women in the late 1950s and several came to see me. I felt it my duty to point out to them that though epidemiology would give them a fascinating and satisfactory life their top salary level would always be much less than that of their clinical colleagues. This problem became acute in the 1960s and almost killed the promising resurgence of British epidemiology which had started in the 1950s. I certainly raised the problem, but I did not shout loud enough. I do not blame Nye Bevan; his bribe was well worth while to help get the National Health Service started.

It was during this period that I really began my official travels, which have continued ever since. I started travelling with Charles Fletcher while he was still director of the unit, serving as interpreter and x ray reader during visits to France,

Germany, and Belgium, "selling" our system of classifying the pneumoconioses. There were some alarming occasions until I learned to diagnose Charles's hypoglycaemia. There were several return visits to Hasselt, Lille, and Lyons. I became particularly friendly with Dr Van Mechelen at Hassalt and Dr Louis Musse at Lyons. There were also two memorable trips to conferences in Lisbon and Copenhagen in the Jaguar. During the latter I visted Bornholm where John Gilson, who succeeded Charles Fletcher as director of the Pneumoconiosis Research Unit, later conducted an interesting epidemiological study of chronic bronchitis.[19] There was also a visit to Nigeria to visit my old friend Kenneth Mellanby, who had become principal of the University of Ibadan. He had previously offered me the professorship of tuberculosis there, which I accepted. Soon afterwards, however, over an expensive lunch, Sir Andrew Cohen asked me to resign to enable a political appointment to be made. I agreed. I learnt a lot about the difficulties of these new colonial universities and the tuberculosis situation there.

The 1950s were for me extremely educational. I developed an entirely new attitude to medicine. Looking back, I think that the main scientific advances were concerned with the determination of the normal distribution of medical variables such as blood pressure and pulmonary function, and the use of the randomised controlled trial to measure the effectiveness of therapies. This latter innovation, which I ascribe to Bradford Hill, at last offered clinical medicine an experimental approach to the validation of its practices and treatments. It was high time that medicine and the National Health Service monitored and accounted for how they were serving the public. Too much that was being done in the name of health care lacked scientific validation. I had always been a supporter of the NHS, passionately believing that "all effective treatment must be free," but there seemed far too little interest in proving and promoting what was effective. In the course of our surveys I had sufficient contact with the working of hospitals and clinics and the delivery of health care generally to be dismayed by what passed for service. I was troubled by the variable and curious prescribing of general practitioners, the all too varied reasons for referring patients to hospital, the attitudes and behaviour of the consultants they encountered there, and the variable ways in which death certificates were completed. I sometimes thought of all this as my Rhondda Fach worm's eye view of the working of the NHS. It was a gloomy picture, but suddenly superimposed upon it were the results of Bradford Hill's streptomycin trial,[20] showing what could be achieved by a really effective therapy. We were then working on the epidemiology of tuberculosis in the Rhondda Fach, and it was not long before streptomycin made its impact on our own findings. It was at this time that I began to wonder and discuss with my colleagues how other forms of medical treatment would stand up to the test of a randomised controlled trial. Looking back, this is undoubtedly the point at which the immense potential of the randomised controlled trial began to dawn on me. It offered clinical medicine, and health services generally, an experimental approach to questions of effectiveness and efficiency, and a massive step forward from "validation" by clinical opinion and essentially subjective observations.

Over the next few years I was to get so hooked on the idea of randomised controlled trials that a few extra words on them might be justified in the hope of helping non-medical readers to appreciate something of my immense regard for them. In fact some colleagues thought of it as nothing short of an obsession. I think it was the simplicity of the idea in relation to the magnitude of the advance it represented that captured my admiration, initially. The idea of a controlled trial in which the value of a new treatment is assessed in comparison to that of an existing one by applying each to a comparable group of subjects was not new, but it was not until the arrival of the randomised controlled trial that major problems of ensuring matched groups were largely overcome. Matching on the basis of human judgment is too open to error and the distortions of bias, but by introducing the random allocation of subjects to groups, the randomised controlled trial transcended such human fallibility and set controlled trials on firmer foundations. Also, where large numbers of subjects are involved, randomisation assists the even dispersion of all the personal characteristics likely to affect outcome. The more I thought about the design of the randomised controlled trial the more I liked it, particularly its wide applicability. Of course, there were limitations to its potential, but these seemed unimportant in comparison with the advance it represented.[21]

Despite all the happiness of this period, a small but growing undercurrent of worry introduced itself into my life in the later 1950s, as it became clear that it was the MRC's intention to transfer pneumoconiosis research to the NCB in the not too distant future. The job of the MRC was to develop techniques and surveillance strategies and then hand them over to the industry concerned. This seemed reasonable, but I could not help becoming increasingly concerned about where this would leave me. I found myself with mixed feelings: wanting to remain in pneumoconiosis research but doubting whether there would be the same kind of role for me when it became the responsibility of the NCB. The prospects did not look particularly good. Stan Roach and I had been testing the possibility of a major project to investigate far more fully the relationship between dust dosage and disease, and although the NCB had found little difficulty in approving it, they had also made it quite clear that they did not want us to take charge of arrangements.[22] This was very much the low spot in an otherwise remarkably happy decade; a time of total uncertainty. The future of the Pneumoconiosis Research Unit was still undecided, but it was likely to be the study of some other industrial disease, and I doubted whether my community approach would be of much use. The technique is really only applicable to industrial diseases if the prevalence is high. The great question was where would I go? I had no other direction or area of research in mind. I had not even contemplated a major transfer to work on another disease. My real love was pneumoconiosis. In fact, deep down, I did not want to leave the Pneumoconiosis Research Unit. I had been really happy there and I was frightened of the idea of leaving.

The solution came when Fred Heaf, the inventor of the Heaf test and professor of tuberculosis in the Welsh National School of Medicine, announced his retirement. It occurred to me that I would have a chance, and that the job would have advantages. Our relations with the Welsh National School of Medicine had never been particularly close, although the latest professor of medicine had been very friendly. I thought that if I became a professor the consultants would be more willing to cooperate in surveys and randomised clinical trials, and I would not need to lose contact with the Pneumoconiosis Research Unit. The professor of pathology had always maintained close links with the Pneumoconiosis Research Unit.[23] Also, the fact that Professor Heaf had spent nearly five months a year travelling for the Colonial Office gave me an idea. If I got the job I would have time to run a small research unit, if I could get the backing of the MRC, and I thought that I might. MRC headquarters had already shown strong support for my work and the team I had built. After consulting Professor Harold Scarborough,[24] who supported the idea of my application for the professorship, I went ahead and applied. Sir George Pickering[25] gave me a reference and I got the job against fairly stiff opposition.

CO-WORKERS

There were four groups of people associated with my surveys. At the base, as it were, were the scientific staff of the Pneumoconiosis Research Unit. All my proposals were criticised by them and often improved. I remain grateful to them. Then there were the medical members of the scientific staff who came on surveys with me. The first of these was Jeffrey Chapman, who was a tower of strength in the early difficult days. He helped me during the surveys at the Haig and Bankhall collieries. He left to fulfil a lifetime ambition – to be the medical officer of a whaling ship – but later turned up as an efficient leader of one of the NCB medical teams, and still later as a member of MRC headquarters staff. He was a great loss and I had difficulty in replacing him, as epidemiology was much less popular then amongst doctors than it is now. There followed a series of short-term appointments – one English, one Indian, and one American. It did not work out and I was often alone but nevertheless managed fairly well. The so-called renaissance in epidemiology did not happen in my world until Bill Miall arrived in 1952. We had the memory of Salonica as a bond in addition to our common interest in epidemiology to help us work together, and Bill fortunately came to Cardiff with a powerful interest in blood pressure.[26] I always wanted my co-workers to have a different interest. After studying the distribution and inheritance of blood pressure in the Rhondda Fach and the Vale of Glamorgan, and making a valuable contribution to the subject,[27] as well as helping me on numerous surveys, he eventually took on the directorship of an MRC unit in Jamaica, which I had helped persuade Sir Harold Himsworth and the Wellcome Foundation to establish there. By that time Bill needed other fields to conquer, and Jamaica had some attraction. It had an established medical school; it was more or less English speaking, and the normal distribution of blood pressure in the population there seemed, on the evidence available, curiously raised. I visited him there about once a year and had great admiration for the way he coped with the incredible difficulties associated with field epidemiology in the Third World. The results of his surveys were probably not quite as exciting as we had hoped, but they were of great interest. We still do not know why the Jamaican population has raised blood pressures[28] and a higher percentage of abnormal Q wave abnormalities in their ECGs than their counterparts in the USA and why its representatives in the UK still have very few deaths from ischaemic heart disease. Bill eventually returned to the UK in the late 1960s, and I was not surprised. Circumstances had not remained quite as they were when first he went to Jamaica. Fortunately, after some searching for the right job, he settled at Northwick Park and took charge of an important trial of therapy for slightly raised blood pressure.[29]

My next recruit came in a different way. Ian Higgins joined the Pneumoconiosis Research Unit originally as a clinical physiologist and only moved across to epidemiology when he became disillusioned about his future as a pulmonary physiologist. He soon, however, became interested in the epidemiology of chronic bronchitis and in particular the effect of smoking.[30] It was possible to study this in the same surveys as I was studying pneumoconiosis, and the symbiosis worked well and helped me a great deal. Later he became especially interested in ischaemic heart disease,[31] and I have already explained elsewhere how his growing research connections with North America assisted his decision to move to the USA in 1960. I had hopes that he would return to the UK, but he did not. After some initial troubles in the USA he soon established himself by his work on coal workers' pneumoconiosis and the effects of smoking. He became a Professor at Ann Arbor. I was never so close to him as to Bill Miall but he gave me great help, for which I shall ever be grateful, and over the years we have continued to keep in touch.

The third in this remarkable series, who arrived at the Pneumoconiosis Research Unit just before the close of the decade, was Julian Tudor Hart, a young doctor whose communist faith had survived Hungary. He came from working in London as a general practitioner and on a part-time basis with Richard Doll as a next step in developing his epidemiological interests, and we had an immediate natural bond, not only through the strength of our research interests but because of my contact with his father's work during the Spanish Civil War. I realised from the first that he was important, as well as likeable, but I doubted whether I could keep him as an epidemiologist. He did one survey meticulously and all too soon departed into primary care. I do not remember his friendly farewell remarks to me exactly, but they were something like this: "Archie, you're OK. You are doing good, but you are not doing it very fast. I think by changing to primary care I can have a much quicker effect." I think he was probably right. He has certainly had an important effect on primary care in the UK. For him it was virtually impossible to stop being a care giver and concentrate predominantly on research. While some of us survived on a more detached, long-term scale of hope for change he could not stand back from the immediacy of the suffering he saw about him in the Rhondda. In a way I think I knew, very deeply, how he felt, but I had known too many days when the immediacy of disease gripped my waking hours, and perhaps this now made it easier for me to view things from a little further off. I still see Julian at intervals and I am grateful for the way in which my views on primary care have benefited from our meetings.[32] I admire him greatly.

The next section was the radiographic one, which was of the greatest possible importance for our studies of chest disease. This was really a subsection of the radiographic department of the Pneumoconiosis Research Unit. In the background were the practical skills of John Gilson, but in control was Bill Clarke, a remarkable ex-Army radiographer. He was undoubtedly mainly responsible for the high standard of the chest films (which is essential to the study of pneumoconiosis) we were able to achieve under field conditions. Under Bill Clarke were three other radiographers. They were, in order of appearance, Megan Pritchard, the late Jim Chambers, and Sheelah Latham. Megan, a charming Welsh-speaking radiographer, bore the brunt of our early difficulties bravely and successfully. Jim was a severe bronchitic and asthmatic but worked enormously hard through the terrible winter of the first Rhondda Fach survey and many other surveys later. Sheelah, with her imperturbable charm and skill, kept our survey populations and the whole team reasonably contented. One of her achievements was to persuade the clergy at Staveley in Derbyshire to pray for the success of our survey when we made a short research excursion there in 1957.[33] Behind the radiographers were the men in the dark-room who were also very important. They were in a position to wreck any radiographer's work, as we knew from the early days. There was one occasion when a temporary got drunk and forgot to wash the films, and they all came out pink and had to be retaken. The chief in the darkroom became Roland Harris, a photographer whom I found one day during the first Rhondda Fach survey. He has been with the MRC ever since as photographer and darkroom specialist. In addition, he took some excellent films of our activities during all our surveys from 1953 onwards. Acting as his relief in the darkroom was the late Roy Rees, a rather dour Welsh speaker who drove our x ray van all round the country with never the suggestion of a mistake. I am deeply grateful to them all.

163

The next group consisted of what was usually termed my "team." As I have already said, it consisted, from a survey point of view, of fieldworkers and headquarters staff. It was a group that grew up slowly and partly by chance. Gwilym Jonathan was its first member. He came as the result of an advertisement. He was an ex-miner from the Rhondda Fach who had made a miraculous recovery from severe tuberculosis in the prechemotherapy days. I employed him originally to teach me how to take coalmining industrial histories and how to persuade miners to be x rayed. It proved a lucky choice. He was extremely successful as a persuader; gentle and slow, but determined. He was a gentle, intelligent, likeable man and even after his eventual retirement he still returned to help me on occasions with major follow-up surveys.

Hugh Bates was the second to arrive, not long after Gwilym. His appointment was, I think, suggested by Charles Fletcher, when we were about to do the follow-up survey at Wattstown Colliery in the Rhondda Fach in 1949. He was an ex-miner of the Wattstown Colliery, an open communist, and an ex-boxer. He looked the part, short and powerfully built. He also had, even in 1949, the largest shadow of PMF in his lungs that I had ever seen. He had been in the Pneumoconiosis Research Unit ward at Llandough Hospital and had heard of our activities, wanted to help, and came to see me. I was surprised and at the same time impressed. In some ways taking him on seemed a bad bet medically but from the first we got on well and I employed him. He was a great success. The most surprising thing about his work on the surveys was that he was as successful in persuading non-miners and women to cooperate with us as he was with miners. Fortunately his medical condition, very surprisingly, deteriorated very slowly and he continued working with me until 1963. Unfortunately his last years turned out to be terrible. Just able to walk, forbidden to drink, he suffered grimly from gallstones, on which the doctors did not dare to operate. I was almost relieved when he died. He deserved a happier retirement. It would have been difficult to find a more loyal friend.

The next to arrive was Fred Moore. He was, in most ways, different from the others. He was small and stocky, with powerful glasses. He had had some contact with the coal industry through his father, who had been a minor official in the industry, but he himself had started out as a grocer before the war. His wartime Army career had been a distinguished one in which he had risen from private to captain. In fact, he held the rank of major for a short time before demobilisation. After the war he had decided on a new career as a male nurse, and when he came to see me he had already qualified with distinction and seemed to be en route for a post of some importance in nursing. I was naturally impressed by his interest in joining us, but also a little frightened. I badly needed someone to bring order into our record system and Fred oozed order and efficiency. What worried me was that I would not be able to keep him interested. I had no idea then how enormously important he would prove to be for epidemiological research over the next 30 years. During that period he organised our records in such a way that they were all available 30 years later. In addition he showed himself better than any doctor in getting blood out of difficult veins; better than most hospital technicians in taking electrocardiograms under difficult conditions; and better than most hospital departments in producing diagrams for slides and illustrations. He could also code death certificates as well as any member of the Registrar General's department of medical records. Later he became a valued colleague, checking my calculations and writings. He has stayed with me long after retirement and into the 1980s and, although very deaf due to war service, and overweight, he is still invaluable. Without him our research output would have been far less, and in spite of his occasional rudeness and bad temper I shall always be deeply grateful for such a remarkable collaboration.

The next to join the team was Louise Roberts. After a series of rather unsatisfactory secretaries Louise appeared in response to an advertisement. She was well educated, with an honours degree in English, and thought she would like the survey life. She tried, liked it, and was first rate. With Fred and Louise at headquarters, I was free to spend long hours out in the field, home visiting or reading x rays at the mobile x ray units.

The last of the team to arrive was Tom Benjamin, a watch

repairer from the Rhondda Fawr. I think Gwilym recommended him. He again was different – a rather mercurial character, not particularly interested in pneumoconiosis but very interested in people and how to persuade them, and even more how to trace them in follow up studies. I never knew him so well as I did the others, but he made a valuable contribution.

It would be wrong not to mention the statisticians, Peter Oldham and the late Bob Carpenter. They were part of the scientific staff of the unit and not part of my team, but they gave invaluable help to everybody. They did not come on surveys with us but were of the greatest importance in the planning of our work and the analysis of the results.

All members of the team except one continued working for the MRC until they died or retired. Fred went on working for the MRC on various grants long after his retirement. The one exception to this pattern was Louise. Quite suddenly, in 1959, she disliked me so much that she could not go on. I never understood how I had sinned, but I was clearly to blame and she left. She was a great loss, but I am grateful for what she did while she was there.

PERSONAL

The population of Rhoose Farm House changed from time to time as bachelors got married. Martin Wright left us in 1952, but his place was soon filled by Dr Bill Briscoe, an Oxford physiologist, full of ideas, some of which I never fully understood. He was excellent company and regularly larger than life. On one occasion, after complaining that his room at the Pneumoconiosis Research Unit had far too little floor space, he went ahead and divided it, horizontally, into two rooms each about six feet high. On another occasion he went to a rather posh dance in full evening dress and Wellington boots. I still remember a breakfast with him when he admitted that he had been charged by the police as being drunk in charge of a stationary motor cycle. He married an American doctor and later became a professor in New York. It was then that Bill Miall joined us for a few months, after which he married and reared a family in Penarth, where I kept in close everyday touch with them until they departed for Jamaica. Stewart Kilpatrick took Bill's place at Rhoose Farm House. At that time he was a medical registrar in the Pneumoconiosis Research Unit's ward at Llandough Hospital. His arrival marked the start of an enduring friendship. I remember giving a large party at Rhoose when he became engaged to Joan. She has, with my permission, been trying to educate me, mainly politically, ever since. Mr and Mrs Barlow served us well throughout these years. At times it must have been hard work for them, but we were away most of the day and they had what I hope was a comfortable home base. I do not think we gave them too much trouble. We were reasonably disciplined and, except for occasional parties, fairly sober.

Personally, I look back on the period with great nostalgia. It was wonderful being able to discuss any ideas I had with people in the same house with the same kinds of interests and scientific background. It was like the atmosphere I remembered from my undergraduate days at King's, but at a much higher and more specialised level. Access to such companionship at the end of what were usually long days was remarkably catalytic, and this may explain why I was able to read so much in this period, despite pressures on time. Possibly it was because of the routine I built up of always reading in bed before going to sleep, no matter what time I turned in. Although this late night literary diet included its share of second rate detective stories, it was in this period that I became addicted to Jane Austen and Trollope. Politically, it was Koestler's writings that had the greatest influence on me and I moved further to the right. I also came across Medawar, who introduced me to Karl Popper, who was to have his great influence on me in the 1960s. For a time I attended meetings of the Fabian Society, of which I had been a member since before the war, but I found the other members unbelievably boring and stopped going.

As food rationing disappeared and the need for our smallholding diminished I decided to try my hand at sport again. For the first time I found myself discovering that I had leisure again. I had been a better than average lawn tennis player and felt that this was my best option, so I joined the Dinas Powys Tennis Club, near Llandough Hospital. I still recall an obviously memorable remark by one of its lady members on my first visit. She asked me where I lived, and when I mentioned Rhoose she replied, "What a pity. All the best people live in Penarth." Fortunately such a remark was generally out of character with the social climate of the club and my membership survived. I enjoyed many hours of tennis there, and even won the open singles one year.

I steadily reverted to my prewar levels of travel, as restrictions lifted across Europe, permitting me to ski at Christmas and explore the Mediterranean in summer. Skiing was usually with George Rink and his family. He had recently married a widow with two sons. Occasionally we were joined by my sister Helen and her family, with whom I also made my first postwar trip to the Mediterranean, to Ischia. This visit was a huge success, leading to more ambitious tours, first of the Greek mainland and then of Rhodes, Crete, Italy, Sardinia, and Malta. I enjoyed them all and became, I suppose, an early, convinced European. Together with all my professional journeyings I was lucky to get such an international education.

I was also fortunate in other interests. I started to buy pictures and sculpture. Originally I think my sitting room walls were covered by reproductions, mainly of works by El Greco – one of my juvenile enthusiasms. In the 1950s they were slowly replaced by original paintings. Among them was the wonderful abstract by Ben Nicholson, "Variations on the Shape of Beer Mugs," and two paintings and a sculpture by Michael Ayrton. I must have had more than a lucky streak in my early ventures as a collector.

TWO MEDICAL INTERLUDES

My health was generally good during this period, but there were two odd incidents. The first started as I was driving back from a visit to Manchester with Bill Miall in 1954. I slowly realised that my left leg was getting weak. I was also feeling generally ill with vague stomach pains and I let Bill drive me home. The next morning I found that my abdominal muscles on the left side were paralysed, as were some of the muscles of my left leg. I had also been constipated for a few days – an unusual occurrence for me. I was soon in hospital and seen by a variety of medical experts, who despite a good deal of uncertainty finally felt that I might be suffering from polio-myelitis and, to be on the safe side, notified the case. Although it was a rare disease in men of my age, the fact that I had recently been on holiday in an area where there had been a few cases possibly settled the diagnosis. Within a week or two, however, I made a complete recovery and returned to work. In retrospect I think the diagnosis was wrong. I believe I had a mild attack of acute porphyria. While in Manchester I had had backache and I think I took a sleeping pill, which may well have contained a barbiturate. I can, however, scarcely blame the doctors for missing such a rarity. They had really nothing to go on. If only I had hallucinated a little they might have got on to it and saved my sister and myself a lot of trouble a few years later.

The second incident was in 1956, while we were preparing to go up to Annandale, in Dumfriesshire, for the second part of a comparative survey[34] of tuberculosis that had begun in the Vale of Glamorgan. I noticed some spots on the back of my right hand which slowly became hard, though not painful. They were seen by all the Pneumoconiosis Research Unit doctors, and there were some jokes about "Archie's syphilis." By chance, several weeks later, I was asked to advise a dermatologist who was doing a survey of athlete's foot amongst miners. The conversation stopped abruptly when I happened to put my right hand on the table. I was taken to a cubicle and had a chunk of skin removed from my right hand, and the pathology showed it to be epithelioma. This was not too serious as such cancers rarely spread, but it marked the start of a series of misfortunes. Firstly, the wound burst and went septic. That was not too serious, but when I recovered I was told that Sir Harold Himsworth, Mellanby's successor as secretary of the MRC, was worried about me. It was thought I might have suffered increased radiation exposure during my x ray surveys and that this might have caused the epithelioma. He wanted me to see the leading specialist in London. This was good of him, but the result was disastrous. I saw the specialist, a charming, intelligent man, who examined me and found a small mobile gland in my right axilla. He asked me how long it had been there and I had to admit that I had no idea. I thought vaguely that it had been there since the time of a septic finger sometime during the Spanish Civil War, but I was not at all sure. He then asked if he could take it out. I was not too keen as I was due to start in Annandale in about a fortnight, but he promised that it would only take a few days, so I agreed. I was then introduced to a distinguished surgeon, the date was fixed for about a week ahead, and I went back to Cardiff.

I returned to London the night before the operation. I think I must have had some unconscious fears, as I made a curious half joke to Martin Wright as I set out. He liked Latin tags, and as I said goodbye to him I quoted: *"Morituri te salutant"*. I was given a side ward and slept well. I came round from the anaesthetic rather late the next day to find, to my surprise, the whole of my chest swathed in bandages, but I was feeling pretty well. The next morning I felt much brighter and ate a hearty breakfast. Then came a visit from the surgeon, who displayed a curious seriousness, so I ventured a fairly penetrating question about the unexpected mass of bandages, whereupon he advised me to prepare myself for less than favourable news: "I must tell you the truth. Your axilla is full of cancerous tissue. I have done my best to excise it and have removed your pectoralis minor, but I may well not have saved your life." Before he turned and left the room he also gave me an impression that further developments might not take all that long. For a moment the world seemed to end.

After a short period of surprise and shock I turned as far as I could on my side and sobbed unashamedly. I do not remember much about the rest of the day. It was full of self-pity, though, chiefly on account of all the effort put into my fight back from the despair of Salonica –

What fool or blackguard gave me eyes to see or ears to hear?

– to a position where I was poised for a successful scientific career. It seemed so unfair. Relief did not come until the early hours of the next morning, in a curious way. I worked out a simple plan of how I would spend my remaining time. I would go back to Cardiff for five or six weeks, just long enough to tidy up, hand over my ongoing research, and sell my house. Then I would go and live with my sister and her family in Galashiels, who had looked after me so well when I returned home from life as a prisoner of war. I could then die in the local cottage hospital which was, I knew, very comfortable. A curious feeling of peace came over me when I had completed the plan, and I fell asleep.

The next day was much better and I slowly regained control and was able to deal with visitors. I had been told that the pathologist had not yet reported, but I never doubted the surgeon's words. Days passed and visitors came in increasing numbers. It was soon clear that they were more embarrassed than I was. The only trouble now was that my temperature began to rise, and for the first time I began to feel ill. A hospital cross infection was diagnosed. It was for this reason that, when the good news arrived from the pathologist that he could find no evidence of cancer cells in the tissue removed from my axilla, I did not quite react as I should have. An informal party was arranged; Sir Harold Himsworth very kindly came over from MRC headquarters, but the surgeon did not come, and unfortunately I was beginning to feel so ill with my infection that I did not enjoy my resurrection as much as I should have. The next few days were hell, as they battled against the infection, searching for pockets of pus in my chest and trying out new antibiotics. To their credit they won, and I am very grateful, particularly to the houseman.

I recovered slowly, but it was clear that the movement of my right arm would be seriously limited for some time. The original physician was kind to me, but I never had the heart to inquire why a "cold" section was not done at the time of the operation. It may be of interest to some that at the peak of my despair I never had any desire to talk to a clergyman of any denomination. It may also help others to know that planning one's last few months on earth gave one man much needed peace and will, I hope, help me when the next time comes. I finally made a complete recovery. The only residual handicap is that if I swim with my eyes shut I tend to swerve to the left because of my pectoral weakness.

Many years later I discovered that I had in this curious period survived yet another fantastic hazard. When I was told that I was, biochemically, a severe porphyric I made inquiries about my anaesthetic for the operation. They had used a barbiturate in the induction phase, and although this is not always fatal to porphyrics in the latent phase it is considered a serious risk. This is no criticism of the anaesthetist. He could not possibly have known. It just shows that I was lucky, as I still am. But there was no luck about the success of the survey in Annandale. The skills and the resolve of the team rewarded me with the lowest refusal rates yet recorded for such a survey.

NOTES

1 See Fletcher C M, *et al.* The classification of radiographic appearances in coalminers' pneumoconiosis. *Journal of the Faculty of Radiologists* 1949; 1: 1.

2 For survey details see Cochrane A L, *et al.* Pulmonary tuberculosis in the Rhondda Fach: an interim report of a survey of a mining community. *Br Med J* 1952; i: 843–53.

3 See Cochrane A L, *et al.* A follow-up chest x ray survey in the Rhondda Fach. *Br Med J* 1955; i: 371–8.

4 Dr Victor Henry Springett, MD, FRCP, consultant chest physician, Birmingham Chest Clinic.

5 For the results of the survey see Cochrane A L, *et al.* Factors influencing the radiological attack rate of progressive massive fibrosis. *Br Med J* 1956; ii: 1193–9.

6 See Oldham P D, Roach S A. A sampling procedure for measuring industrial dust exposure. *Br J Ind Med* 1952; 9: 112–19.

7 A name given to the survey by Dr Philip Hugh-Jones, its co-director, and reflecting his ornithological interests. From the time of his arrival at the Pneumoconiosis Research Unit the use of bird names had become a trend in the nomenclature of experiments and experimental groups. His decision to use the term "Eagle" reflects the perceived importance of this particular survey.

8 Professor Charles Fletcher, who had close contact with the Eagle survey, feels that Archie's concern regarding the lack of portable physiological equipment may well have led him to overcriticise the work on disability being carried out by Pneumoconiosis Research Unit physiologists. He points out that "without the work of the Eagle physiologists there would not have been a clear approach to testing miners' disability. Previously, little had been known about the physiological basis of breathlessness caused by pneumoconiosis. The Eagle survey showed that this was due chiefly to impaired ventilatory capacity, so that the maximum breathing capacity was the best single test. This was subsequently simplified to the forced expiratory volume, which Archie used in his subsequent surveys. Neither the complicated lung volume measurements used in the MRC surveys of miners in 1938 nor the vital capacity measurements used in the first studies of miners in the Pneumoconiosis Research Unit in 1946 were as discriminatory as the maximum breathing capacity test. That the small samples of miners used in the Eagle study were fortunately representative of the populations they were taken from was later established by Archie when he found the same relationship between x ray category and disability in his larger samples of miners as that which had been found in the Eagle study."

9 Gilson J, Hugh-Jones P. Lung function in coalworkers' pneumoconiosis. Medical Research Council Special Report Series No 290, 1955.

10 Cochrane A L, Miall W E, et al. Factors influencing the radiological attack rate of progressive massive fibrosis. Br Med J 1956; i; 1193–9.

11 See Miall W E, Caplan A, et al. An epidemiological study of rheumatoid arthritis associated with characteristic chest x ray appearances in coal workers. Br Med J 1953; ii: 1231–6.

12 Professor Jonas Henrik Kellgren, FRCS, FRCP.

13 Later the Arthritis and Rheumatism Council.

14 A view of this collaboration of the author's team and visiting psychiatrists from the Maudsley Hospital has recently been provided by Professor Ken Rawnsley, one of the psychiatrists who took part in the venture: see Bulletin of the Royal College of Psychiatrists 1988; 12: 8–11.

15 Professor Wilfred Robert Trotter, DM, FRCP, consultant physician, Thyroid Clinic, University College Hospital.

16 See Trotter W R, Cochrane A L, et al. A goitre survey in the Vale of Glamorgan. British Journal of Preventive and Social Medicine 1962; 16: 16–21.

17 See Higgins I T T, Cochrane A L, Thomas A J. Epidemiological studies of coronary disease. British Journal of Preventive and Social Medicine 1963; 17: 153–65. See also Thomas A J, Cochrane A L, Higgins I T T. Lancet 1958; ii; 540.

18 See Cochrane A L. The attack rate of progressive massive fibrosis. Br J Ind Med 1962; 19: 52–64.

19 See Olsen H C, Gilson J C. Respiratory symptoms, bronchitis, and

ventilatory capacity in men. An Anglo-Danish comparison, with special references to smoking habits. *Br Med J* 1960; i: 450–6.

20 The reference is to Daniels M, Hill A B. Chemotherapy of pulmonary tuberculosis in young adults. An analysis of the combined results of three Medical Research Council trials. *Br Med J* 1952; i: 1162.

21 For fuller comment by the author on randomised controlled trials see *Effectiveness and efficiency, random reflections on health services.* London, 1972: 20–66.

22 The intention was to study dust–disease relationships in 20 selected collieries.

23 Professor Jethro Gough, MD, FRCP, FCPath.

24 Then professor of medicine, Welsh National School of Medicine, and director, Medical Unit, Cardiff Royal Infirmary.

25 Regius professor of medicine, University of Oxford.

26 Bill Miall had recently been house physician to George Pickering at St Mary's, Paddington, and had inevitably become involved in Pickering's studies of hypertension.

27 With the help of colleagues, Bill Miall's work confirmed that blood pressure levels were influenced multifactorially and that the familial factor was almost certainly due, in large part, to polygenic inheritance. See Miall W E, Oldham P D. Factors influencing arterial pressure in the general population. *Clin Sci* 1958; 17: 409–44; also Miall W E, Oldham P D. The hereditary factor in arterial blood pressure. *Br Med J* 1963; i: 75–80.

28 Bill Miall found that the distribution of blood pressure in Jamaicans was wider than in Welshmen – more hypertensives and more hypotensives – and that similar factors influence blood pressure levels similarly in the two races. See Miall W E, Kass E H, *et al.* Factors influencing arterial pressure in the general population of Jamaica. *Br Med J* 1962; i: 497–502.

29 See MRC Working Party on Mild and Moderate Hypertension. MRC trial of treatment of mild hypertension: principal results. *Br Med J* 1985; i: 97–104; also Miall W E, Greenberg G. *Mild hypertension – is there pressure to treat?* Cambridge, 1987.

30 Ian Higgins had a broader interest in factors influencing pulmonary function than this indicates. For further reading on his work in this period see Higgins I T T, *et al.* Respiratory symptoms and pulmonary disability in an industrial town. *Br Med J* 1956; ii: 904–9; also Higgins I T T, *et al.* Population studies of chronic respiratory disease. A comparison of miners, foundry-workers and others in Stavely, Derbyshire. *Br J Ind Med* 1959; 16: 255–68.

31 See Thomas A J, Cochrane A L, Higgins I T T. The measurement of the prevalence of ischaemic heart disease. *Lancet* 1958; ii: 540–4; also Higgins I T T, Cochrane A L. Epidemiological studies of coronary disease. *British Journal of Preventive and Social Medicine* 1963; 17: 153–65.

32 Julian Tudor Hart's attitude to research and primary care is well represented in *A new kind of doctor*. London, 1988.

33 See Higgins I T T, *et al. Br J Ind Med* 1959; **16**: 255–68.

34 A comparative study in which members of the author's team were to collaborate with a group that had just completed an initial survey of tuberculosis in Annandale (*Br Med J* 1957; **ii**: 185). The leaders of this group, Drs Jack Cochran and C Clayson of the Lochmaben Sanitorium in Annandale, felt that there were important similarities with survey work already in progress in the Vale of Glamorgan and proposed a collaborative study of tuberculosis in these two regions. Interest in the project shown by cardiologists of the Dumfries and Galloway Royal Infirmary also led to its extension to incorporate studies of cardiovascular disease. In the author's absence, the team from the Pneumoconiosis Research Unit was led by Dr Ian Higgins.

5 The sixties

For the next 10 years I was the David Davies professor of tuberculosis and chest diseases in the Welsh National School of Medicine and honorary director of the new Epidemiology Unit I had persuaded the MRC to establish in Cardiff. It was a period in which I lived in two different worlds and, despite my hopes and intentions, they overlapped far less than I would have wished. It seems almost natural, therefore, to consider them separately.

ACADEMIC LIFE

Firstly, a brief review of my days as David Davies professor. When I came to the chair at the end of the 1950s there had just been the most revolutionary period of change in the field of tuberculosis and chest diseases. There had been unparalleled, almost unbelievable advances in the treatment of tuberculosis, and mortality and morbidity figures had declined to levels unimaginable a decade or so before. In this country, as across the other developed industrial nations, tuberculosis's reign as a major disease had run its course. Streptomycin had shown the way to reliable, effective treatment, and for those whose clinical experience antedated antibiotic therapy it was as though we had seen practice in two different ages. Tuberculous meningitis no longer represented an almost certain death sentence. Miraculously, patients were now expected to live. Patients with severe pulmonary tuberculosis, despite the erosion of their lungs, could look forward to recovery rather than death. This conquest of a disease that had cast a dark shadow over the lives of all too many for so long also had its wider secondary effects. The rapid decline in tuberculosis incidence allowed medical interests to refocus on other forms of chest disease that had formerly lain neglected in the shadow of tuberculosis; diseases as important as chronic bronchitis. Also there had been a considerable expansion of prevention interests, including a national spread of immunisation programmes. Little was as it had been a decade before and yet the design of the course for which I was now responsible bore little relationship to the new order of things. Even accepting that it had been designed to meet the needs of doctors from developing countries it was obvious that major reforms were needed, but what I had not realised was the great inertia against change that existed in academic institutions. It took me nearly three years to negotiate an adequate place in the curriculum for epidemiology and medical statistics. I wanted all the students, many of whom were destined eventually to serve in public health and health service administration, to appreciate the value of good data collection and analysis, and the relevance of statistically astute surveillance to health services everywhere. I believed it important for them to have the right research perspectives, feeling that this might help medicine to become more orientated towards monitoring its own performance. Far greater attention to the epidemiology of chest diseases also figured in this new provision, together with special studies of observer error (in the reading of chest x rays) and factors involved in assessing the cost effectiveness of health care services. I felt that the changes were vindicated just as soon as students began to give greater thought to research methods and the analysis of data, and to appreciate the special place of controlled trials in medical research, as I had done more than a decade earlier during Bradford Hill's lectures at the London School of Hygiene and Tropical Medicine.

I also felt a good deal happier in 1962 when the course moved to much more suitable accommodation at Sully Hospital. This transfer owed a great deal to the hospital's medical director, my old friend from the prisoner of war camp in Salonica, Bill Foreman, and had the considerable secondary advantage of freeing the course's original accommodation at 4

Richmond Road, Cardiff, for my recently formed Epidemiology Unit. This was a more complex achievement than it sounds. It was quite a manoeuvre, involving a good deal of unseen negotiating. The least pleasant aspect of this period of change was the departure of a number of lecturers who had made a contribution to the former course, but whose teaching was no longer required. I also had to change the external examiners, one of whom almost refused to be sacked. Fortunately their successors, Vic Springett and Reg Bignall,[1] proved a great success, and with their assistance I soon changed the final examination paper to a multiple choice questionnaire, which seemed a reasonable step, given the difficulties some of the postgraduates had in writing English at examination speed, and the difficulty their examiners had in reading the scripts.

As well as reorganising the course and transferring it to better accommodation there were also the pastoral challenges of academic life. It would have been difficult not to be concerned about the welfare of quite a number of students arriving with each fresh intake to the Tuberculosis and Chest Diseases Course. Usually they were from the Third World and their problems were characteristically about finance, accommodation, or loneliness, although occasionally they were political or psychological. I did my best to cope with them all and found the opportunities to help highly rewarding. I suspect that I enjoyed the fatherly role in which I often felt cast, and can only hope that my enthusiasm for helping did not make me meddlesome. One way in which I sought to reduce some of the loneliness I saw about me was to organise fairly frequent parties at Rhoose Farm House to introduce students to a range of colleagues and friends. I knew how lonely some of them were and hoped that the idea would catch on with other academics, but the response was minimal.

The end of each academic year brought other problems. There was an unfortunate tendency of a very small minority of the postgraduates to offer me presents before the final examination, which had of course to be refused, but it was difficult to do this without giving offence and damaging good relationships that had sometimes taken a fair time to establish.

Another problem was interviewing those who failed the examination. They typically claimed that they could not return to their countries disgraced by a shameful result. On occasions there was literally "wailing and gnashing of teeth," but no one attempted violence, although a sort of bribery was suggested occasionally. I explained that the final decision had to be that of the external examiners and advised them to resit. Such interviews were emotionally exhausting. Another more serious problem was my discovery that an important percentage of those attending the course had no intention of returning to their own countries to cope with tuberculosis problems there. They were using the course as a means of entry into the UK to obtain a job in the NHS in an unpopular speciality such as geriatrics. This annoyed me, and I am pretty sure I reduced its incidence, but it was hard to tell from the application form what were the applicant's intentions. The technique was more prevalent amongst the Indians and Pakistanis than the others.

It was only when the course was better organised and I had the assistance of a senior lecturer that I got around to really considering the relevance of what we were providing for future medical specialists of the Third World. It did not take me long to realise that the UK was the wrong place in which to teach doctors from developing countries about tuberculosis. Although in my lectures I used to argue the need to rely on sputum smears for diagnosis, and on domiciliary treatment, this was not what they were witnessing at the Sully Hospital, where diagnosis often included sputum culture and determination of resistance, lateral and oblique x rays, and occasionally tomography. Opportunities for inpatient care were also remarkably good. The contrast we were demonstrating seemed illogical and possibly dangerous. I felt that it would be much better to have their studies based in Africa or Asia, with lecturers flown out from the UK and elsewhere, but also using local teachers. My rough calculations suggested that the cost to the World Health Organisation and other supporting bodies would be less. I thought I had a good case, which I argued in London with little success. The Ministry was against my idea. They wanted the course to remain in the UK

179

on political grounds. The World Health Organisation, on the other hand, thought the idea impracticable. This body was chiefly interested in establishing a course in Prague to keep the East–West political balance. It did, however, start a course in India, at Madanapalle, but it was not a great success. Eventually I gave up trying to do anything about the problem but remained convinced that it was inappropriate to prepare postgraduates for the chest disease problems of the Third World by way of a course in Cardiff. The disillusionment I felt, despite the popularity of the course and the pleasure of helping many of its student, was one of the major reasons why I eventually retired from the chair at the age of 60. At that point I felt that I had done a reasonably good job in reorganising the course and looking after the postgraduates, but knew there were others who could have made an equally useful contribution and a few who could have done the job much better. Looking back though, I realise how much I enjoyed knowing those young postgraduates from the developing world, and suspect that I learnt far more from them than they did from me.

The other aspect of my academic life really consisted of attending the Senate of the Welsh National School of Medicine and its satellite committees, which I did regularly. Initially I kept fairly quiet and tried to discover how the Senate worked, while being as helpful as I could. In the longer term I hoped to negotiate a senior lectureship for my department. What I found most fascinating was the ongoing debate, nationally and in the Senate, about the future of medical training. There was a strong motivation towards change in the air, with good opportunities for new initiatives. Although the major lines of the curriculum were laid down centrally by the General Medical Council, and there were inevitable financial constraints imposed by the University Grants Committee, each medical school still had considerable scope for developing its own approach to medical training. There seemed, however, to be one critical limiting factor. No one anywhere seemed to have a clearcut idea of the kind of doctor they wanted to produce or how changes in the curriculum or methods of student selection would affect the end product.

Here was an issue crying out for in-depth consideration and investigation.

The senate of the Welsh National School of Medicine was probably no better and no worse than other medical school senates. Its work was made rather more complicated by the fact that the training for the 2nd MB examination came, for historical reasons, under Cardiff University College, which like the Welsh National School of Medicine was a constituent institute of the University of Wales. The provost and chairman of the Senate, Dr Trevor Jones, was an exceptional medical administrator. He had been a senior administrator both in the Emergency Service during the second world war and in the embryo NHS. He was a good chairman but lacked an academic background, and he failed to control the most powerful figure on the senate, who was the professor of pathology. In many ways, the professor had every right to be powerful. Pathology, since the time of Virchow (as doctors during this period were predominantly interested in diagnosis) had always held the status of a last court of appeal. Also, in addition to having been a professor in Cardiff for longer than anyone else, he was the only member of the senate at that time with an international reputation. Among his achievements he had invented a technique for mounting thin sections of whole lungs, which was a real advance in studying pulmonary conditions. Unkind people whispered that his chief technician deserved all the credit, but they only dared to whisper. He had also published an interesting pathological finding suggesting that "focal emphysema" causing pulmonary disability was associated with simple pneumoconiosis, which unfortunately brought him into direct conflict with MRC findings and myself. He was also Welsh, born and bred, in a senate where there was a majority of Scots and some English. He deserved our respect and got it to some extent, but he abused his position disgracefully. At nearly every Senate meeting he was good for a 20 minute speech, and sometimes touched 30 minutes. The content was often rambling, but woe betide anyone who disagreed. As the years went on his interventions became longer and vaguer, but it was only towards the end of this period that the cause of this aberration was discovered. There was also another time waster in the Senate of a very different type. He was a charming Scottish professor of bacteriology, who had become rather paranoid through some accident of administrative change concerning the Department of Bacteriology and the Public Health Laboratory Service that had not assisted his position. I am afraid I have forgotten the details, though I heard them often enough. He was good for a 10 minute speech at most senate meetings. The most rational voice in that assembly was that of Harold Scarborough, the charming, somewhat neurotic, professor of medicine, who tried hard to control the excesses of the professor of pathology. There was little time for the rest of us.

In the early days I made great efforts to establish better relations with the professor of pathology in the hope of a more useful association. I visited him several times to discuss our conflict of views regarding focal emphysema and its possible association with simple pneumoconiosis. I admitted freely that we had not carried out all the possible physiological tests, largely because they were not portable enough to figure in our surveys. I also discussed with him at length the aetiology of PMF, in which he had a strong interest, and asked him to suggest further epidemiological approaches. He really thought epidemiology to be irrelevant, however. He considered that pathology had established the facts, and that was final.

The two main subjects we discussed at the senate were the allocation of money and changes in the curriculum. Later the building of the new teaching hospital had prominence. I found discussions about changes to the medical curriculum depressing. Enthusiasm for change without a corresponding concern for investigating its validity seemed ridiculous, but this did not prevent me from arguing fiercely for more epidemiology and statistics, with particular reference to encouraging the evaluative skills of future doctors. Despite the difficulties confronting a body dissected by so many vested interests, we did, on the whole, make progress. Often this surprised me. I was much helped in the latter half of the period by Ron Lowe's arrival as professor of social and preventive medicine. He became a great friend and was a far more effective academic than I was. I can only remember making two interesting proposals as a member of the senate. One was a very simple one – to evaluate the teaching of anatomy, which I thought too detailed and time consuming. I had been first in anatomy in the Cambridge 2nd MB, and it had never been of any use to me. I suggested that there should be a questionnaire about anatomy applied to medical students in their last year of the course to see how much detailed anatomy they remembered. The idea was blocked by the professor of anatomy. I cannot remember how or why, but his tactics won the day. The other idea was very ambitious. The basic problem was the value of changing from the classical curriculum (9 o'clock lecture, two hours in the wards, 12 o'clock lecture, 2–4 o'clock in laboratories, 5 o'clock lecture) to a more "with-it" programme of teaching in small groups and seminars, time off for reading in the library, projects and trips abroad, etc. The latter was more attractive but almost certainly more expensive, and no one knew what the effect would be. Therefore I suggested randomising the students between the medical schools in Cardiff and Bristol. This would have been fairly ethical as between 80 and 90 per cent of the would-be students applied to both schools. One school would run a fairly classical curriculum and the other adopt a more with-it approach. The external examiners and examination papers would be the same, and some randomising of teachers could be achieved, now that the Severn Bridge was open. The follow up of students would have been easy, and we would certainly have learned something of the relative merits and disadvantages of the different approaches. It would, however, have been difficult to organise and probably too expensive; and it was laughed out of court.

I also remember being deeply interested in the senate's allocation of money. I really needed a senior lecturer, not only because an isolated professor is an absurdity but because I desperately needed more time in my newly created Epidemiology Unit, where a new line of research – health services research – was beginning to take off. The prospects in the senate were very gloomy, however, and in despair I turned to the MRC for help. Could they finance a senior lecturer for me for a short time until the school could take over this provision? To my delight and surprise the MRC agreed, partly I think because of a growing interest on the part of the DHSS in health services research. I presented this offer to the senate, and to my surprise it aroused immediate, intense opposition, led by the professor of pathology. The main argument was that there was another professor, senior to me, who still lacked the assistance of a senior lecturer. He had come up the hard way, through appointments as lecturer and senior lecturer. It would be monstrous he argued, if I, who had taken a short cut to a professorial chair through the MRC, advanced to having a senior lecturer before my colleague. It was "Buggins's" turn and if he did not get a senior lecturer no one should. I was furious and compared the senate to a group of hungry prisoners of war who preferred no one getting more food to a few who were ill getting the extra. There was a delay, but my turn did eventually arrive, and I was rewarded by having an excellent senior lecturer. It was Stewart Kilpatrick, who had lived with us at Rhoose Farm House for a time while working at the Pneumoconiosis Research Unit in the 1950s. In addition to being a first rate chest physician he was very much on my wavelength where research was concerned. As I write, he is now dean of the Welsh National School of Medicine, and David Davies professor of tuberculosis and chest diseases.

In my early years as a professor I had another idea which for a time worked out well. It was an attempt to build easier lines of communication with the undergraduate medical students with whom I felt out of touch. Certainly there seemed too much of a gulf between us. My idea was to meet them socially by arranging a series of supper parties at Rhoose Farm House. The annual intake to the medical course was only about 55 per year, so I calculated that if I had four or five to dinner once a week during term time I could get to know all of them in their first year in the school. The students chose who should come each week. I merely drove my Jaguar up to the medical school to collect them, and then drove them out to Rhoose, where I hope I wined and dined them well. They were a little shy at first, but when the word got round that I seemed human they used to decide beforehand who should drive the Jaguar out to Rhoose. I always drove them home, having drunk very little myself. We talked of politics and medicine, sex, and books. My taste in pictures and sculpture was fiercely criticised. They were rather shocked to hear that I had been to a public school but forgave me when I said that I had won a scholarship there. They liked my stories about the Spanish Civil War and prisoner of war camps. In fact they seemed to enjoy those dinners almost as much as I did. I remember that about 20 years later, during a visit to the MRC Epidemiology Unit by a group of medical officers from the DHSS, one of the visitors who had been a medical student in that period caused me some embarrassment by recalling with great clarity some of the provocative remarks I had made at the time of his excursion to Rhoose Farm House. The dinners clearly made their mark, but whether for better or worse I could never tell.

The students were very different from those I remembered from my own undergraduate days at King's College Cambridge, or later at University College Hospital. In the first place there was no obviously first class intellectual minority. The best students went elsewhere. There was also a far higher proportion of women amongst them, although University College Hospital had been considered a leader in its proportion of female entrants in my time. There were also fewer on the far left politically. They were replaced by the Welsh Nationalists – a lively group I rather liked. I used to tease them about Welsh culture, arguing that it consisted of inefficient hill farming and narrow Calvinism in the North and West, and beer, sex, and Rugby football in the South, the priorities varying in the various valleys. They fought back admirably. Unfortunately it could not last. The intake of students to the medical school increased, and I found that I could not cope, although I did try for a time to have 10 or more students to parties to meet my friends. It did not work. Under these circumstances there was little chance to get to know them, and I found it far more difficult to control their drinking. The end came when, at such a party, one drunken student nearly knocked over my disabled sister and two of his colleagues were caught trying to pocket bottles of whisky and gin.

One curious outcome of that first happy period when they came to dinner in fours or fives is worth recounting. It was that period when oral contraception was just becoming widely practised and every amorous young man thought that every young woman was on the contraceptive pill. The inevitable result was a small epidemic of unwanted pregnancies amongst the medical students. I suppose it was inevitable that one day a student, whom I knew well, and liked, appeared at Rhoose. He looked ghastly, and soon broke down in tears. He felt as though the end of the world had come. I finally managed to get him talking and it soon became clear that he deeply loved his girlfriend who had become pregnant, but without qualifying he did not know what the future could hold for their marriage. What he felt he could not do was to admit to his parents that he had been involved in premarital intercourse. He could not rely on their assistance and believed that they might make the situation even worse. He asked for help and was obviously thinking about abortion. I guessed that there was an easier way out but needed time to contact friends outside Cardiff who could advise me, so I invented, on the spur of the moment, a routine that served me well during the next few years. I promised him help, and complete confidentiality, but said that I must first interview his girlfriend alone before talking to them together and making any definite suggestion. During the next few days I got a great deal of advice from friends outside Cardiff who were much more experienced in such affairs than I was. I do not think anyone else in Cardiff knew what I was doing. I then saw the girl, who was also a student whom I knew well. She was very distressed but clearly loved the boy and wanted to marry him. She thought that she had "sinned" and felt unable to face her parents. I asked her to come back with her boyfriend in two days' time. After some discreet phoning and one visit I was able to suggest that I should motor them up to a party in the house of the girl's parents, where the boy's parents would also be. They were going to discuss the date of their marriage and the pregnancy would never be mentioned. I gathered that it was a good party. I did not attend. I did not want to be the ghost at the feast. There were, over the years, perhaps a dozen such cases, most of them ending in marriage. When marriage seemed unlikely to be a happy solution I suggested abortion, and, if both parties agreed, I helped them to arrange it by means of a telephone number and sometimes with financial help. Religious and legal authorities would have condemned what I was doing, but I felt a need to do more than leave such students in what seemed like a hopeless situation. The most difficult problem arose when I considered abortion the best solution but the girl refused to consider it. I remember all too well one pathetic case when the girl was abandoned by her boyfriend and her family and eventually gave birth to her baby in a rather unfriendly hospital, which I had found for her in another city. I was her only visitor, which I found rather embarrassing. The child was adopted and she continued her studies, but at what a price? I was relieved when the students found other ways of solving their problems.

My academic career was in many ways not a particularly profitable one, but it gave me a much needed contact with the younger generation and, strangely enough, provided a respectable camouflage while I negotiated the curious and difficult transition from my love of pneumoconiosis to enthusiasm for health services research.

THE NEW MRC EPIDEMIOLOGY UNIT AND DEVELOPMENTS IN RESEARCH

The setting up of the new MRC Epidemiology Unit proved as complicated as reorganising the Tuberculosis and Chest Diseases Course. Initially there were difficulties in securing accommodation, and we undertook our first survey as a new unit while still under the roof of the Pneumoconiosis Research Unit, where John Gilson kindly allowed us temporary accommodation. It was an interesting survey, involving two quite distinct investigations, one of them resulting from a rather doubtful bonus to our 1958 follow-up survey in the Rhondda Fach. In this survey we had taken blood samples from a somewhat limited section of the population, to assist Stewart Kilpatrick's studies of anaemia. It was when these samples passed to the haematologists for analysis that an unexpected problem began to emerge. Unknown to me they added blood grouping to the tests specified and found a fairly significant relationship between simple pneumoconiosis and blood group A. Here I was in real difficulty. As well as finding it hard to believe that genetic factors could be important in a condition I already regarded as essentially due to the mechanical retention of dust, I realised the complications there would be for the NCB and NUM if the results were published. What position would be adopted in relation to the recruitment of men of blood group A? Thoughts of the overreaction that might result worried me. Charting associations between disease and such common genetic traits as blood group was much in vogue at that time, and our findings would almost certainly have attracted more attention than they merited. Under such circumstances I decided that we should refrain from any publication of our findings until they had been validated by a more substantial survey; a decision that some of the haematologists found difficult to accept. Nevertheless, it was a decision that stood. It was the grafting of this larger investigation onto plans already in preparation for a further study of PMF in the Rhondda Fach that gave the new unit's initial survey its curious hybrid character. Originally the intention had been to make the unit's first initiative a final attempt to show whether or not tuberculosis played a part in the induction of PMF. This resulted from my immense dissatisfaction with what the two valleys scheme had achieved in this direction. I now proposed to approach the problem from another angle, using the Mantoux tuberculin test. Through its indication of how far individuals had experienced tuberculous infection, this test provided another means of investigating the hypothesis linking PMF with tuberculosis. Could we discover a significant difference in the extent to which PMF sufferers in the mining population had experienced tuberculosis? Certainly we should, if tuberculosis had an aetiological role in their disease. Hart and Aslett had applied this idea to the question over 20 years earlier but had not studied a statistically relevant sample of the mining population. Only 151 miners had been involved in their tests.[2] Our intention was to extend this approach to a representative cross section of the Rhondda Fach's mining population, involving over 1200 miners and ex-miners; a cross section drawn from census lists compiled only two years earlier.

Although Ian took charge of the survey as a whole he had in Julian Tudor Hart and Stewart Kilpatrick two very effective lieutenants, Julian taking responsibility for the Mantoux testing and chest x raying of the subjects involved in the study of PMF and Stewart conscientiously collecting the blood samples needed to extend our picture of blood group distribution. Both projects required a good deal of effort over several weeks, and I got off lightly on this occasion. What assistance I gave consisted largely of persuading miners and ex-miners to attend the centres we had set up for this survey and motoring them there when necessary. Each man taking part in the PMF study needed to attend on at least two occasions; first for a high quality chest x ray and the initiation of the Mantoux test, and then, approximately 72 hours later, for an assessment of his skin reaction to tuberculin, which merely meant measuring, to the nearest millimetre, any reaction zone arising around the point of the Mantoux injection. When all the subjects had been tested, and we had radiologically diagnosed all the cases of PMF among them, we were then in a position to compare the overall tuberculin sensitivity displayed by PMF sufferers with that of non-sufferers. The fact that the two groups displayed very similar levels of tuberculin sensitivity made it highly unlikely that tuberculous infection played even a minor role in the induction of PMF.[3] This finding virtually laid to rest a question that had troubled me for far too long, and I breathed a sigh of relief. There was also further comfort in the results of the blood studies, which vindicated my decision to delay the publication of earlier findings. They did not show any association between blood group A and simple pneumoconiosis.[4] I felt greatly relieved.

The minor part I played in this survey left me a fair amount of time for thinking about the future research of the unit. My most immediate problem was to help Ian, my chief assistant.

He was keen to branch out into the epidemiology of ischaemic heart disease, and although we had already involved ourselves in preliminary studies in the Vale of Glamorgan and the Rhondda Fach[5] it was clear that we needed a new idea to take us beyond mere measurements of incidence. The only one I came up with was that of evaluating the effects of exercise on the heart disease experience of the inmates of long-term prisons in the UK by providing special incentives and first-rate facilities for exercise in a random half, third, or a quarter of all such establishments. I realised that the population would not be typical of the UK population as a whole, but its advantages greatly outweighed any disadvantages and brought a difficult investigation within the bounds of possibility. It was a wonderfully captive population for initial examination, as well as follow-up studies. Long-term prisoners were also associated with a relatively high incidence of ischaemic heart disease, and I felt that it would be worth while using their ranks to demonstrate whether or not exercise had the potential to change heart disease statistics. I was sufficiently enthusiastic about what might be achieved to approach the prison authorities, but they responded with a curious form of dismay, all said to be bound up with ethics. I have had various contacts with the Home Office over the years and its civil servants have consistently exhibited hysterical reactions to the mention of randomised controlled trials. This can only be seen as regrettable. If William Whitelaw had, for example, subjected his "short, sharp, shock" strategy for dealing with young offenders to a randomised controlled trial then we might, by now, have known its true worth and be some way ahead in our thinking. Intuition alone carries a very low guarantee of worthiness. The failure of our approach to the prison authorities left us very much at square one, still looking for a worthwhile means of advancing the study of heart disease, and there was little to prevent Ian from pursuing a growing interest in working in the USA. It was a great loss to me when he left Cardiff in 1963, although for quite a time I continued to hope that he would return.

Although we drew a blank with the prison authorities, it is just possible that my thinking about prison populations assisted a new line of interest, for it was around this time that I found myself wondering increasingly how far randomised controlled trials and the kind of cross-sectional surveys in which we specialised might be of value in sociological research. This soon became an important preoccupation, and it was not long before I had persuaded Sir Harold Himsworth that the MRC should finance the addition of a sociologist to the unit's staff. This was when John Palmer joined us. My idea was that we should start by studying the impact and relevance of the punishment awarded in a number of simple disciplinary situations. This interest probably reflected something of my Calvinistic background, as well as the extent to which corporal punishment had made an impression on me in my days at Uppingham. Since then I had often wondered about the value of such "correction," which so many extolled and yet so few had sought to validate. My first idea was to investigate the practice then common in schools of caning boys who were caught smoking. Was there any evidence that it had a deterrent effect? Our chance to look into this came only after protracted negotiations with a number of secondary schools in the Rhondda, when one headmaster eventually offered us the confidential access we needed to his punishment book. John Palmer's initial survey of the smoking habits of the boys in years 2, 3, and 4 of this school may have seemed on the face of it a fairly trivial beginning, but it was very much in the spirit of a pilot investigation and more to test the difficulties than break new ground. He merely conducted a short, confidential interview with each boy, asking just two main questions: "How much do you smoke now?" and "How much did you smoke a year ago?" Then he checked the punishment book to find which smokers had been caned. Although the study was far too simplistic to yield major conclusions it did show an interesting lack of any downward trend in the smoking of those who had been punished.[6] In general they were smoking more, although it would have been reasonable to argue that they might well have been the very boys whose smoking was increasing fastest and who may well have smoked even more in the absence of a deterrent. It was clear that the relevance of caning as a deterrent could only be tested by a randomised controlled trial, but I held back on such a suggestion, recognising that randomised controlled trials of corporal punishment were almost certainly going to raise a lot of opposition. At this stage I felt it best to keep our approach to schools as simple as possible and merely sought an opportunity to randomise and investigate the effects of two common disciplinary reactions to lateness: detention or a talk from the head teacher. To my surprise it took only a few inquiries to locate a headmaster willing to cooperate, and John Palmer made an impressive start to the project. After only one term the results were already indicating a possible difference in the effectiveness of the two measures, with a reprimand from the senior master seeming somewhat more effective in preventing further lateness.[7] Unfortunately John Palmer moved to another post before we could take this trial any further.

Another area of interest during John Palmer's time at the unit was that of juvenile delinquency in the Rhondda, and we made a good start. My team had already amassed a fair amount of information on the population there during the time when we were helping Ken Rawnsley's team of psychiatrists in the 1950s, and despite initial difficulties we soon negotiated access to local police records. It was unhappy data, but it did give us a flying start to examining the family factors associated with delinquency. Without such assistance we would have needed a difficult and costly survey of Rhondda families. Little in our findings surprised us. The main factors associated with delinquency seemed to be virtually as we had expected: sex, position in the family, numbers of siblings, unemployment of parents, and broken home background. My main interest was from the point of view of prevention and "treatment." As regards prevention, I suggested randomising social workers to families where there were at least three children, one of whom had been delinquent. That was turned down at once. As regards "treatment," I had a good idea of what was going on from the literature and the papers, but I attended a few magistrates' courts in the Rhondda, just to be sure. What I found was rather like general practice, with a wide variety of "treatments" being given for what seemed to me identical "diagnoses." For instance, a boy of 10 caught breaking and entering could be given either a warning or probation, or his parents fined; although just occasionally he might be referred to his headmaster for summary punishment. There seemed little in the way of rhyme or reason in the way such punishment was awarded, and I discussed the problem privately with a number of magistrates I knew. I suggested to them the value of controlled trials, but was horrified when they reacted like elderly physicians and headmasters. They too suffered from the God complex. They knew what to do without the help of any trials. It was depressing.

Even after John Palmer's departure I went on hoping for an opportunity to demonstrate the relevance of controlled trials to sociological research. I even continued visiting schools in the hope of locating a headmaster prepared to assist with a randomised controlled trials of corporal punishment. Almost predictably, few were prepared to listen for long. My only breakthrough came with a head who weakened very briefly and actually considered collaboration, but then he went the way of the rest, suddenly turning to me and saying "No. I just can't do it. When a boy is caught smoking, I know whether he should be caned or not!" He did not know that I knew many of the boys in his school, and some of their parents. I checked up. All the boys caught smoking were caned. After that I can remember talking to a large number of boys about the effect of caning. Their opinions varied considerably, but at that time a majority felt that it would have been impossible to run an efficient school without it. I can also remember that among those who had been caned it was characteristically the tough ones who said that it had no influence whatsoever, while the more sensitive ones generally admitted a preventive effect.

Unable to develop the kind of collaboration I needed in schools, I tried next to investigate John Bowlby's ideas about the effects of parent loss on young children.[8] I decided to look at what had happened to boys who had suffered the loss of a father. Boys had the advantage of being easier to trace as they did not change their names on marrying, but I am less sure of the reason for deciding to look at those who had lost fathers. Perhaps I felt that most of the work already carried out in this field concerned maternal loss, and there was room for a change. I suppose it is also possible that somewhere in the back of my mind I was also influenced by the fact that I had experienced such a loss. My idea was to list all the men in the Rhondda who had died between the age of 24 and 35, 20 years ago, find out if they had any sons under 5 at the time and, if so, investigate what had happened to the youngest. They would be compared to controls selected on the basis of their names being a randomly chosen distance apart in the Rhondda birth register and the credential of having a father alive at the age of 5. We were chiefly interested in how the two groups fared as regards marriage. Although laborious and quite time consuming, the work seemed to be going well until we ran into an unexpected snag. It turned out that the local registrar disliked giving us access to the birth registry, as a result of which relations deteriorated and an official complaint from him brought arrangements to an end. This seemed like the last straw. I had never imagined that sociological research could prove so difficult.

Fortunately, while the doors of sociological projects seemed forever closing another avenue of research came into view. Since setting up the unit I had been looking for the right kind of challenge for the team I led, preferably one connected with the delivery of health care, and like manna from heaven came the 1960s rash of enthusiasm for screening. There was, I must admit, some excuse for it. Several workers, including Jerry Morris and, I suppose, myself, had shown what an iceberg of disease there was below the surface, if apparently healthy populations were examined. There was increasing dissatisfaction with the effectiveness of treatment, and the hope that earlier diagnosis would improve the chances of cure was not altogether unreasonable. I cannot remember exactly how I got involved, although I have an impression that it resulted from my contempt at being called a screener. I remember someone referring to me in this fashion at a meeting, and the trouble I took to point out the purpose of my surveys, and the fact that though they sometimes led to the early detection of disease I had no evidence that this had ever enhanced the prospects of cure. This set me thinking, and I suddenly saw that underlying all screening was a hypothesis that earlier diagnosis meant better prospects of effective treatment. I also realised that this hypothesis could only be tested by surveys, followed by randomised controlled trials: work particularly suited to my own unit. At this point I began negotiations with MRC headquarters and the Ministry of Health, and eventually had their approval for a first series of investigations to evaluate various forms of screening.

We began by investigating the benefits of the early detection and treatment of iron-deficiency anaemia, a disease all too common at that time in adult women. A study of anaemia we had carried out in the Rhondda Fach in 1958 had already generated a good deal of interest at the unit, and Peter Elwood, a new member of the team, was particularly enthusiastic about looking at screening and any benefits it offered. I remember the long hours we spent discussing the kind of survey and randomised controlled trial we required, out of which came a model that was to form the basis of our approach to randomised controlled trials (see figure 12).

When thinking of screening for some unacceptable condition relating to a biological variate, such as blood pressure or haemoglobin level, the need is to define a region on the population's normal distribution of that variate where it is ethically and practically reasonable to intervene and conduct a randomised controlled trial of a proposed remedial treatment. This is often a complex question and one far removed from the simplistic view on which early aspirations for screening seem to have been based – that there are clear boundaries between "healthy" and "unhealthy" levels of a variate. What our early model recognised was that it is clearly unethical to involve subjects at the extreme end of the distribution, and clearly requiring treatment urgently, in a randomised controlled trial where there is only a 50:50 chance of receiving more than a placebo. It is equally unreasonable to intervene in the lives of those whose position in the distribution reflects no great risk. At the very least the validity of a screening strategy has to rest on finding the point or points on the distribution where intervention is capable of doing more good than harm.

Peter took charge of this investigation of screening for iron-deficiency anaemia and did an excellent job in surveying several large populations of women in the Rhondda Fach. He studied over 18 000 subjects in all, and with a refusal rate of less than 5 per cent. In one of these studies the distribution of haemoglobin levels was plotted and those suffering from other diseases that might have affected the haemoglobin level eliminated from the study. Although there was no clear point on any distribution curve to indicate where anaemia actually began it was generally accepted that haemoglobin levels below 12 g/dl of blood were suspect, and Peter's first investigation concerned those immediately below this threshold, with haemoglobin levels of between 10 and 12 g/dl. He gave everybody in this category a questionnaire covering all the symptoms of anaemia listed in standard textbooks of medicine, and then randomised the group, arranging for half to receive a conventional course of iron tablets while the other half took only a placebo. The questionnaire and the haemoglobin measurements were then repeated eight weeks later,

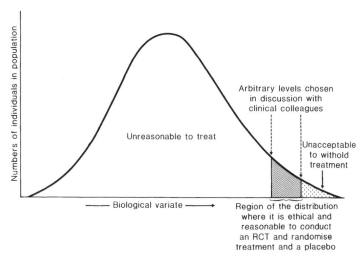

Figure 12 Possibly the first model to crystallise out of my early discussion with Peter Elwood on ethical and practical issues relating to certain randomised controlled trials. It looks a good deal easier than it is to apply.

with some interesting results. The haemoglobin levels in those receiving iron had risen as expected while those not on iron showed just a slight reversion to the mean, but when it came to reviewing symptoms little had changed. There was no evidence of a beneficial effect by either the genuine tablet or the placebo. Findings were similar when the exercise was repeated on a group of subjects with haemoglobin levels between 8 and 10 g/dl. The provision of iron clearly made little difference to the symptoms of the women in the categories investigated – a situation which set a question mark over this particular aspect of screening.[9] Of course no one investigation answers all questions. We could not exclude the possibility that supplementary iron helped in a more subtle way than we could detect, or in the longer term.

Next in the progression of screening studies came a survey of glaucoma in the Rhondda, followed by a randomised controlled trial of its early treatment. How all this arose is interesting. I had always thought that by becoming a professor I would get good contacts with other academic medical departments and increase the prospects of collaboration in the mounting of surveys and trials. I was, in general, sadly wrong in this assumption, and the origin of the glaucoma survey and trial demonstrate how these things happen in real life. It all began with the growing worries of Irene Calford, my secretary, about the medical treatment being received by her mother, who was becoming blind. Irene was dissatisfied with the action being taken in the outpatients department at the Cardiff teaching hospital, and I said that I would ring up and complain. I spoke to the senior registrar. He said, in a rather cheerful Australian voice, that he would look into the situation right away, but went on to point out that he knew something of my work and that we might have research interests in common. He also felt that I might be able to help him with a project he had in mind. We met, and I discovered that he was Fred Hollows,[10] a likeable, difficult, New Zealander. He had been trained first as a priest, then as a doctor in Australia, and he was rather left wing. He is now deservedly well known because of his unique ophthalmological survey of Australian aborigines and his general battle to improve their way of life. When we met he wanted me to help him do a glaucoma survey. This suited my ideas fairly well, if not perfectly. At that time glaucoma was "top of the screening pops," with letters demanding glaucoma screening clinics appearing in most newspapers and journals. No evidence was available, however, about the probable effectiveness of such a provision. It was clearly important to get an evaluation going as soon as possible, so I agreed to provide whatever help I could with the survey, just so long as it was linked to a randomised controlled trial.

Our next meeting carried us a good deal further. We had the help of Fred's colleague Peter Graham,[11] a senior ophthalmo-logical consultant, and Peter Sweetnam, a young statistician, who had recently joined the unit. The discussions that followed were easy and practical. On the clinicians' side there was no trace of the God complex. We listed the tests to be carried out during the survey, any evidence we had on their reproducibility, and any problems likely to arise from differences in the length of time they required. One of the tests was certainly a problem. It was far lengthier than the rest and could only lead to a bottleneck in the flow of patients. We needed to find the best way round this hurdle. Our greatest problem, however, turned out to be a time limit on the survey itself. Peter Graham, like most of the ophthalmological consultants in the country, had only a part-time appointment with the National Health Service, and had other practice interests to maintain. This meant that it would be impossible to secure his undivided assistance by the provision of an NHS locum. His only opportunity to help in a major survey would be by sacrificing his summer holidays, but this still meant a clearcut time limit.

The study we eventually planned had three main aims. Firstly, to collect reliable data on the distribution of intraocu-lar pressure in an unselected population of adults; then to subject a group of the population's typical glaucoma suspects to a randomised trial of medical therapy; and while doing all this we intended to chart the overall incidence of glaucoma and other eye diseases in the survey population. There was little reliable evidence about the prevalence and incidence of glaucoma at that time. Those taking part would be subjected to five tests. In addition to an examination of their visual field there would be slit lamp examination of the anterior segment of each eye, applanation and Schiøtz tonometry to determine intraocular pressure, and ophthalmoscopic examination of their optic discs. Because of the problem that visual field examination took so long, however, we were finally forced to restrict this examination to a random third of those tested.

When all our preliminary calculations were completed it was decided that we should examine about 4000 people in the 40–74 age range. As we had only eight weeks available for the entire survey this meant examining an average of about 100 people a day. In fact we needed to see closer to 200 a day in the earlier weeks to compensate for the inevitable slowing down of the response rate. This was some task. Almost everyone had to be persuaded and then picked up and deposited at the clinic at five-minute intervals. A good many of them also needed motoring home because their pupils had been dilated. I saw there was going to be a major administrative problem and decided to take charge of the whole survey myself. What I did not know was that this would be the last time I ever took charge of a survey.

I am glad to say that it all went very well indeed, because of the devotion of the team. The weather was good, and we had lunch-time picnics in the hills above Blaenllechau and steaks in the upper room at Myrtle's in Pontygwaith in the evening, and talked about the future of ophthalmological epidemiology. Even more seriously, we discussed the difficulties of mounting a randomised controlled trial of early treatment for glaucoma. It was the very same problem that we had run into in our randomised controlled trial of anaemia treatment. Between what limits on the normal distribution was it ethical to inflict a randomised controlled trial on subjects? The findings of our first cross-sectional study of glaucoma, shown in figure 13, illustrated this dilemma particularly well. Above what level of ocular pressure were subjects exposed to significant risk of developing vision field defects? Cases of glaucoma featured across a wide spectrum of pressures. This survey also showed little in favour of glaucoma screening, as calculations based on our results showed how small the protective effect would be, assuming that pressure could be adequately controlled by treatment. Nevertheless, we went ahead with the controlled trial, randomising the provision of medicated and placebo eyedrops to all those who registered ocular pressures of 21 mm Hg or more; a level that had somehow become commonly accepted as a convenient borderline between normality and abnormality.

At the review two years later there was no significant difference between the average drop in ocular pressure in the control and treated groups, though they showed a slight regression to the mean. The lack of benefit was possibly due in part to the great resistance of those with normal sight to putting drops into their eyes regularly. Some women were unhappy about the eyedrops interfering with their makeup. Our impression was that less than half the subjects took the drops regularly. We had therefore thoroughly tested the value of screening for preventing glaucoma by tonometry, as widely demanded, and shown that it was really not on. We also showed, in the course of this work, that existing literature had

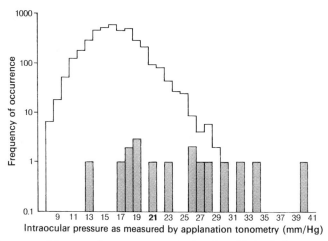

Figure 13   The 1963 glaucoma survey in the Rhondda Fach demonstrated the lack of a clear cut association between elevated intraocular pressure and risk of glaucoma. Cases of glaucoma (stippled) occurred widely across the pressure distribution, even below the mean.

grossly overestimated the incidence rate of glaucoma. On the basis of our findings the attack rate seemed merely of the order of 5–10 cases in every 10 000 of the adult population per year.[12]

Whatever the outcome of the glaucoma survey I came out of it bitten with the idea of ophthalmological epidemiology. The methods of ophthalmologists seemed so beautifully quantitative, and there seemed so much that might be gained by the study of the aetiology and possible prevention of cataract and glaucoma. (On one occasion I pointed out, rather cynically, that the reason why so little work had been done on the prevention of these two diseases was the fact that they were both to some extent treatable, as well as being responsible for a high proportion of ophthalmological incomes.) I discussed the idea with the senior colleagues at MRC headquarters and with advisers at the DHSS, and it went across well. As a result I got an eye clinic in the Rhondda, and a salary for an ophthalmologist, at about the senior registrar level. I still think it was a good idea, but it did not work out. There were two main reasons. One was technical. We could not discover any quantitative method of measuring the extent of cataract in an eye. Estimating the extent to which the cataract interferes with vision is a very doubtful measure. We sought advice from a range of experts distinguished in this field, but in vain. The other problem was the nature of young ophthalmologists. They all had the ambition of becoming a 9/11ths or 7/11ths National Health Service consultant, and the MRC had no comparable carrot to attract them in the direction of epidemiology. The situation was made even worse by the fact that if senior registrars in ophthalmology did transfer to epidemiology for a time this lessened their chances of becoming consultants. Fred Hollows did boost my hopes that we might surmount the various difficulties and establish a solid vein of worthwhile epidemiological research in this field when he joined us for a short period before becoming a professor in Australia. Then came John Wallace. He was really promising. He had been soundly trained in Glasgow, was really interested scientifically, and had that rare capacity of being able to lead an epidemiological team in the field. He was not with us long enough, however, and in the end the only products of the whole idea were a survey of glaucoma and intraocular pressure in Jamaica,[13] and a survey of lens opacities among steelworkers.[14] When John left us to become a consultant in the Highlands ophthalmological epidemiology died. I still think it was a good idea to try to start it, and I hope someone will come along and resurrect it.

Our next adventure was with cervical cytology. By 1964 major vibrations from North America about what could be achieved by regular smear tests were rocking prevention lobbies in the UK and it would have been difficult for any epidemiologist not to have been caught up in the groundswell of interest. The great question at the Ministry of Health, which had been monitoring developments in North America throughout the early 1960s, was how far to accept the claims being made for this kind of screening. Max Wilson,[15] one of the ministry's principal medical officers, had already spent time in the USA and Canada, particularly Vancouver, taking a first-hand look at some of the major screening and associated research programmes. Such surveillance had a natural degree of priority as there were considerable implications for the NHS in the success of any such development. In my own unit and the University Department of Obstetrics and Gynaecology in Cardiff colleagues regularly discussed the published facts and figures and the questions they raised. Beyond all the hopes that this was indeed a breakthrough in cancer prevention, and the natural support any move in this direction commanded, there were a great many unanswered questions. In fact, despite the euphoria of some of the literature, there were far more questions than answers. Even my natural scepticism was extended by the total failure I experienced in trying to find hard evidence that this form of medical surveillance reduced cancer registration and mortality rates. No matter how laudable the basic idea looked, one longed for evidence that it really was on firm foundations. This is why, when the DHSS, in a preliminary sounding of senior figures in epidemiology and social medicine, asked my view of how far we should be looking to incorporate this kind of screening within future health service provision, I suggested, as far as I remember, beginning by making cervical cytology free in one or two regions of the UK and monitoring the outcome in terms of subsequent levels of cancer registration and mortality. Even if we failed to demonstrate significant levels of cancer prevention there was at least the prospect of knowing more about the natural history of the disease itself. This seemed essential. I liked the idea of differential provision and monitoring. In my view this seemed perfectly ethical. It could hardly be considered a case of withholding validated care from a section of the population. This was a potential care process needing to be validated, and that validation we could attempt. This would have been more difficult in North America, where popular opinion already saw cervical cytology as an established form of prevention.

Overall I got into a good deal of debate locally about what should be done in the UK, not least in my own unit where Hubert Campbell, my statistician, had considerable interest in the possibilities for further research. He had recently returned from a sabbatical study leave in North America, where he had seen several cervical cytology studies in progress, in particular the one in British Columbia, and he was convinced that there were special opportunities for research in this country, within the context of the NHS. He also felt that Cardiff would be a city suited to the requirements of a survey. Although the prevalence of positive smears was at that time believed to be low, Cardiff's population of approximately 350 000 looked as though it might have the right number of subjects for a relatively short-term study, possibly of around five years' duration. It was not long before I found myself round a table with Hubert Campbell and colleagues from the University Department of Obstetrics and Gynaecology discussing the prospects of getting a local study under way. I am not sure how many of us took part in that meeting, but we were certainly joined by Professor Archie Duncan and consultant James Lawson, whose enthusiasm for a major research initiative I still remember. Cardiff did have a good deal to offer. In addition to population size, it had a medical school with active departments of gynaecology and medical statistics, a unified pathology service in good collaboration with the then separated Public Health Service, as well as its own epidemiology unit. It was at this meeting that we decided to form a Cardiff Cervical Cytology Committee bringing together relevant agencies and specialities, and to draw up a research protocol for MRC and DHSS approval and funding. Just as soon as we had that support we were able to appoint a very sound epidemiologist, Dr Joyce Landsman, to take charge of the scheme, and by Autumn 1965 things were moving, although not with instant ease. My memory of those early days is not particularly clear, but there were difficulties in a number of directions, not least through some of the quarrels that arose, some of the worst involving the cytologists. By this time I had largely retreated to the sidelines but I understood the pressures on Joyce. This survey was a colossal undertaking. As well as surmounting the difficulties of achieving the high degree of interdisciplinary and interservice collaboration necessary for the project's success, she had before her the task of interesting all the married or previously married women of an entire city in cervical cytology, not by mass media publicity but by a massive programme of home visiting.[16] As I write, in the 1980s, the results of this major study involving the cytological surveillance of many tens of thousands of Cardiff women are still being analysed and slowly published. Just how far they make a case for the benefits of this form of screening I shall leave to the full analysis. I suspect the results will prove far less impressive than the efforts of Joan Landsman's team.[17]

On a personal note, I recall one particular incident in the course of this survey that caused me some anguish. It occurred when we had completed the first round of the project. Despite the inevitable difficulties of bringing in certain population groups for examination, the study still represented the best on a defined population anywhere. We had the names of all the cases of invasive cancer of the cervix diagnosed by other means. This was clearly a beautiful set up for a case-control study, and we were in touch with an American research group interested in the possibility of this being a transmissible disease initiated by a virus. There was even an offer to do antibody work for Herpes (which at that time was under consideration as a possible causal agent) if we could supply the blood. It may be that I became too excited about the possibility of adding studies of causality to what was already going on, but I persuaded the chairman of the main survey committee of the acceptability of a questionnaire, which contained, not too blatantly, questions on the frequency of intercourse and number of sexual partners. (We had been somewhat doubtful about these questions and had done, in secret, a pilot survey in a neighbouring town. Dr Landsman interviewed the women, and I talked to any husbands who had questions about the survey and what we were about. There were no objections.) On the strength of this I sold the idea to the Cardiff general practitioners, through their general committee, without a problem. I got the first whiff of resistance when I started talking to consultant gynaecologists. One really surprised me by stating that it was insufficient to get the general practitioner's permission to interview a patient. If she had ever been under the care of a consultant the consultant's permission must be obtained as well. This seemed the greatest extension of the God complex I had yet experienced. Soon afterwards, at a public meeting in Cardiff, where I was billed to talk about the progress and development of the cytology survey, my research plans were denounced from the floor as unethical by a senior gynaecologist, and I was forced to take the proposal to the local ethical committee before I had time to talk to the gynaecological consultants generally. The ethical committee turned the proposal down flat. I had to accept, but I was angry.

I found this whole "screening" period of my life bewildering. The idea we were selling was so simple: "One cannot assume that diagnosing a disease earlier will help." Yet I had the greatest difficulty in convincing a host of fairly senior people to take our arguments seriously. I published and lectured a great deal about screening during this period and never ceased to be amazed at the resistance I met. My biggest disaster was in Cardiff, in 1967. I had been asked to lecture on screening but had not been warned of the presence of the press, though I do not think I would have altered the lecture if I had known. "Inter alia," I said, "there is at present no hard evidence that cervical smears and subsequent medical attention prevent deaths from carcinoma of the cervix, although such evidence may appear in the future." Most scientifically minded people would have accepted this as Holy Writ, but for some reason it enraged my audience. I was lampooned in the local press in banner headlines, and to my horror no one could be found in the medical school to say a word in my defence. My mail was swollen for quite a time by abusive letters, many of them anonymous. One of the rudest came from a senior gynaecologist. I felt very lonely, but fortunately MRC headquarters gave me full support. I never really understood the public and medical reaction to our reasonable reservations.

Fortunately there were a good many others who felt a need for caution, and I was relieved when Gordon McLachlan of the Nuffield Provincial Hospitals Trust, who was to be a great friend of mine in the future, set up a committee on screening to bring many of us together. It was chaired by my old friend Tom McKeown, professor of social medicine at Birmingham, and included other old friends. The most important for my future were Dick Cohen, who had been at King's College, Cambridge with me, and Max Wilson, an old colleague from University College Hospital days. They were now very senior medical officers at the DHSS. The committee considered screening in all its aspects and ways of assisting its validation. From this work came a good deal of invaluable discussion, a small book on various aspects of screening, and fresh impetus from its DHSS members, who played their part in the setting up of a screening committee at the DHSS to provide a degree of ongoing surveillance. I was naturally delighted that concern for surveys and randomised controlled trials advanced as a result. There was also a good deal of satisfaction in this for the unit. We felt that we had already made a real contribution through our investigations of anaemia, glaucoma, and cervical cytology.

In the middle 1960s, while the unit was heavily focused on screening, I had the opportunity to begin thinking about what I wanted to do next. I was involved personally only with the glaucoma survey on a full-time basis. Through my contacts with Max Wilson and Dick Cohen I had become increasingly concerned about health services research and felt that the unit could make a special contribution to the evaluation of established health-care practices. They had grown up randomly and variously, with few attempts at validation. I felt increasingly strongly that they should be subjected, as far as possible, to the scrutiny of randomised controlled trials, but realised that progress in this direction would be difficult. Established practices are difficult to challenge without causing concern amongst those who have helped to establish them. By the time they are established they are firmly believed to serve the patient's interests and therefore it is not an easy matter to walk in from the comfort of an epidemiology unit and start suggesting withholding them from some individuals because you want to apply something called a randomised controlled trial. One day, though, I wrote down my plans for making a start.

To show that it is ethically acceptable and practically possible to randomise
(1) place of treatment between
    (a) hospital and home,
    (b) outpatients clinic and home, and
    (c) hospital and outpatients clinic.
(2) length of stay in hospital.

None of these ideas was new, but the combination gave me an interesting programme, which was probably the first of its kind for health services research in the UK. I do not think I proved very successful, but I learnt a great deal. I got off to a quicker start than I had anticipated when I discovered by chance that all patients who had cataract operations stayed in Cardiff Royal Infirmary for 13 days. I found this absurd, as most of the possible complications occurred in the first two days. I teased the ophthalmologists about this. I knew them fairly well by this time. I suggested that it all stemmed from a matron in 1940 who wanted to change the sheets once a fortnight! They finally capitulated and agreed to randomise five and 10 day stays. Unfortunately they insisted on conducting the trial themselves, without our help. This posed a serious problem. I was certain that the trial would be more scientific if we controlled it, but it became clear that the trial might not be done at all if we pressed the point, so I gave in. They did it, although not very well, but it had the effect I wanted. I also learnt how important it was to increase the number of operating theatres if one wanted to take full advantage of a reduction in length of stay.

My next adventure was in randomising inpatient and outpatient treatment. By chance we met a charming surgeon, Hugh Jones, who was interested in discovering whether his varicose vein patients should be injected in outpatients or treated surgically as inpatients. (He also had a wonderful wife with whom I enjoyed some happy and informative discussions.) We started negotiations at once. This time it was much easier, as he wanted our help. All that we needed was a sound statistical design and a liaison officer from the MRC, acceptable to the surgeons, to supervise its implementation. Peter Sweetnam, who had succeeded Hubert Campbell as my statistician, provided the design and Jean Weddell, another recent addition to my team, took charge of the work on the ground. At that time she was in the final phase of recovering from a road accident and the project seemed to me just right as a rehabilitation exercise. We got off to a flying start, but there was one unfortunate incident. After the preliminary arrangements had been completed and about 50 cases had been randomised, Jean and Peter fortunately noticed that something was wrong with the randomisation. There was a definite excess of serious cases on one side of the trial. We traced this problem to an innocent surgical registrar, who apparently knew nothing of the trial and was abstracting "interesting" cases from one side. We tore up the first 50 records and started again. The depressing effect of this setback was more than atoned for by my idea – I think it was my idea – to cost the two sides of the controlled trial. I had been introduced to Brian Abel Smith, professor of social administration at the London School of Economics, by his brother, then a barrister, at the top of the Parsenn Lift, when skiing at Davos. He said he thought we might have something in common. This was an underestimate. I have enjoyed his company ever since and learnt a great deal from him. It was natural, therefore, when thinking about costing the sides of this trial to ask his help, and he sent down to Cardiff an intelligent and charming young economist, David Piachaud, who educated me about the practical side of measuring cost effectiveness, and was to remain a good friend ever after. The immediate results of this costing exercise were negligible. Effectiveness could only be measured after a longer-term follow-up, but the fact that such a study had been completed by medical staff within the NHS excited the interest of economists.[18] Dick Cohen had for some time been encouraging economists to take more interest in the NHS, and this trial acted as a catalyst in bringing epidemiologists in touch with the economists, particularly the group associated with Professor Alan Williams at York University. Alan proved a lively and effective pioneer of health service economics, and he has been a good friend and adviser ever since that first encounter. It gave me immense pleasure, some years later, when receiving an honorary degree at York, to have him introduce me at the degree ceremony.

The next randomisation of place of treatment we attempted was the most traumatic. Max Wilson of the DHSS had drawn my attention to the fact that coronary care units, one of the most expensive recent developments in inpatient care, had not yet been evaluated despite their considerable status. It was Max who put me in contact with Gordon Mather, a cardiac consultant in Bristol, who was already asking questions about the effectiveness of these units. Gordon and I were very different. He was a part-time cardiologist with a flourishing private practice; but we got on well together. He had become worried that coronary care units might be doing more harm than good. We both felt, therefore, that they should be subjected to a randomised controlled trial and discussed possible strategies. We both distrusted local ethical committees. At that time they consisted almost entirely of leading elderly consultants strongly affected by the God complex. We decided, therefore, to ask the DHSS and MRC to set up a special ad hoc committee centrally to decide whether the kind of trial we had in mind was ethical. To our surprise they agreed. I filled in time by talking to the Cardiff general practitioners about the trial and securing their support in case the research should go ahead. I also started talking to the cardiac consultants about the idea. They seemed interested and not particularly antagonistic, particularly as there was a chance of their getting a new coronary care unit through the plan.

The ethical committee meeting in London was a fascinating affair. There was, as far as I remember, a long, rather narrow table. At one end sat Lord Platt, the chairman. I had been on the opposite side to him in the great Pickering–Platt[19] battle over the normal distribution of blood pressure, but I do not think he bore me any ill will. Sitting to the right and left of Platt were Sir George Godber and Sir Harold Himsworth, while along both sides were "the ranks of Tuscany," the consultant cardiologists who were determined to stop the trial. Lord Platt, in a remarkably good opening speech, made it clear that he was interested to hear whether there was any hard evidence that coronary care units altered the natural history of the disease for the better. The cardiologists, he said, should produce their evidence, and it was then up to Gordon Mather and myself to refute it. This was, of course, too easy, as I knew their case already. It consisted mostly of figures suggesting that there had been a reduction in mortality from ischaemic heart disease among those admitted to hospitals that had installed coronary care units. They did concede under questioning, however, that they had admitted many more patients into their units, of which the majority had been mild cases. This was as good as engineering a success story. They really did not have any hard evidence of beneficial provision. I was not really surprised (but was secretly delighted) when Lord Platt ruled that the trial we proposed was ethical, and I returned almost triumphant to Cardiff. But my triumph did not last long. The very next day the cardiac consultants made it clear to me that whatever Lord Platt had said there was going to be no randomised controlled trial of coronary care units in Cardiff. I was at first disbelieving, then furious, and cursed the day I had become a professor in the hope of better cooperation with consultants. Later I became fascinated by the psychology underlying the decision. The consultants whom I knew personally were ordinary, reasonable, intelligent people. They knew that the Platt committee had completely outflanked them intellectually and ethically, but they still felt a sacred right to treat patients as they wished. I was horrified. Fortunately I had many other interests at that time, and Gordon Mather encouraged me to take a continuing interest in his trial in Bristol, where he had no such troubles. The fact that a trial could be ethical in Bristol and unethical in Cardiff did not seem to worry anyone in Cardiff. In Bristol, Gordon went ahead, with cooperation from his colleagues and with valuable results for all those who view technological advances with unrestrained enthusiasm.[20]

The only other story about the trial which falls into this period is the report Gordon Mather and I had to give to the "Platt committee" after the trial had been running for, I think, six months. The results at that stage showed a slight numerical advantage for those who had been treated at home. It was of course completely insignificant statistically. I rather wickedly compiled two reports; one reversing the numbers of deaths on the two sides of the trial. As we were going into the committee, in the anteroom, I showed some cardiologists the results. They were vociferous in their abuse: "Archie," they said, "we always thought you were unethical. You must stop the trial at once. . . ." I let them have their say for some time and then apologised and gave them the true results, challenging them to say, as vehemently, that coronary care units should be stopped immediately. There was dead silence and I felt rather sick because they were, after all, my medical colleagues.

Getting medical colleagues involved in randomised controlled trials proved far more difficult than I could ever have imagined, and I knew it would not be easy. On occasions I felt drained by my efforts and that I was getting nowhere. Perhaps this is because I was so emotionally involved in trying to focus attention on validation, which I saw as fundamental to any care process. This may also explain why I have given so much space to this aspect of my work in the 1960s and neglected reference to other things going on in the unit, which certainly deserve mention. My colleagues were involved in a number of valuable lines of research, in some of which I managed to play a small part. One small study was an interesting example of the use of an epidemiological technique in health services research. The idea was to compare the logical and the actual use of medication. We chose the prescribing of vitamin B_{12}. This is only effective in the treatment of pernicious anaemia, whose prevalence in England and Wales is known, as is the optimum dosage of vitamin B_{12}. The result is shown in table I. We thought it threw a dreadful light on prescribing in general practice. We later discovered that the situation was even worse in Northern Ireland, and very much worse in France. It was even more depressing to discover when we repeated the investigation a year later that the consumption of vitamin B_{12} had increased even further.

Table I Observed and expected prescribing of parenteral vitamin B_{12}, if all cases of pernicious anaemia had been treated within the NHS in 1966.

	Expected requirements (1000 µg)	Observed amount prescribed (1000 µg)	Ratio Amount observed/ amount expected
Reasonable	716 318		3.2
		2 313 717	
Ideal	270 182		8.6

Source: British Journal of Preventive and Social Medicine 1971; 25: 147–51.

I also became involved in an interesting observer error study in dental diagnosis. Two professors of dentistry had been, of necessity, appointed before the building of the new dental school was completed. Because this left them in something of an interim position I suggested that they might like to take part in an observer error trial, which the unit could mount. My idea was that the two professors would record, by way of a questionnaire study, the dental state of a random sample of Rhondda Fach adults. They agreed. They drew up the questionnaire and we arranged to motor in the random sample to a dental clinic in the Rhondda for examination by the professors. The survey was carried out by my team, with some interesting results. We assured possible participants that they would only be examined; that there was no question of any treatment or pain, but that they would receive advice if they asked for it. Despite such reassurances, the team still had great difficulty in persuading the population to cooperate, and the response rate proved much lower than we had ever had before

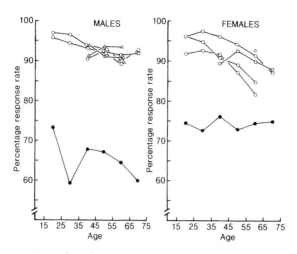

Figure 14 Persuading the public to come forward for dental examination proved a special challenge. Response rates were more than 20 per cent down on the levels usually achieved by the author's team.

Attendance for chest radiograph ($\bigcirc$); for intraocular pressure measurement ($\square$); for surveys that included blood sampling ($\triangle$); and for dental examination ($\bullet$).

(see figure 14). One tough young policeman fainted when he sat in the dental chair. The results of the survey were never published. This was reasonable as it was only a pilot study, but I saw the figures and, as far as I remember, the only question the two professors consistently agreed on was the number of teeth in the mouth!

Becoming interested in dentistry, we did two case-control studies using our Rhondda population data: one which suggested that the edentulate was the same weight as the non-edentulate and had similar expectations of life. We also helped a charming New Zealander, Mike Harkness, to do a survey of a random sample of Cardiff schoolchildren from the orthodontic point of view. He took casts of a high percentage of them. He then asked a distinguished panel of dental experts to say whether or not orthodontic treatment should be advised, and how they should be treated if treatment was advised. The results were rather frightening, as the observer error rate was so high.[21] (Still in the early 1980s, as I am drafting these notes, I am trying to help a young Scottish dentist, Bill Shaw,[22] to solve the orthodontic problem. It is a serious one.)

While all this was going on, and when they were not assisting me in my various projects, my colleagues were extending their own interesting lines of inquiry. Peter Elwood made excellent progress in his studies associated with the epidemiology of anaemia, and in particular the fortification of bread by adding iron. I think my only contribution was in eating a radioactive breakfast to help him. I was also delighted when Estlin Waters, a young epidemiologist who had joined the unit in the 1960s and given help with a number of surveys, established himself as an authority on migraine. He used all the established techniques – surveys, case-control studies, and randomised controlled trials – and finally established that migraine was not really a syndrome, just the extreme end of a spectrum of headache conditions.[23] As a chronic sufferer I found this hard to believe, initially, but this did not prevent me from feeling specially pleased by Estlin's success. He had worked particularly hard to help others before this breakthrough in his own research, and well deserved success. He is now professor of community medicine at Southampton.

Also important in this period were the close links I formed with Professor Ed Kass, an academic clinician at Harvard with strong interests in epidemiology, whom I first met in Jamaica when visiting Bill Miall's epidemiology unit there – the one I had helped to persuade the MRC to set up. Bill served as its director from 1962 to 1971, and I greatly enjoyed visiting him from time to time to keep in touch with his progress and ideas. Like Bill, Ed was to become a lifelong friend. He was an impressive man of ideas, which we enjoyed long hours discussing, particularly those he wished to test on defined populations. Over the next few years, with the help of his financial resources, we tested a number of his hypotheses on our survey populations in Wales, particularly ideas concerning bacteriurea and the use of automatic blood pressure machines. Unfortunately the results were not very exciting, but the increasing association with Harvard was to prove useful, both for me and the unit.

From a personal point of view the period can only be viewed as a highly interesting and important one in which I recovered from my addiction to coal workers' pneumoconiosis and found a new interest in health services research. The MRC and DHSS were tolerant in allowing me to try out a fair number of odd ideas, which I cannot say always proved successful. My biggest success, I suppose, was with screening, but even that was disappointing when we could not take the research further and look at aetiology, as in the case of glaucoma. On the other hand, I had shown that a variety of new types of investigation were ethically acceptable, and practically possible. I hoped that others would follow in the wake of what we had begun. Above all I suppose that the chief thing I had gained was far greater insight into the working of the NHS. I had learnt a lot from the Rhondda Fach in an earlier decade, but these 10 years had raised my intellectual understanding to a much higher vantage point. I suspect that I could only underestimate how much my contacts with Dick Cohen and Max Wilson at the DHSS, Gordon McLachlan at the Nuffield Provincial Hospitals Trust, and the scientists of my own unit made all this possible.

COLLEAGUES AT 4 RICHMOND ROAD

I have mentioned a number of co-workers with whom I was associated in the 1960s, but some of my colleagues at 4 Richmond Road deserve better introductions than they have received. In fact I have said all too little about the contribution made to my work and piece of mind by the constant support and assistance I received from my personal secretary Irene Calford, without whose help I would have accomplished much less. I have also shortchanged the part Hubert Campbell played in the years when the unit was getting off the ground.

Hubert joined the team towards the end of 1962, just a few

months after we had moved to Richmond Road. As a statistician he proved that he had a great deal to contribute to the planning of surveys, and as a colleague he made a good job of criticising many of my ideas and initiatives. Like me he had strong political views, and something of a mixed background in getting to where he wanted to be. He had served as a scientific officer with the Royal Navy in the second world war, and then worked as a statistician in Newcastle, where we first met in 1950 when I was there talking about the Pneumoconiosis Research Unit's radiographic system of classifying stages in the development of pneumoconiosis. Later he undertook medical studies in Newcastle, and after qualifying spent a year or two with the Registrar General's department as a statistician. It was after contact with my team in the Rhondda Fach, while assisting with a private census there, that he applied to join us. He arrived just ahead of preparations for the new unit, and gave considerable assistance at that critical time. I also recall his influence in helping to bring about the Cardiff cervical cytology study, as well as a range of fairly sharp exchanges in our discussion of epidemiological strategies. We were never close, though, fundamentally because we commonly viewed and reacted to situations differently. In fact if Hubert had gone to Spain in 1936 we would have found ourselves on opposite sides in that argument too.

As Hubert steadily became more involved with the medical school in the later 1960s, eventually taking the chair of medical statistics there, his place was taken by Peter Sweetnam, one of the first cohort of postgraduates to emerge from Cardiff's new MSc course in statistics, who came to us in 1966. His ideas had been turned in the direction of medical statistics by Charles Rossiter of the Pneumoconiosis Research Unit, who taught on the MSc course, and the outcome was a letter asking about the possibility of a job. Peter has been associated with my work ever since. In addition to his credentials as a medical statistician he has a special ability to listen to my various ideas, and quickly debunk the bad ones. This has been an invaluable service. We also share interests in gardening and sport. Monday mornings would not have been the same without the prospect of our quick review of the weekend's rugger or cricket results. Peter also gave me the benefit of his gardening know-how during his fairly frequent visits to Rhoose Farm House, where we spent a good many relaxing evenings toasting prospective gardening strategies.

Peter Elwood also came into my life through a letter asking about the prospects of a job. He was then a junior member of a Department of Epidemiology in Belfast, where he had studied medicine at Queen's University. He came over to Cardiff at my suggestion that we should talk over his career interests – and we went on talking for three days. It was a good association from the first. While we argued about religion and alcohol, that first meeting showed how closely our wavelengths related regarding epidemiological research and its role in clinical medicine. Peter was clearly a lateral thinker, and someone we needed at the unit. In addition to experience of occupational medicine in the flax industry of Northern Ireland, he had already conducted studies on tuberculosis, iron-deficiency anaemia, and vagrancy. In particular, we both felt that there was important mileage in further studies of anaemia, and we shared ever more expansive ideas of field studies on prevalence, clinical opportunities, and prevention. Over the next 10 years Peter turned all these ideas into completed studies and publications. There can be few areas of research where so many ambitious ideas have been put so fully to the test. It was very special to have the two Peters there for the rest of my years at the unit. There was a remarkable feeling of partnership. Perhaps this is why I found the task of handing over the reins to Peter Elwood when I retired far easier than I could ever have anticipated. It was really more like handing on the baton in a relay in which we all shared. I am pleased that this Ulsterman did cross the Irish Sea and make his home in South Wales. What he has done for the unit has my deepest admiration.

Estlin Waters, who arrived in 1964, about a year after Peter Elwood joined the unit, proved another valuable addition to the team. In the five and a half years that he spent at 4 Richmond Road he showed first a considerable capacity to involve himself widely in helping other colleagues, and later went on to the fascinating work on migraine I have already mentioned. Brought up initially in Toronto, a son of Welsh parents working in Canada, he had returned to this country for his later schooling and medical studies, and I had first come into contact with his work when he spent six months at Llandough Hospital as a senior house officer – his first job after coming down from Bart's. By that time his parents were back in Cardiff. Some while later, after he had been away and completed national service, he answered an advertisement we had put out for an epidemiologist, and it did not take us long to make up our minds. How I enjoyed his enthusiasm for work and life generally. In opportune moments we seemed to chat about everything under the sun, but I have a feeling that Rugby football surfaced more than any other topic during conversations with Estlin. I had divided feelings when he went off to Southampton in 1970; pleased for his progress, but aware of our loss.

Jean Weddell, who joined the team in 1965, did so in a less conventional way. She had been one of my students on the Tuberculosis and Chest Diseases Course at Sully Hospital in 1962–63, when I had developed a liking for her ready humour and capacity for penetrating criticism. It was towards the end of that academic year that she had the bad luck to be struck down in a severe road accident, which left her immobile for quite a time. In the months that followed, our friendship developed through a series of Sunday afternoon hospital visits, which my calendar accommodated surprisingly well, although at one time the illness of my sister in Edinburgh meant visits to Jean only on alternate weekends. It was in 1965, towards the end of her convalescence, that I had the idea that here was just the person we needed to take charge of the randomised controlled trial of outpatient and inpatient treatment of varicose veins that we were then planning. It turned out to be one of my better ideas, and Jean stayed on for several years and developed a number of interesting epidemiological projects. She has the kind of critical mind I much admire, and a refreshing directness of comment which on occasions has stopped me in my tracks when it has been directed against prized innovations in the Rhoose Farm House garden. It is lucky that we have never shared a garden, but we have shared in a very happy friendship over many years.

The last of my colleagues to be recruited in the 1960s was David Bainton,[24] who although only fairly recently out of medical training had well established interest in epidemiology. On joining the unit he worked first with Jean Weddell, assisting with an incidence study of stroke she had begun a little earlier in 1969. Later, in the early 1970s, he went on to design and conduct an important study of the incidence of gallstones in a local population (Barry), and then a randomised controlled trial of treatment of gallstones, which is mentioned in the following chapter. David brought with him a massive enthusiasm for epidemiology and social medicine, and it was the impetus of this that led to his moving on from Richmond Road far sooner than we would have wished.

Any review of the support I received from colleagues in this period would be seriously incomplete without due tribute to all that Irene Calford, my secretary, did to keep my day-to-day life in order. She has supported so many aspects of my work with exceptional caring, and time and time again has shown a remarkable flair for anticipating what I might need or neglect. It was lucky for me that she applied to transfer from the Pneumoconiosis Research Unit when I first moved to Richmond Road. She has been an important member of the Epidemiology Unit ever since. She also has the distinction of being the only person I have met in recent years who could read my writing.

FAMILY, HOME, AND LEISURE

The main features of this period were the rehabilitation of my great-great-step-aunt, Florrie Leman, and her "tweeny"; the explosion of my gardening instinct; interests in various committees serving the arts; and my more detailed discovery of Karl Popper. There was a lot that seemed to be changing on the domestic front, and I still felt that I was growing up in my appreciation of domestic comforts. Rhoose Farm House became more and more a home from which I disliked being away.

The Aunt Florrie incident was my only venture into what might be called family social work. Florrie Leman was the youngest daughter of my great-grandfather's second marriage. I first met the family when I was a Cambridge undergraduate. My sister had visited me for a May week ball, and we were encouraged by my mother to motor home through Chipping Sodbury to see the Lemans. After all, my second name was Leman. We were given a warm welcome, in a beautiful Queen Anne house, which proved rather primitive in its internal arrangements. The general set up was of two fairly large houses on an impressive plot of land. In one, the more modern house, lived Dr Curtis Leman, Florrie's brother. He had been married but, as I discovered later, had had to dissolve the marriage on discovering that his wife was already married. In the old family house Aunt Florrie reigned supreme, helped by an aged domestic home help. We were well fed and kindly treated and left rather fond of the curious set up we had encountered.

My sister and I discussed what I should do about this odd family connection when I settled in Wales after the war. Nothing was known about their fate in wartime, and it was thought that I was their nearest living relative. In retrospect I am ashamed that I took so long to contact them, but for quite a number of years my life left few opportunities to journey to Chipping Sodbury. At that time travelling by car meant crossing the Severn by ferry, and braving its notorious queues. That did not help.

It was not until the early 1960s that I made my first visit to Chipping Sodbury. My great-great-step-uncle had died and Florrie, now 85, was living alone with the domestic "tweeny" Louie, aged 75. They gave me a boiled egg with my tea and I came away feeling that they were coping quite well. It was only after a later visit that I suddenly became worried. I thought they were starving, though they were by no means poor. I consulted the local doctor. He said that he too was worried. He had had great difficulty in getting into the house; and he pointed out that they had quarrelled with everyone in the village and were now buying very little food. I challenged Aunt Florrie about this and she finally admitted that they had become bored with cooking. I suggested that a holiday at Rhoose might help to restore their appetites, and to my surprise they eventually agreed. I told them to pack while I telephoned Rhoose, and in an amazingly short time Aunt Florrie and Louie were installed in the back of the Jaguar, on their way to South Wales. The Barlows supported me magnificently, doing everything they could to help our rather special guests settle in. I was surprised how quickly they regained their appetites. They ate surprisingly well when someone else was doing the cooking. They also seemed to lose any sense of wishing to return home. This placed me in a difficult position. It could have been argued that I had kidnapped a possibly wealthy relative (I had no idea of the extent of her wealth), so I arranged an experiment. I explained to my aunt that at the end of their "holiday" I would motor them back to Chipping Sodbury and leave them there for two weeks. I would then visit them and ask whether they would like to come to Rhoose permanently. Finance was never mentioned. When I returned to see them at the end of the experiment they were already packed and waiting. In fact I don't think they had unpacked. The door of Rounceval House was locked, and Aunt Florrie's reign at Rhoose Farm House began.

It was fascinating to see what simple care could do for two old ladies. They came back to life; Aunt Florrie emerging as a quite definite character, with wonderful stories which included the Bristol Riots, dinner with Dr W G Grace, and her brother's bigamous marriage. She took over Martin Wright's old sitting room, where she insisted on receiving guests at my parties, wearing some remarkable Victorian jewellery. Later I wheeled her into parties in her wheelchair, and always we were expected to drink her health, which we did dutifully. The party I gave for her 90th birthday was a great success. I had had her portrait painted, secretly, and presented it at the peak of the feast. She enjoyed the gift, but didn't think the painter had done her justice!

My only modest medical intervention in this period came when Aunt Florrie began complaining of sleeplessness. She had been a lifelong teetotaller, but I put some diluted brandy in a medicine bottle and she thought I was a wonderful "doctor." She continued the therapy until she died. I have possibly given too much space to this simple act of family care, but it gave me great satisfaction.

Unfortunately the story had a tragic end. She became paranoid, thought my housekeeper was poisoning her, and kept demanding that I should taste her food, drink, and medicine. This proved difficult for someone as busy as I was then, but on Ken Rawnsley's advice I did not hospitalise her. Although she later began to show signs of recovery, an unfortunate reaction to a penicillin injection given for a respiratory infection brought her interesting and not always easy life to an end.

I had, fortunately, talked with her solicitor several years before, after one of his regular visits to Aunt Florrie. I had made it clear to him that I did not want a legacy, but I thought she should leave a considerable sum to the Barlows, who had done most of the caring. Unfortunately she changed her will during her paranoia, in spite of the solicitor's efforts. She left me £1000, which I gave to the Barlows, to whom she had left nothing. After a legacy to Louie, she left the bulk of her estate of about £50 000 to some Leman relatives who had not visited her for 20 years. Louie's survival presented further problems, which were eventually solved, but I have spent enough space on this family social problem.

My other great interest during this period was the improvement of Rhoose Farm House and its garden. I had done a certain amount to improve the house in the previous decade. In the 1960s I continued buying sculpture and paintings, including two Hepworth's and works by Duncan Ferguson, Josef Herman, and Michael Ayrton, all fairly cheaply. However, I bought them all because I liked them, not because of their possible value. I like to think that any success I had in picking out successful artists resulted from good taste rather than purposeful investment. I would also like to think that I inherited something of an artist's instinct from my mother. Judging by the one picture of hers that I possess, she might well have become a competent artist if she had continued. As regards the alterations to the house, I had always known what I wanted since first setting foot there. Now the time had arrived to go ahead. All that I needed was a competent, sensitive architect who liked this sort of work, and I was lucky in finding John (later Professor John) Eynon, who helped me greatly.

In the garden it was different. I drew up a plan: sculpture there; rose garden here; swimming pool over there; shrub gardens over that rise; pool with sculpture along there; etc. What I did not know, though, was enough about plants. I needed advice. This I sought locally with little success, but fortunately I soon met Dennis Woodland of Hillier's. I was home and dry. He gave me sound advice to get me started and then came down once a year to tell me what I had done wrong in the interim and to discuss future developments. As a result of this happy collaboration it did not take long for the western side of the garden to take form – about an acre in all. It has been a delight to me ever since.

I must interpolate some explanation of this sudden new interest. Basically it was made possible by the death of my step-father, which made me much wealthier. In addition I found myself with more hours at home, now that my participation in surveys was reducing. I had also decided to give up tennis, preferring to go out while I was still winning. Then there was another curious factor, which arose out of the blue, and remarkably rapidly: a determination to make my immediate environment as beautiful as possible.

There were many difficulties, in particular the alkaline nature of the soil, but I soon became confident and decided to buy the farmyard buildings adjacent to my existing holding, to extend its eastern side. With John Eynon's help the barn and farm buildings, which formed three sides of an open quadrangle, were converted into a house, flanked by colonnades of eighteenth century arches. I considered that only a sculptor could use this setting, and looked round for one to come and live there. After a considerable exercise in persuasion, Peter Nicholas, a young sculptor whose work I greatly admired, accepted my invitation to come with his family for a trial period in the new barn complex. It was an experiment

223

that worked, and to my delight they stayed. Peter had been more than a little reluctant to come at first, and I can understand this. He had recently spent a highly successful year in Italy on an Arts Council award, after which he had put a lot of effort into establishing his first studio, near Raglan, in Gwent. He had every reason to be reluctant to try another experiment at that stage when his own efforts were blossoming well.

Turning the rest of the farmyard into a garden was a problem. There was only a thin layer of soil over solid limestone. I decided to risk a scree garden, and Dennis Woodland finally agreed. Although there were serious early difficulties it is now something of real interest and beauty.

During this period, in addition to serving on many medical committees, I also served for three years on the Broadcasting Council for Wales,[25] the Visual Arts Committee of the Welsh Arts Council, and the Selection Committee buying pictures for the Welsh National Museum. I do not think I was of much use, but I learnt a great deal. At the BBC I was educated about the Welsh language problem. My one suggestion was that we should measure how many people used the broadcasts and telecasts in Welsh. I was supported by a majority of the council, but the secretariat killed the idea. My final conclusion was that the Welsh language was dying and would die whatever was done. My reasons for this were largely based on what I knew about a comparable situation in Eire and the fact that various legal, educational, and broadcasting measures already taken in Wales had had little effect. Also, the Welsh language is socially and politically divisive and is having a disastrous effect. It is always sad to watch someone or something die, and even harder to arrange a satisfactory funeral. Perhaps the trial period of the Welsh television channel will do the trick.[26]

There was an unfortunate incident some three or four years after I had left the Broadcasting Council for Wales. I was interviewed on Welsh television about the "wine paper" I had recently written.[27] The core of its argument concerned a strong negative correlation between the amount of wine consumed in 18 developed countries and death rates from ischaemic heart disease. This had been well represented, diagrammatically, in the paper (see figure 15), and I took the main graph with me to the interview in the hope that it would assist the interviewer. It did not. The interviewer clearly did not understand what I was trying to get across. This I could forgive, but not her audacity in allowing another diagram to be used in the broadcast programme. This had only three or four points on it instead of 18, and far from assisting my argument was actually good enough to destroy it. I complained, naturally enough, and to my surprise the Welsh BBC would not even apologise, so I had to take the matter to an official BBC complaints committee in London, where I won a public apology on television. I haven't appeared on Welsh television since!

My first discovery, as I sat on the Visual Arts Committee in the late 1960s, was about myself. I no longer reacted to trends in the visual arts field with excitement, as I had done in discovering all the various developments that had taken place

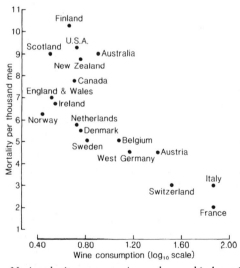

Figure 15   National wine consumption and annual ischaemic heart disease mortality rates for males (40–65 years) in 18 developed countries, using data for 1976–77

from the time of the impressionists. As painting became more and more abstract, and sculpture abstract and plastic, I found that I was bored. I particularly disliked the pictures of one well known lady, consisting of wavy, parallel lines, which made me feel migrainous. Clearly something had happened to the visual arts . . . or to me? In earlier years I had looked forward to discovering new artists with new ideas, but now I felt rather lost.

I also received something of an education about the status of opera in Wales. Wales has had a deprived history so far as its generation of painters, sculptors, and architects is concerned. It badly needs a big investment in those who might develop the visual arts there but, alas, most of the money from the Arts Council goes to the Welsh National Opera. I am not very musical, but there are a number of operas I have enjoyed hearing performed, especially "The Marriage of Figaro" and "Salome." I also enjoy a number of symphonic works and the songs of Schubert, but in general I prefer plays to concerts. I had an interesting experience in Vienna, hearing Verdi's *Otello* at the opera house and seeing Shakespeare's "Othello" at the Burgtheater on consecutive nights. The former was doubtless well sung, but I could not hear the words, and the libretto takes terrible liberties with the text. I was scarcely moved by it, while the next night I was moved to tears. The opera cost, I think, five times as much as the theatre. For me music alone does not communicate feeling concisely, compared with the spoken or even written word, although in some cases I find that it intensifies the meaning and feeling aroused by words. Therefore when I hear opera lovers going into ecstacies about an opera sung in a language they do not understand, and with a farcical libretto, I am somewhat suspicious. Anyone feeling in this way would have to regard the Welsh National Opera as having too much of the cake.

At this point, too, I want to interpolate some remarks about two societies which have meant a great deal to me during my medical, scientific career. They are the Society of Social Medicine in the UK, and the International Epidemiological Association. I was a founder member and a constant attender at both. Each has grown considerably in size and importance since its foundation years in the 1950s. I think the most important factor in their success is that their membership is not limited to those who are medically qualified. Many statisticians, sociologists, economists, and others have joined. This has enriched their discussions greatly. It also has possible dangers. The UK Society of Social Medicine was at one time nearly overrun by sociologists, whose scientific attitudes were rather different from those of the epidemiologists, but the danger passed. I have enjoyed the meetings of both societies and through them have made a very large number of friends throughout the world. I am grateful to both of them.

The other major change in this period was that instead of being interested in Popper I became fascinated and almost taken over by some of his ideas. I had first been attracted to him by his solution of the problem of induction. As I read more I found that he produced a logical justification of all my doubts about Freud and Marx. I continued to read him, almost daily, and became more and more convinced of his general views.

As the decade moved towards its close there came an unexpected cloud over what had been largely happy days at Rhoose Farm House. Mrs Barlow developed rheumatoid arthritis. I knew quite a lot about the condition and saw that she was in expert hands, not that much could be done. I knew the general prognosis was bad but that there were often long stationary periods. The Barlows had been good to me for many years and I was loth to lose them. I engaged a daily to reduce their pressures and hoped for the best.

ANOTHER MEDICAL INTERLUDE

One morning in January 1965 I found myself at 9.00 am with Professor Ken Donald in the Medical Unit of Edinburgh Royal Infirmary, beside my sister's bed. She was hallucinating freely and appeared weak. I was not feeling too good myself. The day before I had rushed up from Wales to a mental hospital in the south of Scotland in response to a telephone call telling me that my sister, aged 58, was suffering from severe senile psychosis.

The hospital where I found Helen presented an unusual picture. It was an "open" one, concentrating on the rehabilitation of neuroses and psychoneuroses. It was socially orientated. There were bright curtains, music, and people dancing and playing cards. The place seemed in a whirl. I had nothing against this, but there in a corner I found my sister, who looked desperately out of place. Although periodically hallucinating, she recognised me and talked to me freely. Almost her first words were: "Archie, can you get me out of here? I think I'm in the wrong sort of hospital." For an hallucinating patient I thought the remark showed great perception, although I still needed a clear picture of what had been happening. The story started with backache, followed by severe constipation, abdominal pain, and increasingly abnormal behaviour, leading to hallucinations. She was moved to the local cottage hospital but was found to be uncontrollable and was transferred to the mental hospital. The whole history spanned about seven days, with very low blood pressure and an absence of knee and ankle jerks the only abnormal physical signs.

The two consultants in psychiatry and general medicine were patient with me when I queried their diagnosis of "senile psychosis." They agreed that the case was atypical, with its short history, missing knee and ankle jerks, and very low blood pressure, but argued that there was no other obvious explanation. As an epidemiologist I was in a weak position to challenge the views of two experienced physicians but remained convinced that my sister would die if she remained there, and that she was not dying of senile psychosis. They finally pointed out, rather coldly, that I was free to move my sister if I signed the discharge form. I said that I must first go and discuss the situation with her family. I drove slowly to her home and on the way decided to raise heaven and earth to get my sister into the Medical Unit at Edinburgh Royal Infirmary and if possible into a bed in full view of the sister. It seemed the safest place for such a bizarre case. My brother-in-law agreed. I rang the professor in Edinburgh, Ken Donald,[28] whom I knew slightly, and he, out of the kindness of his heart, agreed to help. I hired a private ambulance, signed the discharge papers, and set off with my sister and her daughter for Edinburgh.

It was a terrible journey. It was snowing and the road was slippery; my sister was having extraordinary hallucinations; her paralysis was increasing; and at one time I thought that she was dying; but we got there, very late. Ken Donald examined her, agreed that a diagnosis of senile psychosis was unlikely, ordered a lot of tests, and said that he would see me at 9.00 am the next day. So, after a sleepless night of much telephoning, in a hotel in Edinburgh, there I was.

Fortunately we did not have to wait long for the diagnosis. The houseman appeared with a urine bottle, in which the sample had a definite port wine colour, and we all muttered "Porphyria," though I knew practically nothing about the condition. Ken said that there was an expert on porphyria in Glasgow, Dr Abe Goldberg,[29] who would come over, and I went off to educate myself about the disease. I discovered that it was a dominant, inherited disease; one in which an affected parent has a 50:50 chance of transmitting it to an offspring. It is due to an enzyme abnormality in the liver, which affects the biosynthesis of haem, although the ramifications of its effects on metabolism are far from understood. Porphyria is symptomless in its characteristically long latent phase, but acute attacks can be caused by porphyrics taking certain drugs, usually barbiturates and sulphonamides. My sister's case was quite typical. It started with abdominal pain after taking barbiturates; then came the hallucinations and then the paralysis. There is really no treatment. The objective is to keep people alive until they recover spontaneously. On the whole I was relieved. The situation was a good deal better than if a hopeless cancer had been diagnosed, and I was relieved that I had transferred her to the Medical Unit. I now felt that she had every possible chance of recovery. She would certainly have died in the mental hospital.

I searched medical bookshops that day for something about porphyria and found Geoffrey Dean's book *The Porphyrias*.[30] While reading it I suddenly realised that although I had got my sister diagnosed and given the best available treatment I still had other serious responsibilities. In *The Porphyrias* there is the sad story of a letter being sent to a close relative of a recently diagnosed porphyric warning her of the dangers of taking barbiturates. The letter arrived a week too late. She had taken barbiturates and had died. I realised I had a job to do, and quickly. Both my parents were dead, so I sat thinking which side of the family to start on. There were really no clues, but information on the Cochrane family seemed more accessible, so I decided to have a look at them first. Dr Abe Goldberg agreed to do the tests, and I staged a curious sherry party in Galashiels for all available Cochrane blood relatives. It was an emotional meeting, with everyone believing that my sister was dying in Edinburgh. I gave a short lecture on porphyria, explained the situation, and finally asked them all for specimens of urine and faeces. They responded well. The specimens were sent to Glasgow, but all were negative, except for those from two of my sister's children, so we were no further on. Next I started on my mother's side. Oddly enough, the first test on myself, carried out in Cardiff, proved negative, and it was not until several months later that Professor Rimington asked me for a sample of faeces and later wrote a polite letter telling me I was, biochemically, a severe porphyric.

The next few months were busy. As a professor, I was running a course on tuberculosis and chest diseases for doctors from developing countries; and as a director of a research unit there were other interests commanding attention. I tried to spend weekends in Edinburgh with my sister, who remained desperately ill in intensive care, and left the urgent task of tracing my mother's family tree to every spare minute I could find. I began by examining the faeces of those I knew, but did not get very far until one member of the family came up with my great-grandmother's Birthday Book. During the period that followed I received enormous help from Fred Moore, who became as interested in the family tree as I was. He designed a beautiful "do-it-yourself" kit, in which samples of faeces and urine could be sent to Cardiff from all over the world. After six months we found that we had seriously underestimated my

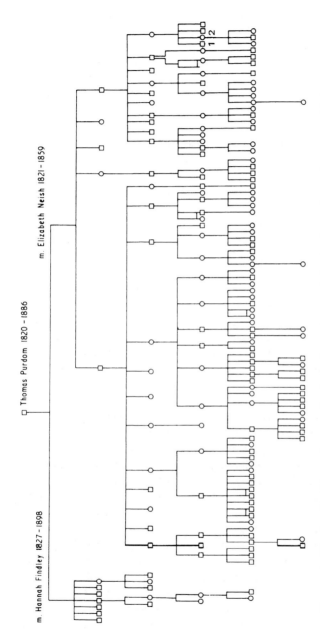

□ Thomas Purdom 1820 - 1886

m. Hannah Findley 1827 - 1898

m. Elizabeth Neish 1821 - 1859

1 2

Figure 16   The first family tree drawn up by the author in his search for the descendants of great grandfather Thomas Purdom. A copy was sent to each descendant located, with information on the dangers of porphyria, acute or latent, and a request for samples of urine and faeces. Further information led to the expansion of this family outline, the details of which appear in the paper by Cochrane and Goldberg.[31] 1, Archie Cochrane; 2, his sister.

great-grandfather's capabilities. He had 153 living descendants, of whom we finally examined 152 (see figure 16). Contrary to some suggestions by cynical colleagues, no one was in prison or in a mental hospital.

Meanwhile, in Edinburgh, the battle for my sister's life was being fought in the intensive care unit. She seemed almost completely paralysed, being for a time only able to move one eyelid. She appeared to remain fully conscious, but communication was difficult. She had numerous complications: collapsed lungs, septicaemia, and severe constipation requiring the manual removal of faeces. But the team battled on and after a long period of renal dialysis she slowly started to recover. After a lengthy convalescence she eventually emerged with only slight neurological defects in her thumbs and one leg. I am deeply grateful to Ken Donald, and particularly to Harry Rees, for the skilled, devoted care they provided.

Slowly the results came through from this scattered family, with members living as far away as New Zealand, and we were able to begin the analysis. As I have explained elsewhere, I had become interested in distributions. General medical opinion had in the past assumed a bimodal distribution separating the healthy and the sick – that is, a distribution of characteristics that had two peaks – but our research on the distribution of characteristics in populations had shown that it was unimodal, though sometimes a little skew. Theoretically, however, I had every reason to assume that a characteristic controlled by one dominant gene should give that rare phenomenon, a true bimodal distribution. Unfortunately this did not happen when we measured faecal porphyrin levels in our attempts to trace relatives with latent porphyria. The distribution was just very skew, making it difficult to decide which members of the family had inherited the gene.[31] To some extent this was probably due to the insensitivity of the test, but at that time I could not be sure that I was examining descendants of the right great-grandfather. On the preventive side, however, we have been reasonably successful. All of the descendants and their general practitioners have been warned about the possibility of porphyria and the dangers of barbiturates and sulphonamides.

There were, of course, moments of fun amid all the worry and hard work of this episode. I remember a conversation with a distant Cochrane relative, of the upper middle class in Edinburgh, who had heard that my sister was suffering from "the South African type" of porphyria. After criticising me for allowing Helen to be admitted to the Medical Unit instead of an expensive nursing home (where she would certainly have died) she stated that she always thought there was a "touch of the tarbrush about the Purdoms!" Another amusing moment came with a letter from a dear old uncle in New Zealand. He replied to my first letter explaining the situation by saying that he was surprised that any member of the "runt" of the family left in the UK had become a medical professor but not surprised to discover that he was a very ignorant professor, who clearly did not realise that the good air and good food of New Zealand had long ago got rid of all the diseases inherited in the UK. (New Zealand death rates from all causes were at that time rather higher than our own.)

There was another service I felt I had to do to help my sister. She was advised after her recovery to be teetotal. Though not really a drinker she clearly enjoyed her glass of sherry, and so I examined the evidence against taking alcohol. This was far from conclusive, so I set up an experiment. I was going to drink my usual amount of alcohol for a month, and collect my faeces for examination. I would then do a month without alcohol, with a similar collection, and then a month with increased alcohol consumption, just before Christmas. There was no difference in the distribution of faecal porphyrin levels in the three months. A paper on these results was turned down when I tried to publish it, but I advised my sister that she could have her sherry, and I continued drinking. Neither of us, or my sister's two daughters, have so far suffered any ill effects.

It was a curious, emotional, interesting, and exhausting interlude, which in a way I enjoyed. As a result I altered the natural history of one person's disease for the better, and possibly prevented other incidents. As one Cardiffian wit put it when I retired from my professorial chair: "There would always be my stool to continue the interest!"

233

NOTES

1 Dr John R Bignall, MD, FRCP.
2 Hart P D'A, Aslett E A. MRC Special Report Series No 243. London, 1942.
3 See Hart J T, Cochrane A L, Higgins I T T. Tuberculin sensitivity in coal workers' pneumoconiosis. *Tubercle* 1966; **44**: 141–52.
4 See Higgins I T T, *et al*. Blood groups of miners with coal-workers' pneumoconiosis and bronchitis. *Br J Ind Med* 1963; **20**: 324–31.
5 See Higgins I T T, Cochrane A L, Thomas A J. Epidemiological studies of coronary disease. *British Journal of Preventive and Social Medicine* 1963; **17**: 153–65.
6 See Palmer J W. Smoking, caning and delinquency in a secondary modern school. *British Journal of Preventive and Social Medicine* 1965; **19**: 18–23.
7 See Palmer J W. Punishment – a field for experiment. *Br J Criminol* 1967; **7**: 434–41.
8 Dr John Bowlby, CBE, MD, FRCP, consultant psychiatrist, Tavistock Clinic and Institute, London. See Bowlby J. *Child care and the growth of love*. London, 1953; also Bowlby J. *Attachment and loss. Vol I*. London, 1980.
9 See Elwood P C, Waters W E, Greene W J W, Sweetnam P, Wood M M. Symptoms and circulating haemoglobin level. *J Chronic Dis* 1969; **21**: 615–21.
10 Professor F C Hollows, FRCS, associate professor of surgery, University of New South Wales, Australia.
11 Peter Anderson Graham, FRCS.
12 See Hollows F C, Graham P A. Intra-ocular pressure, glaucoma, and glaucoma suspects in a defined population. *Br J Ophthalmol* 1966; **50**: 570–86; also Cochrane A L, Graham P A, Wallace J. Glaucoma. In: *Screening in medical care*. London, 1968; also Graham P A, Hollows F C. A critical review of methods of detecting glaucoma. In: Hunt J. *Glaucoma*. Edinburgh, 1969.
13 Wallace J, Lovell H G. Glaucoma and intra-ocular pressure in Jamaica. *Am J Ophthalmol* 1969; **67**: 93–100.
14 Wallace J, Sweetnam P, Warner C J, Cochrane A L, Graham P A. An epidemiological study of lens opacities among steel workers. *Br J Ind Med* 1971; **28**: 265–71.
15 Dr James Maxwell Glover Wilson, FRCP.
16 See *The Cardiff cervical cytology study*. HMSO, 1966; also Evans D M D, Hibbard B M, Jones J M, Sweetnam P. The Cardiff cervical cytology study: prevalence of cytological grades and initial histological findings. *Br Med J* 1981; **282**: 689–91; also The Cardiff cervical cytology study: enumeration and definition of a population, and initial acceptance rates. *J Epidemiol Community Health* 1980; **34**: 9–13.
17 The Study has never answered the initial question it was set to resolve.

18 See Chant A D B, Jones H O, Weddell J M. Varicose veins: a comparison of surgery and injection/compression sclerotherapy. *Lancet* 1972; 1188–91; also Piachaud D, Weddell J M. The economics of treating varicose veins. *Int J Epidemiol* 1972; 1: 287–91; also Piachaud D, Weddell J M. Cost of treating varicose veins. *Lancet* 1972; 1191–2.

19 The Pickering–Platt controversy concerned the nature of essential hypertension. Platt supported the older view that essential hypertension was a disorder transmitted by single gene inheritance, with features of Mendelian dominance. According to this view it was a discrete disease entity caused by a specific chemical fault and any search for its causation should be directed towards defining that fault. Pickering challenged this concept on the grounds that evidence from many sources suggested that blood pressure was a graded characteristic and that essential hypertension represented merely the upper end of a continuous frequency distribution. The disorder was determined by polygenic inheritance but much influenced by environmental factors. The controversy went on throughout the 1950s and the early 1960s. The data collected from the Rhondda Fach and Vale of Glamorgan surveys were an important contribution to the eventual acceptance of Pickering's views.

20 See Mather H G, *et al*. Acute myocardial infarction: home or hospital treatment. *Br Med J* 1971; iii: 334–8.

21 See Harkness E M, Brown W A B. Clinical cephalometric standards: a radiographic study of 12-year old British girls. *Orthodontist* 1972; spring: 25–34.

22 Now Professor Bill Shaw, professor of orthodontics, University of Manchester.

23 See Waters W E. Community studies of the prevalence of headache. *Headache* 1970; 9: 178–83; also Waters W E. Headache and blood pressure in the community. *Br Med J* 1971; i: 142–5.

24 Recruited in 1969, David Bainton actually joined the Epidemiology Unit in January 1970.

25 Member, Broadcasting Council for Wales, 1971–74.

26 Since the time of writing a Welsh television channel has been successfully launched, run jointly by the BBC and Harlech Television.

27 St Leger A S, Cochrane A L, Moore F. Factors associated with cardiac mortality in developed countries, with particular reference to the consumption of wine. *Lancet* 1979; i: 1017–20.

28 Professor Kenneth W Donald, OBE, DSc, MD.

29 Now Sir Abraham Goldberg, KB, MD.

30 Dean G. *The porphyrias, a story of inheritance and environment*. London, 1963.

31 See Cochrane A L, Goldberg A. A study of faecal porphyrin levels in a large family. *Ann Hum Genet* 1968; 32: 195–208.

6 Into the seventies

TWO UNEXPECTED DEVELOPMENTS

I had expected a fairly peaceful period in the last few years before I retired, but it turned out rather differently. Two events early in 1972 considerably changed my life. First, by a short head, came the publication of my little book *Effectiveness and Efficiency*, which made far more impact than I could have ever imagined; and soon afterwards I found myself the first president of the country's newly formed Faculty of Community Medicine. I still remember the shock of finding myself in the chair at the inaugural meeting of the new faculty,[1] and my swift retreat to my sister's home in Scotland just as soon as I could get away from London. Even there, however, I could not escape some of the publicity generated by *Effectiveness and Efficiency*. In fact *The Sunday Times* carried a full page article on the book that weekend, with comment that my sister felt rather overpraised it.[2]

Both these events altered my life considerably, and both require some aetiological explanation. *Effectiveness and Efficiency* is the easier to explain. Each year the Nuffield Provincial Hospitals Trust invites a specialist from some branch of medicine or medical science to give the Rock Carling Lecture, in memory of the famous surgeon Sir Ernest Rock Carling.[3] It involves writing a book, giving a lecture based on its text, and receiving a fee of what was then £1000. I was, I suppose, a possible choice because of my interests in health services research, a field beginning to attract a good deal of attention, but I suspect that my selection owed more to Dick Cohen's support. Looking back, it was an invitation that I accepted with insufficient thought. I was very busy at that time and the Rock Carling commission took a back seat for too long, leaving me with an almost impossible challenge as the deadline for publication drew near. I ended up writing the book almost entirely between the hours of 10.00 pm and 1.00 am at Rhoose, when I had finished everything else. I date the real beginnings of my love of whisky to this period. I had to give myself something to keep going. I slowly made up my mind about the public I wanted to influence, and decided on medical students and non-medical intellectuals. I decided to concentrate mostly on one simple idea – the value of randomised controlled trials in improving the NHS – and to keep the book short and simple, with a few jokes to assist its palatability. Even so, I did not meet the deadline of the Nuffield Provincial Hospitals Trust, and it was fortunate that they agreed to give me an extra year to tie things up. During that period Fred Moore was a great help in cutting superfluous detail from the drafts. When I did finally forward the typescript to Gordon McLachlan I understand that he did not particularly like the first sections of the book but that his wife persuaded him to give it a go. Gordon and I both disliked the title but could not think of anything better. After all this the excellent reviews that followed came as something of a surprise. The book was a far greater success than we could have imagined. It was translated into Spanish, French, Italian, and Polish, and the interest it generated led to a large number of invitations to travel and lecture.

The other development was more complicated and far more a result of chance. Its background was the proposed reorganisation of the NHS. This had previously been a tripartite affair, involving hospitals and consultants, public health departments and medical officers of health, and general practice and general practitioners. The new proposal was to unite, as far as possible, the hospital and public health sectors to provide, in association with general practice, a new two-tier structure to local health service administration. I would have liked a completely unified NHS, but half a cake is better than nothing. In the new two-tier structure, former medical officers of health could look forward to much wider administrative responsibilities as they added hospitals to their field of surveillance. In fact the future need was for a much wider specialist in community medicine, and discussion soon focused on the future training requirements and professional representation of this new speciality. Quite early on in this debate there emerged the idea of setting up a new faculty of the Royal College of Physicians to serve such interests.[4] I first heard about this at the Society of Social Medicine, where there was general disapproval of a situation likely to serve only those who were medically qualified. It was thought that an organisation serving community medicine needed wider than merely medical representation. Nevertheless, the Society of Social Medicine did appoint people to serve on the committee to discuss the founding of the new faculty, and for some reason I was appointed alternate to one of its representatives. I cannot even remember who he was, but I did attend in his place at a fairly late stage in negotiations and, rather belatedly, realised how important the outcome would be. For the first time the full importance of finding the right kind of specialist to assist health service development and administration struck me. It was clear that we needed specialists equally skilled in administration and epidemiology and with a broad view of social medicine and its research. Then we would have a chance of making the NHS more effective and efficient. Here I felt very much at home. I had just spent 18 months trying to write a book on ways to greater efficiency. My main concern, however, like that of many others on the committee, was how to get things under way without undue delay. We needed a new kind of specialist, and as soon as possible; not in the distant future. This urgency, as much as anything else, assisted our resolve to establish the new faculty.

It was while arrangements were in progress that I was asked to contact Sir Richard Doll about the possibility of his becoming the faculty's first president. He, I think, agreed, and I went off on my scheduled skiing trip to Davos pleased that I had at least been of some help. I had two enjoyable weeks on the slopes and never gave the matter another thought, and so it was a great shock to come back and find myself faced with a difficult unexpected decision. Richard Doll had withdrawn from the presidency because of his preoccupation with the big battle that was just breaking out between the MRC and those interested in implementing the recent proposals of the Rothschild report. I was asked to take the place he had vacated. The invitation clearly had a lot to do with the impact *Effectiveness and Efficiency* had had. A few weeks earlier I would have been too remote a figure to have even been considered. Now, after a remarkable rash of publicity, I was the best alternative to Richard Doll. It was a surprising position to be in, and it is difficult to describe the kind of pressure such an invitation put me under. I had very mixed feelings, not least about my capacity to do a good job, and I found it difficult to make up my mind. I had so little experience of chairing committees and even less of the kind of diplomatic and negotiating skills such a role required. It was only after telephoning a lot of friends that I finally came to a decision, but I never realised what I was taking on, although I recognised that the job to be done was a critical one. This is how I became the first president of the Faculty of Community Medicine of the Royal Colleges of Physicians of the UK.

Launching a new faculty in the space of about two years is a fairly tall order. Reorganisation of the NHS was scheduled for 1974. Before then we needed to draw up a constitution for the new faculty, arrange admission and examination procedures for members and fellows, successfully recruit enough members to ensure financial viability as well as credibility, and assist in planning courses of training for the new specialists in community medicine. Throughout this process of formulating a constitution and admission and examination standards we also needed to command the approval of the royal colleges of medicine. This was the essential basis on which recognition of the new speciality depended.

The recruitment of members to the new faculty was particularly challenging, even after we had organised a system allowing suitable people to become founder members and fellows. The two groups in which we were interested were medical officers of health and epidemiologists, particularly those with an interest in health services; but the response was curiously unbalanced. On the whole the medical officers of health responded well, but the epidemiologists tended to hold back. Some of my closest friends, in spite of personal appeals, refused to join. Usually their argument was essentially that of the Society of Social Medicine: they did not approve of joining a faculty which excluded other health service scientific workers, particularly statisticians. In point of fact, when I discussed the problem with medical statisticians they appeared to have no objection to the epidemiologists joining a purely medical faculty. After all, the statisticians had their own societies. Trying to persuade those we needed to join proved a major toll on my time over the next two years. I lectured on the work and interests of the new faculty all over the UK, from the Orkneys to Cornwall – I hope persuasively.

There was a great deal to do to get things under way, but at the end of three years, when I resigned as president, we could claim to have completed the job. The structure of the faculty and the examination system had all been accepted by the royal colleges of medicine. Recruitment had been good, and the faculty was financially viable. Two annual general meetings and the first round of examinations for membership had been held. We had also appointed referees in connection with the large number of appointments in community medicine being made at the time of NHS reorganisation in 1974.

It was this latter commitment that led to the only really unpleasant experience of my days as president. Together with Wilfrid Harding, the vice-president of the Faculty of Community Medicine, I was acting as one of the Secretary of State's assessors on a local health authority appointment panel involved in making a very senior appointment. The chairman of the panel, a very well known man, had given us instructions on the way in which the performance of the various candidates should be scored, and I was just totalling my results and recording a few additional comments when, out of the blue, to my horror the chairman said, "That last man we saw was a Jew. We can't have him here." I reacted slowly I am ashamed to say, but not Wilfrid Harding, who had left Germany in 1933 as a matter of conscience. He challenged the statement fairly swiftly. I just felt stunned. I had not heard a remark like that since 1937. I had also not noticed that the man was a Jew. The whole meeting ended most unsatisfactorily, with the chairman resorting to claims that he had been misunderstood, that what he had said was merely a throw away comment not made seriously. Wilfrid returned to the importance of what had been said, but the meeting ended on an uncomfortable note, with an important issue being played down all too obviously. No appointment was made.

After talking with Wilfrid, who subsequently resigned as an assessor on the basis of what had happened, I took responsibility for contacting the chief civil servant in charge of the appointments for that area and made an official complaint. He said that he found my story unbelievable but promised to check it out. A day later he contacted me to say that other members of the panel had confirmed that the words had been said, but that some of them felt that the representatives of the Faculty of Community Medicine were making too much of a minor issue. He asked me what I wanted to do. I said that I wanted the chairman sacked. He replied that he would consult his superiors. Some time passed, but I was finally summoned to Whitehall to see the minister. He treated me with great courtesy and considerable understanding. He agreed with me that as president of a faculty I had every right to complain when I had evidence of an NHS chairman showing anti-Semitic bias against a member of my faculty. He assured me that he was as opposed to anti-Semitism as I was, and that he was just as horrified by what had happened, which he referred to as a "lapsus linguae" of one of his chairmen. At this stage he offered me an abject written apology from the offending one. He then went on to discuss our mutual interests in the improvement of the health service and argued that he could assure me that the resignation of the chairman in question would have a deleterious effect on the NHS in that part of the country. I thought he was on very thin ground there. I had done some checking. The general opinion was that the man was an experienced, forceful chairman, who generally got his own way. There were, however, many who doubted that "his own way" was the best for the health service. Now that his anti-Semitism had been unmasked there was every reason for sacking him. I said as much, but the

241

minister argued that with all his advisers he must know more about the administrative problems of the NHS. I suggested that he might be underestimating the president of the Faculty of Community Medicine. He was, however, clearly not going to give up. He was obviously under some very strong pressure. I could not decide whether it was party or local politics or possibly personal friendship. I thanked him for the time he had given me and said I was sorry but I would have to pursue my end by other means.

The next day I saw my trusted lawyer in Cardiff and asked him to study the Race Relations Act and advise me. He was fascinated by the case and promised a speedy opinion. In the meantime, to be on the safe side, I wrote to a senior medical Jewish friend, giving him details and asking advice.

My lawyer's opinion was interesting in two ways. The action, if it did take place, would be not only against the well known chairman but also against the minister, his employer. The other more difficult point was that I would have to get the written agreement of the man about whom the remark had been made. This latter requirement put me in a difficult position. The man had no idea of what had been said, and I did not particularly want him to know. It was not difficult, though, to get in touch with another doctor who was a friend of his and get advice. I was very glad that I did. I was told that I really must not approach the doctor at present. He was depressed at not having got the jobs he wanted in the reorganised NHS. It was strongly argued that I should not approach him until he got a job. I checked the information from another source and received roughly the same reply. I arranged to be informed when he got a job.

This left me in an unhappy position. I wanted to do something to help kill anti-Semitism, which had haunted most of my early life, but my hands seemed tied. Even inquiries to the Jewish Medical Association and a leading Jewish member of the House of Lords proved depressingly unhelpful. The response was virtually the same in both cases. I was thanked for my efforts but advised against taking any legal action. Nevertheless, I might well have gone ahead when I heard that the doctor had got a job, but by this stage the time limit for taking the action had passed. I had failed again, but I still do not understand under what pressure the minister acted, because he must have been briefed about the Race Relations Act and the risks he was running.

But let me return to the last days of my presidency, and happier memories. One of the greatest rewards of this period came when we at last received confirmation that community physicians would be eligible for merit awards. A damaging oversight in earlier provision had been put right. I also had the great privilege and pleasure of giving Sir Austin Bradford Hill honorary fellowship of the faculty. I think Nye Bevan and Sir Austin have done more for British medicine than anyone else in my lifetime.

There remains the question of who deserves the credit for the creation of the faculty. I would like to make it very clear that I played a limited role. As a figurehead I was useful because I had just written *Effectiveness and Efficiency*, and as a Scot working in Wales I was useful in coping with the growing nationalistic tendencies of these countries. I was a fairly competent general chairman, who never minded having his ideas outvoted. I remember once being in a minority of one when I suggested abolishing grace before faculty dinners. I worked hard; never, I think, missing a meeting or turning down an opportunity to give a lecture in my capacity as president. But I was not the powerhouse behind the development of the faculty as I never had a really clear idea as to the characteristics of the ideal community physician.

The real driving force behind the idea of the Faculty of Community Medicine was Max (Lord) Rosenheim.[5] He had failed to teach me clinical medicine when I was a student at University College Hospital, but we had maintained some contact ever since, helped by our mutual friend Rosie Pitt-Rivers. It would be unfair to say that I became his willing puppet when I became president, but he was always there to advise and help if I needed him. He attended nearly all the critical committee meetings, and solved many problems, behind the scenes, at small dinner parties. I think he was the first to see that some such faculty was essential but I suspect that he, like me, never formed a clear idea of what sort of mix this epidemiological administration doctor should be. Apart from Max's relentless driving pressure the necessary administrative burden was borne by the officers of the faculty. They were: vice-president, Dr Wilfrid Harding; registrar, Dr T M Galloway; academic registrar, Professor Michael Warren; and treasurer, Dr F J Fowler.[6]

It would be invidious to separate them by name, but I might say how much I appreciated the hard work of Professor Warren, the academic registrar; Tom Galloway, an old friend from my Diploma in Public Health days; and Wilfrid Harding, who had been closely associated with the idea and development of a Faculty of Community Medicine from the very beginning. These people did the hard nitty-gritty work. One other important character was our secretary Mr Luke, whom I was instrumental in appointing. With his assistants he played a most important part in getting the faculty off the ground. All these deserve enormous credit.

The future of the faculty is still a little doubtful. Most people agree that such a faculty is essential to draw together the right interests in medical administration and associated research. Developing the right kind of community physician has immense implications for the NHS. We have made little progress, however, in deciding what kind of people we should try to attract into the faculty, or how we should train them.

There was another innovation around this time that further diverted my attention from my real love, the Epidemiology Unit in Cardiff. This was the government's decision to set up an Office of the Chief Scientist in the Department of Health, to stimulate and organise health services research. There had been considerable discussion after the Rothschild report on who should control health services research. There was general agreement that much more research should be done, and there were three possibilities. Firstly, there was the MRC, which had a worldwide reputation for first class medical research, and the little health services research that had been done had been carried out in units like my own MRC unit, though most of the money involved was refunded to the MRC by the DHSS. Against the MRC running it was their well known bias towards pure research and their reliance on spotting winners on the basis of the research protocols they received. They had a limited record of initiating research into problems of immediate importance, although they had set up the Pneumoconiosis Research Unit in 1946. The main alternative to the MRC was the DHSS, which certainly had the best view of the problems most urgently requiring investigation. There was much to be said for health services research being led by the DHSS. Dick Cohen had already done much to stimulate this field of interest while at the DHSS. (I knew Dick well and possibly assumed that when he retired there would be others like him in the DHSS to follow. This did not happen.) A third alternative, suggested chiefly I think by the Nuffield Foundation, was that of establishing another body rather like the MRC specially to run health services research.

Politically the result was never in doubt. The Office of the Chief Scientist was set up in the DHSS. Dick Cohen retired and Sir Douglas Black was appointed chief scientist. I had high hopes that health services research would finally take off. I was given a position on the senior advisory committee, but the whole set up was a flop and was for me and many others a most depressing experience. There were many reasons for this failure, and the ones I list here are possibly biased. There has so far been no detailed analysis. Firstly, to my great surprise, I discovered that, apart from Max Wilson, there seemed to be no one left at the DHSS after Dick Cohen's departure who really believed that health services research could help them solve their problems. They thought that all problems, if ever solved, were solved administratively. They considered the Office of the Chief Scientist as a "cuckoo in their nest," and starved it of staff. Then there was the chief scientist, a charming, intelligent man, whom I liked; a distinguished figure, hopelessly miscast. He was later a most successful president of the Royal College of Physicians. In self defence, finding himself in a hopeless position, he then misused his brilliant capacity for procrastination. He also made a real mistake in choosing to be in an advisory rather than an executive position. Then there was the curious political directive that priority was to be given to psychiatry, mental deficiency, and old age. I was never able to see the order giving this directive, but I have no doubt that it existed. Generously, one could admit that these were areas where one would like advances made, but they were not areas where rapid advances were likely, given the state of research at that time, whereas if we had focused on general hospitals and general practice there were techniques available to carry us much further. The advances could have been considerable. I was shocked that such ministerial edicts about priorities should be accepted so lamely. It suggested that the DHSS was a dangerous place to house a research organisation. Then there was the size of the main advisory committee, about 30 as far as I remember, including medical economists, sociologists, administrators, and epidemiologists. It was far too large and there was of course a continuous internecine war between the subgroups. They all wanted the money. There were endless meetings at the DHSS and weekend meetings at York. I was always discussing resigning with my friends at York, but to my shame never did. I had a misplaced loyalty to Sir Douglas Black. I was wrong.

I imagine health services research will finally return to the MRC, where, after all, it started, but I feel sorry for members of the council who will have to adjudicate on all proposals, ranging from molecular biology to those involving cost-effectiveness studies of treatment programmes. I do not envy them. I also suspect that health services research will suffer if the MRC maintains its spirit of cautious respectability in funding research projects. I remember the answer to one of my proposals: "Archie, I have no criticism of your protocol. I am sure it would be very useful, but it's not quite the sort of thing the MRC does."

RESEARCH

After this discussion of interests away from Cardiff it may seem an afterthought to mention what was going on in my own unit, but this is far from the case. In fact the early 1970s brought an important milestone in my own research, for in 1971 we conducted a 20 year follow-up study of the men we had first met in the Rhondda Fach in 1950–51. A small team of us went back there to find out what had been happening to miners and non-miners, and those we had radiographically diagnosed as suffering from various categories of pneumoconiosis when the two valleys scheme was launched. Fred Moore and I were surprised how easy this follow-up exercise proved. We used letters, telephone, and local registers, but I always took on the final home visiting. I enjoyed this very much. Knocking on a door you have knocked on 20 years ago and wondering who is going to answer is a rare experience. Some of those I contacted were kind enough to say they recognised me at once, but I am afraid they lied. What they said, however, was of minor importance compared with our success in tracing them, and in the end we managed to locate and determine the fate of all but 10 of them, a success rate of over 99.8 per cent.

Above all, our findings showed something of the excess mortality affecting the miners and ex-miners of the survey population (see table II) in contrast to mortality among the non-miners we had examined in 1950–51. Also, the data clearly endorsed the view that there was little pulmonary disability among men of all categories of simple pneumoconiosis and the primary category of PMF. After 20 years only those who had originally been diagnosed in categories B and C of PMF showed a high incidence of disability.[7] It was quite

Table II The 20 year follow-up of miners, ex-miners and non-miners of the Rhondda Fach, 1971. Mortality experience related to pneumoconiosis category: percentage surviving after 20 years.

Age group in 1951	Non-miners	Miners and ex-miners according to pneumoconiosis category					
		0	1	2	3	A	B and C
25–34	93	95	96	94	90	96	81
35–44	82	81	75	76	78	75	47
45–54	64	50	54	55	67	53	29
55–64	31	22	25	24	30	15	12

possible that the mass of data yielded by the survey would also reveal other interesting findings, but the necessary statistical analysis looked pretty daunting given the number of statisticians at the unit and the fact that my retirement was due in 1974.

Whatever I have said of interests away from Cardiff these preretirement years were predominantly research orientated. This was inevitable. My main concern was for the development of the unit, which was, after all, a research unit. I hope I even continued to help some of my colleagues. I liked to keep close contact with their research interests.

The most important piece of work going on at the unit was Peter Elwood's randomised controlled trial of aspirin on the mortality of men who had recently had a heart attack. It was entirely his idea, but he convinced me of its importance and I backed him as much as I could. The design was roughly to continue the trial until there had been a predetermined number of deaths within the sample population. The Cardiff consultants were on this occasion very cooperative. Peter Elwood was clearly better at gaining cooperation than I was. In fact everything was running well when out of the blue came a curious interruption. I was at my desk in the Epidemiology Unit one morning when a telephone call came through from the USA, asking if I was Archie Cochrane and whether my unit was conducting a controlled trial of aspirin? I confirmed that such a project was in progress under the direction of my colleague Peter Elwood. "Can I see you both, tomorrow?" said the voice, and after a quick glance at my diary and a brief word with Peter I arranged a time for us to meet. Little further was said, leaving us 24 hours in which to speculate as to the purpose of the visit, which was clearly of some urgency.

Hershel Jick, a charming intelligent North American epidemiologist, arrived with us as arranged, and slightly jet-lagged. His story, in brief, was that he was conducting a large-scale drug study of the drugs which had been taken by patients prior to their admission to hospital. An analysis had shown that there was a marked deficiency of aspirin takers amongst those who came into hospital diagnosed as suffering from myocardial infarction. This could be interpreted as meaning aspirin either killed people with an ischaemic heart disease attack before they came to hospital or that it prevented or reduced the severity of the attack so that they were not hospitalised. He argued that it was important to discover as soon as possible whether aspirin was killing or curing. I found it a fascinating story, as did Peter Elwood and Peter Sweetnam. Hershel showed us the figures, which were very convincing. We asked, "What do you want us to do?" He replied, "Break your code, and check what your results are showing." Randomised controlled trials are characteristically "blinded" to prevent the investigator knowing which subjects are involved in which treatment, and all subjects were coded for this purpose. I could see that it was a reasonable request, but those who know the difficulties involved in setting up clinical trials are not easily persuaded to break the randomisation code in the middle of a project. We looked to Peter Sweetnam for guidance and he explained that premature breaking of the code once could reasonably be ignored when we eventually came to test the significance of the final results. We were strongly influenced in our decision by the possibility that aspirin was harmful and broke the code that very day. I remember the anxious waiting while findings were checked. The result was that there had been six deaths amongst those originally assigned to aspirin and 11 amongst the controls. The difference was not of course statistically significant, but the direction and magnitude was such as to make it highly unlikely that aspirin was killing people. We felt rather relieved, the American was grateful, and the trial continued.

We all thought that this would be the end of the story, but it was not to be. A few weeks later I got a letter from the secretary of the MRC asking me and the two Peters to attend a meeting at MRC headquarters to meet what sounded like a rather high power group from the USA who wanted to suggest some alterations to our aspirin trial.

The meeting was very high powered. Present were the secretary of the MRC, very senior representatives of the DHSS and the Office of Population Census Statistics, Sir Richard Doll, and a senior statistician. The American delegation consisted of our original visitor, Hershel Jick, a well known epidemiologist, and a statistician. The American proposal was simply that our trial should be rapidly enlarged and that its results should be secretly monitored by an independent group so that if a massive protective effect was occurring in relation to ischaemic heart disease, this should be known as soon as possible. They argued that any unnecessary delay could cost many thousands of lives. In return Hershel Jick promised to postpone the publication of his observations and results on hospital admissions. There followed considerable round the table discussion in which we three played little part. Finally the secretary of the MRC asked the British advisers to state their opinions. They were unanimous that the American proposal should be accepted. Then, characteristic of the way in which the MRC treats its directors, I was reminded by the secretary that the final decision would of course be mine and given the opportunity of further discussion with my colleagues in private. I already knew that a decision not to cooperate would be difficult. The Americans had argued their case well and, despite a curious gut reaction against messing about with Peter Elwood's carefully designed trial, somewhere in the back of my mind I could hear that old saying of my step-father's, "You can't fart against thunder." The three of us withdrew and talked, but not for long. The decision was inevitable, but in the end it was mine.

With generous assistance from the MRC, Peter Elwood soon expanded the trial to cover a number of other areas of the country, with Peter Sweetnam making the necessary arrangements for an independent panel of colleagues to receive and monitor all the resulting data. We then waited anxiously, knowing how important the results might be, but our prayers for a speedy conclusion were not answered. There was no message from the monitoring group that an overwhelmingly beneficial effect had been recorded for aspirin. Even when the trial had passed the point at which the original Cardiff-based project would have been stopped there was still no word. When at last the trial did come to an end its results were some way below our expectations. Although they did show an overall reduction in mortality of 24 per cent for those taking aspirin daily, this benefit was not consistent across the trial areas. There was a curious and inexplicable difference between the results in Cardiff and those in other places. Subjects in Cardiff taking aspirin, who constituted just over half of the trial population, showed a 35 per cent reduction in mortality, whereas death rates for those on aspirin elsewhere were marginally increased. This was a curious and confusing outcome rather than one of impact, and we were left trying to account for the very sizeable differences in the effects of aspirin we had recorded. All the factors that might have led to such inconsistencies were examined, but even though there was some evidence of local variations in compliance this was not enough to clear up the mystery. We published our results at the same time as the Americans published their overall findings,[8] but of course the interest was far less than we had hoped for. Indeed, we felt somewhat slighted when the *British Medical Journal* published our papers under the heading "For debate."[9]

Since then there have been a number of large trials of aspirin in the prevention of myocardial infarction and related conditions. Overall, the results are impressive and confirm the findings of our first trial – namely a reduction by one tablet of aspirin a day of about 20–30 per cent in the number of deaths and non-fatal infarctions. In retrospect I feel a shade guilty. If I had stuck with my gut reaction at the time of the MRC meeting – and I am capable of being very obstinate – I think that Peter Elwood and Peter Sweetnam would have come out of the whole episode very much better. My view is that the changes we made, under pressure, eroded a well designed trial rather than adding to its potential. From a personal point of view my last association with aspirin trials was ironic, as when assigned to aspirin in Richard Doll's aspirin trial with doctors I had to give up after a series of most unpleasant vomitings.

There were a great many other activities in the unit in this period, many of which I could only support much more marginally. Peter Elwood continued his excellent work on various aspects of anaemia. Possibly the most interesting was the demonstration that prognostically a high haemoglobin level was much more serious than a low one.[10] David Bainton completed the first survey of gallstones on a randomised sample of the population and followed it by a randomised controlled trial of the treatment of gallstones.[11] There were many other randomised controlled trials, including one looking into the therapeutic effect of vitamin C on the common cold,[12] another assessing the value of anti-mite measures in relation to mite-sensitive adult asthma,[13] and one examining the effect of taking elderly patients off diuretics.[14] In another field, the 20 year follow-up study of the Rhondda Fach males was completed.[15] It was, all-in-all, a very productive period.

During this period I received three rather undeserved honours: doctorates from York University, England, and Rochester University, in the USA, to whom I am grateful, but the greatest surprise of all was an invitation to give the Dunham lectures at Harvard, one of the highest honours that can be conferred on non-American scientists of all kinds. The list of previous lecturers, which included Willem Einthoven (1925), Sir Joseph Barcroft (1930), Sir Frederick Gowland Hopkins (1937), Jacques Monod (1959), and Lord Florey (1965), made me blush with modesty. I imagine the invitation was engineered by my friend Ed Kass. It was for me to talk about "Health Services of the World." By then I knew a great deal about the NHS but not very much about North American and other health services. Although I had started collecting data about the medical, economic, and other characteristics of a range of health services, with the idea of relating them to mortality, this work had not progressed far enough. I considered asking for a few years' delay and concentrating on that analysis, but I did not know what would emerge, and decided to accept. The lectures were fair, but not good enough. I decided that they should not be published. I also felt that I had let Ed Kass down badly. However, I did spend one of the happiest fortnights of my life in Cambridge, Massachusetts, with so many interesting people, in perfect surroundings. In retrospect I realise I should have delayed. The lectures would have been much better.

"RETIREMENT"

In 1974 I retired to a desk in the attic at 4 Richmond Road and Peter Elwood became director of the unit. It was largely as a result of his kindness that I stayed on. He was very encouraging, hoping that I would continue with two main lines of research: the 20 year follow-up studies of the various populations on which we had done cross-sectional surveys in the 1950s, and the investigation of factors associated with mortality in 18 developed countries, which I have already mentioned. For my part, I arranged for Peter to receive enough money from the Abbotshill Trust, with which I had a close association, to employ an additional statistician for three years. I had not succeeded in persuading the MRC that an epidemiological unit needed as many statisticians as epidemiologists, with programmers to support them.

Domestically, arrangements at this time were slightly less sure. Mrs Barlow, my housekeeper, had become severely disabled by rheumatoid arthritis and reached a stage when she could no longer cook. She had looked after me so well for so many years that I had accepted the situation for more than a year before I realised that a better solution was required by both of us. Fortunately, with a little financial help, the Barlows were eventually settled in a small but comfortable bungalow in Rhoose, close enough for Mr Barlow to continue giving me a little help in the garden. He also managed other jobs, and he and his wife made the best of this major change in their lives. The major change in my life came when I managed to persuade my nephew, Joe Stalker, a freelance engineer, and his wife Maggie to come with their four children to live at Rhoose. In my last presidential address at the Faculty of Community Medicine I quoted Jane Austen, when addressing this aspect of my future: ". . . he [Mr Dashwood] invited and received into his house the family of his nephew, Mr Henry Dashwood . . . In the society of his nephew and niece, and their children, and the old gentleman's days were comfortably spent. His attachment to them all increased. The constant attention of Mr and Mrs Henry Dashwood to his wishes, which proceeded not merely from interest, but from

253

goodness of heart, gave him every degree of solid comfort which his age could receive; and the cheerfulness of the children added a relish to his existence."

Possibly because I enjoyed these early years of semiretirement so much I failed to recognise the dangers in the arrangements I had made, both at home and for my future research. My happiness prevented me from recognising that they might not be permanent. Then came a dreadful day in 1977. It followed a routine MRC review of the unit that had not gone particularly well. There was already something of a cloud over the place. Knowing a little about the review body, it was not difficult to suspect a degree of unhelpful personal bias in some of its reporting. Eventually Peter Elwood gained the necessary permission to show me the report, and to my horror it recommended that I should cease to work there. The committee felt that my presence was having a deleterious effect on the unit. For a while my world, the only world I knew, was shaken. Number 4 Richmond Road and Rhoose Farm House were the cornerstones of my life. All the paperwork and cards relating to the long-term follow-up studies were at the unit, and so was Fred Moore, without whose assistance my future research would have been crippled. I returned home that evening deeply depressed.

By an awful coincidence it was that evening that my nephew and niece told me that they wanted to return to their home in Dorset. What I had not realised was that while we all got on remarkably well together there was still an important part of the Stalker family that wanted to be back in the Dorsetshire they loved. Joe and Maggie had never been totally happy about the transfer of their children to schools in Rhoose, which they felt lacked some of the qualities they valued in schooling back home. There was no animosity in their decision, just a wish to get back to where the family had already put down roots. Nevertheless, this double blow to my work and my home made me even more profoundly depressed. The next few days were dreadful. I had, as far as I remember, a lot of silly ideas. I also drank too much. I considered selling Rhoose Farm House and buying a flat in Cardiff or Galashiels. I got an offer of a desk in another research unit, but the problem of moving all the material basis of my research and the inevitable loss of Fred's help would kill the research dead. I fortunately decided to do nothing for a few months but wait and see what would happen if I continued working there. Slowly the clouds lifted. The MRC finally ruled that I could continue working at 4 Richmond Road. I am very grateful to some unknown friends who gave me support at such a critical time. I am particularly grateful to all members of the unit who signed a letter supporting the view that I should be allowed to stay on.

The domestic situation also healed itself fairly rapidly. Following an interim contingency, when a young doctor, Ian Baker, and his family came to share the accommodation and the running of the house, I found a local family prepared to move in and give me help. It was an excellent arrangement that lasted for several years and Robert, Pat, and their daughter Kate derived as much pleasure from being at Rhoose Farm House as I did from having their company and Pat's cooking. I also developed, from conversations with Robert, the idea of dividing the house into two, so that when he and his family eventually had the home he intended to build I would have the right kind of accommodation to let to other families I might like to have at Rhoose.

Research, once the crisis was resolved, continued satisfactorily in the Richmond Road attic. There I shared a large room with a transient number of young non-medical scientists, whom I tried to stimulate by introducing them to Karl Popper and *Effectiveness and Efficiency*. The most memorable were Hugh, Tony and Janet, and later David and "Andrew the mole." The following peaceful years have been reasonably successful. My analysis of the factors associated with mortality in 18 developed countries produced two interesting papers. The first, with the help of Selwyn St Leger, a medical statistician, showed that GNP per head of population was the most important factor associated with mortality levels – that is, an increase in GNP per head decreased mortality.[16] The most surprising finding was that increases in the numbers of doctors per 1000 of the population did not correlate with decreased mortality in younger age groups. Our findings indicated that an increase in the prevalence of doctors was not associated with improved life expectancy for the young. This "doctor anomaly" has still not been satisfactorily explained. The other published paper on this data set related death rates from ischaemic heart disease inversely to alcohol consumption, and in more detail to wine consumption.[17] Such correlations alone do not of course mean very much, but they are a stimulus to further inquiry, and there is already a fair amount of other evidence in support of our findings.

In the later 1970s Fred and I, with the assistance of a number of colleagues and friends in and outside the unit, also managed to complete 20-year follow-up studies of the miners in Leigh, Lancashire, and the coal miners and foundry workers in Staveley, Derbyshire, we had first studied in the 1950s.[18] The results significantly extended our view of the dangers of long-term exposure to dust in the workplace. Also, before the decade was out we produced a fuller analysis of the data resulting from our 20-year follow-up survey in the Rhondda Fach.[19] To do this we needed a fair amount of outside assistance, given the limited availability of statistical help at the unit, and friends such as Richard Peto, Tim Cole, and Mike Campbell have all responded gallantly to our calls for help over the years.

The later 1970s turned out to be a very pleasant period of my life. I enjoyed the company of the young men and women in the attic. I also continued to travel and lecture a good deal, both at home and overseas. Internationally I was chiefly interested in discovering why some countries did randomised controlled trials and others did not. In *Effectiveness and Efficiency* I pointed out that it was the Protestant North West that predominantly did the trials, while the Catholic and Communist South and East did not do them. I thought at that time that some element common both to communism and and catholicism might be the explanation. My travels convinced me that catholicism and communism have very little to do with it. I am now convinced that the answer has much more to do with medical education. Medical education in the Protestant North West has for some time been more scientific than elsewhere. There are, however, still problems. There is resistance to the idea of randomised controlled trials in West Germany. An attempt was made to have them declared illegal. After lecturing in Germany on the value of randomised controlled trials in cardiovascular medicine, and after a rather violent discussion, I was taken aside by the chairman, who said, "Dr Cochrane, you don't seem to understand. Controlled trials are done by the pharmaceutical industry. Gentlemen don't do them." It is difficult to interpret this particular remark, but I suspect that the feeling of shame about the Nazi medical pseudo-experimentation may be a factor. The other exception, undermining my hypothesis about the influence of medical education, is Sweden, where medical education is very scientific, but they do few trials.

Of all the lectures I gave in this period I feel that the best was that given on health economics at the request of my friend and distant relative Professor George Teeling Smith. It was published as a chapter in a book which, disappointingly, few doctors bought.[20]

In this period of semiretirement my garden, which I have neglected mentioning for too long, underwent two phases, one of relative neglect and one of recovery. Certainly the rate of improvement fell when the Stalker family arrived and Barlow left. Due attention had to be paid to the needs of the children, and Joe and I merely managed to keep up the standard and introduce some labour-saving devices. Joe's skills as an engineer and capacity for invention were a great help in this respect. When Joe and Maggie and the family left Barlow came back to help me and steadily we returned the story to one of improvement again. The most striking advance was the introduction of a series of seventeenth century troughs with alpines. My role essentially centred on doing the planting, weeding, and pruning – and I loved it.

As the decade drew to a close I was again remarkably happy. The balance between research interests, travels, and life and gardening at Rhoose seemed about right. I had also started to look forward to a 30-year follow-up study of the Rhondda Fach population. I was not to know that a number of clouds were forming over the horizon.

NOTES

1 15 March 1972.
2 *The Sunday Times.* 19 March 1972: 17.
3 The Rock Carling Fellowship.
4 A collegiate body for community medicine was recommended in the Report of the Royal Commission on Medical Education, 1968. Informal discussions between academic and service community physicians followed, leading in 1969 to a working party led by Professor J N Morris. Largely guided by Sir Max (later Lord) Rosenheim, president of the Royal College of Physicians, the ground was prepared for the formation of a Joint Faculty of Community Medicine of the Royal Colleges of Physicians in the UK. A provisional council was formed in February 1971 under the chairmanship of Dr Wilfred Harding, president of the Society of Medical Officers of Health. Despite a vast majority of practising community physicians among potential members of the faculty, there was strong consensus at the centre that the first president should be a distinguished academic whose status would confirm the standing of the new discipline.
5 Lord Rosenheim of Camden KBE, FRS, President of the Royal College of Physicians, 1966–72.
6 Other members of the inaugural faculty board were Professor Thomas Anderson, Sir John Brotherston, Drs William Edgar, A J Essex-Cater, G D Forwell, and M A Heasman, Professor W W Holland, Drs John D Kershaw and J F Kirk, Professor C R Lowe, Drs W J McGinness, Maud P Menzies and J R Preston, Professor T A Ramsay, Lord Rosenheim, and Drs H M Stewart and H Yellowlees.
7 See Cochrane A L. Relation between radiographic categories of coalworkers' pneumoconiosis and expectation of life. *Br Med J* 1973; ii: 532–4.
8 Boston Collaborative Drug Surveillance Group. Regular aspirin intake and acute myocardial infarction. *Br Med J* 1974; i: 440–3.
9 Elwood P, Cochrane A L, Sweetnam P, *et al.* A randomised controlled trial of acetyl-salicylic acid in the secondary prevention of mortality from myocardial infarction. *Br Med J* 1974; i: 436–40.
10 Elwood P, *et al.* Mortality and anaemia in women. *Lancet* 1974; i: 891.
11 Bainton D, *et al.* Gallbladder disease: prevalence in a South Wales industrial town. *N Engl J Med* 1976; **294**: 1147–9.
12 Elwood P, *et al.* A randomised controlled trial of vitamin C in the prevention and amelioration of the common cold. *British Journal of Preventive and Social Medicine* 1976; **30**: 193.
13 Burr M L, *et al.* Effects of anti-mite measures on children with mite-sensitive asthma: a controlled trial. *Thorax* 1980; **35**: 506–12.
14 Burr M L, *et al.* The effect of discontinuing long-term diuretic therapy in the elderly. *Age Ageing* 1977; **6**: 38.

15 Cochrane A L, *et al*. The mortality of men in the Rhondda Fach, 1950–1970. *Br J Ind Med* 1979; **36**: 15.

16 Cochrane A L, St Leger A S, Moore F. Health service "input" and mortality "output" in developed countries. *J Epidemiol Community Health* 1978; **32**: 200–5.

17 St Leger A S, Cochrane A L, Moore F. Factors associated with cardiac mortality in developed countries, with particular reference to the consumption of wine. *Lancet* 1979; 1017–20.

18 Cochrane A L, Moore F. Preliminary results of a twenty year follow-up of a random sample of an industrial town. *Br Med J* 1978; i: 411–12; also Cochrane A L, Moore F. A 20-year follow-up of men aged 55–64, including coal-miners and foundry workers in Staveley, Derbyshire. *Br J Ind Med* 1980; **37**: 226–9.

19 Cochrane A L, Haley T J L, Moore F, Hole D. The mortality of men in the Rhondda Fach, 1950–1970. *Br J Ind Med* 1979; **36**: 15–22.

20 Cochrane A L. 1931–1971: a critical review with particular reference to the medical profession. In: *Medicine for the Year 2000*. London, 1979.

7 Into the eighties

I shall keep my recollections of the 1980s short. There has been less work and more illness, and this is not a good balance to reflect upon. I entered the 1980s with high hopes of achieving far more than has been accomplished, and though there are compensations in spending more time at Rhoose Farm House this was not my intention. As at many other times in my life things did not quite turn out as I had expected.

Whatever the difficult days that were to come, Fred and I did get off with a good start to the 30-year follow-up of the men of the Rhondda Fach. We were well on the way by the time we took a break at Christmas 1981, but my schedule of home visiting came to a temporary halt when I had a coronary, just two months later. It was a curious experience. I had lectured in many countries and all over the UK on Gordon Mather's trial of home versus coronary care unit treatment after such an attack. Nearly always I was asked the same kind of question after the lecture: "But Dr Cochrane, won't you go into a coronary care unit when you have your first coronary?" My answer had never varied. I had always pointed out that I had discussed the problem with my general practitioner and he had agreed to do his best to see that I was treated at home, although there was always the recognised chance that this might prove difficult. What actually happened is possibly worth recording. I had been lecturing in Barcelona, and came back from Spain very tired. Three days later, at about 10 pm, when I was about to go to bed, I suddenly felt very ill. There was little that was specific, except vague abdominal pain. I examined my abdomen and found nothing interesting. Then I started retching and wanting to vomit. I diagnosed "abdominal migraine" and went to bed. I did not feel too well over the next two days, and eventually asked my general practitioner to visit me, when he found a fall in blood pressure and suggested an ECG. This was done at a clinic in Barry, where I read the electrocardiogram myself as showing reversed T waves in one lead and realised I had had a coronary. Fortunately this late diagnosis meant that hospitalisation was not considered, and the position I had taken in lectures was never at risk.

It is unpleasant to have reversed T waves in one's ECG, for there are obvious prognostic implications. However, I was never short of breath and experienced no angina. In fact I soon felt very much my old self. Nevertheless, I still had to accept a more limited role in the 30-year follow-up programme, and it was mainly due to Fred Moore and Marian Jones that we were finally so successful in tracing those we needed to locate.

The next disaster followed in December 1983, when I was operated on for cancer of the colon. Fortunately the problem had been diagnosed reasonably early and the prognosis was fairly good. I was surprised how quickly I recovered. Within just a month or two I was back tidying up the data collected in the course of the Rhondda Fach 30-year follow up. We had finally traced the fate of 99.9 per cent of the 8000 or so men in whom we were interested, to the extent of knowing whether they were alive or dead, and if dead of what they had died. I finally arranged for the analysis to be done by Mike Campbell in Southampton, who had already proved a great help on other occasions.

The next medical setback came in December 1984, when a non-cancerous bowel blockage that had formed at the site of the previous operation required attention. I was told that the surgery went well, but the postoperative period is said to have proved rather stormy. I cannot express an opinion. I have complete retrograde amnesia for the whole of the time between the operation and returning home from hospital. I came "back to life" on the divan in my sitting room with my niece Maggie in marvellous attendance. She helped me through some difficult weeks, and slowly I began to feel better.

It was while convalescing that I became obsessed with the

idea of holidaying in the sun and was eventually allowed to go off to Kenya, accompanied by my great nephew Simon. Despite all the tribulations of a rather tiresome journey I recovered quickly in the warmth and comfort of the setting I had chosen in Mombasa. I did little but sleep, eat, and swim in warm coastal waters and within days I was feeling very fit indeed. I was, in general, favourably impressed by Kenya. The racial harmony is remarkable, and I gained the impression that there was much less corruption than in some African states I knew about.

I returned to the colder climate of Wales and went to work, helping to draft the papers arising from the analysis of our 30-year follow-up survey, but my new impetus did not last long. A few weeks after starting I was seized by a fearful attack of abdominal pain after a pleasant weekend in the Rhoose Farm House garden. I did not have the option of moving even as far as the telephone, and without assistance I slowly lost consciousness. Fortunately rescue came in the form of a visiting neighbour. It is difficult to account for what actually happened. In hospital the pain slowly diminished, together with plans for investigative surgery, and I returned home with a new priority, the acquisition of an emergency answercall system.

To bring the whole family together we decided to meet in the Lake District at Easter 1985, where I swam and walked "uphill and down dale," and particularly enjoyed a visit to Levens Hall and its famed topiary gardens. It was only a short step from all the joy of this Lakeland break to accept my sister's invitation to return home with her for a further holiday in Scotland. But this was not to prove my happiest visit to Galashiels. I had only been there for two days when I suddenly experienced the considerable loss of breathing power that results from a spontaneous pneumothorax. This diagnosed, I felt much happier. I had treated several such cases when I was a prisoner of war, and the lungs had always "come out" easily. In my case, however, developments were not so helpful. In spite of gallant efforts on the part of the staff of the small general hospital to which I was admitted, the lung was not extended and I was transferred to Edinburgh's

City Hospital, where a major chest operation was required to put things right.

This parade of debilitating events was to continue, curtailing so many plans and limiting everyday aspirations. I even arrived at the point where one starts asking, "What have I done to deserve this?" I can even remember reflecting on those two verses by Robert Louis Stevenson:

It's a different thing that I demand,
Tho' humble as can be.
A statement fair in my maker's hand
To a gentleman like me.

A clear account writ fair and broad
An' a plain apologie,
Or the deevil a ceevil word to God
For a gentleman like me.

Although the uncertainties of my bill of health were not to diminish, there were more positive sides to my experience of illness and health services. Certainly there have been valuable opportunities to test my earlier scepticism regarding the effectiveness and efficiency of the NHS. The consumer's view proved far more favourable than I could have ever imagined, and I am grateful for all the therapy and caring that has kept alive a man in his advancing seventies, despite such a range of problems. Everywhere there was kindness and friendliness on the part of staff, even where the pressures of work might reasonably have intervened. The food, also, was much better than I had expected.

Turning to technical points, I have just two observations to make. The first concerns bedpans. Twice I was offered a bedpan for an acute attack, when little assistance was required to deliver me to a lavatory. Have nurses ever used bedpans? They are a real horror and should only ever be used for bed-bound patients. The other point is more technical. It concerns nasogastric tubes. I suffered agonies after both my abdominal operations. The tube kept coming out and requiring reinsertion. Later I discovered that there had been an excellent randomised controlled trial showing that these tubes are of remarkably little value. I foresee something of an argument arising if ever I return for abdominal surgery.

The most positive outcome of all this illness, oddly enough, has been a marked improvement in my garden, partly due to the increased time I have been able to give it during periods of convalescence and partly the result of a redirection of my energies. As I became progressively less caught up with epidemiological research, devotion to the Rhoose Farm House garden became the compensatory commitment I needed. Certainly the garden has been the great consolation prize of the 1980s. As I pen this chapter it is looking particularly fine. I have introduced several new features in recent years, including a pheasantry and a delightful collection of Phormiums, now rivalling the national collection at the Somerset College of Agriculture and Horticulture at Cannington. I often regret that so few people share in the delights of this rather special couple of acres, and I have now arranged annual open days through the National Garden Scheme in the hope of partly redressing this concern. Now there are a good many visitors each year, and recently additional attention has been focused on the plant collections at Rhoose through a descriptive entry in a guide to 200 British gardens published in 1985.[1]

I have often wondered about the source of my deep interest in gardening as I am neither a botanist nor a horticulturist and have had little real contact with plant life until relatively recently. Both my grandparents had impressive gardens, but the main factor, I suspect, is a curious visual sensitivity, inherited from my mother, which makes me unhappy until my immediate environment is visually satisfactory. I felt almost instinctively the kind of vegetation I needed in the garden and how it should be distributed. Unfortunately I did not know enough about plants to know which to plant. It is lucky that I have had Dennis Woodland's help in overcoming this difficulty.

The problem of making the most of the opportunities provided by the 30-year follow-up survey in the Rhondda Fach was not to be so easily solved, and I am disappointed by the overall outcome. It is true that two papers have already been published covering the more obvious findings, but I still feel that a good deal more could have been achieved if I had been at full stretch and able to play a real part. Above all I had hoped to add something, at last, to our meagre knowledge of the aetiology of PMF, but my attempt has merely fizzled out. My aspirations were for so much more when first I set my sights on the Rhondda Fach in 1949. Now I have the disappointment of finding that my last papers will do nothing to advance my contribution to the PMF story. In fact they may well turn out to be amongst my poorest.

With my dreadful medical record of recent years I cannot look forward to a very long retirement, but this worries me little. Given my expectations of death in the 1930s and 1940s, I have had a rich bonus. With relations, friends, gardening, books and whisky, whatever the fates decree will not be too bad. I have a vague fear of being disabled and having to watch my garden return to the jungle, but my most serious fear is nicely expressed in an anonymous sad geriatric ditty quoted by Alex Bean to an Anglo-American conference in 1984 (which I have slightly modified):

> I can cope with my bifocals.
> My dentures fit me fine.
> I can live with my porphyria,
> But, my God, I miss my mind.

NOTE

1 Plumtre G. *Collins book of British gardens*. London, 1985: 215.

Archie died on 18 June 1988. I had visited him that May at the home of Joe and Maggie Stalker and enjoyed a lively exchange of news, but the clouds were moving in. A remarkable story had run its course.

MB

Appendix A
A L COCHRANE (1909–88)
A biographical outline

1909   Born on 12 January at Galashiels, Scotland, first son of Walter Francis and Emma Mabel (née Purdom) Cochrane.

1916–22 At preparatory school at Rhos-on-Sea. Scholarship to Uppingham, 1922. (Father killed at Battle of Gaza, 19 April 1917.)

1922–27 Scholar, Uppingham School, Rutland. School Prefect and member of rugby football 1st XV. Scholarship to King's College, Cambridge, 1927.

1927–30 Scholar, King's College Cambridge. 1st class honours in Parts I and II of the Natural Sciences Tripos. Also completed 2nd MB studies.

1931   Research student, Strangeways Laboratory, Cambridge. Tissue culture studies under supervision of Dr N Willmer.

1931–34 Psychoanalysis with Theodor Reik in Berlin, Vienna, and the Hague. Some medical studies in Vienna and Leiden. (Published a first paper, "Elie Metschnikoff and his theory of an 'instinct de la mort'.")

1934–36 Medical student, University College Hospital, London. Formally commenced clinical studies.

1936–37 Service in Spain with the Spanish Medical Aid Committee's Field Ambulance Unit. Served with the Spanish Medical Aid Field Ambulance Unit on the Aragon front and at the siege of Madrid, serving at the battles of Jarama and Brunete. Returned to England in August 1937 to resume medical studies.

1937–38 Medical student, University College Hospital. Qualified MB, BCh(Cantab), 1938.

1938–39 House physician, West London Hospital, with Dr Konstam.

1939	Research assistant, Medical Unit, University College Hospital.
1939–46	Captain, Royal Army Medical Corps. Served in Egypt as hospital medical officer, then posted to serve as medical officer to D Battalion, Layforce. Taken prisoner of war on 1 June 1941. Prisoner of war camp medical officer at Salonica, Hildburghausen, Elsterhorst, and Wittenberg-am-Elbe. (MBE (military), 1946, for services as prisoner of war camp medical officer.)
1946–47	Student, Diploma in Public Health Course, London School of Hygiene and Tropical Medicine. DPH, 1947.
1947–48	Rockefeller fellowship, with clinical attachment to the Henry Phipps Institute, Philadelphia, USA. Developed research interests in the x ray study of pulmonary tuberculosis and observer error in the interpretation of x ray films.
1948–60	Member of scientific staff, Medical Research Council Pneumoconiosis Research Unit, Cardiff, South Wales. Main interests: the x ray classification of coal workers' pneumoconiosis; the relationship between dust exposure, x ray category of pneumoconiosis, and disability; the aetiology of progressive massive fibrosis. Responsible for the Rhondda Fach ("two valleys") scheme launched in 1950 to investigate the aetiology of progressive massive fibrosis.
1960–69	David Davies professor, Welsh National School of Medicine, Cardiff, and honorary director, Medical Research Council Epidemiology Unit, Cardiff. Main research interests: the application and promotion of randomised controlled trials, the validation of screening strategies, and health services research. (MRCP, 1961; FRCP, 1965; CBE, 1968.)
1969–74	Director, Medical Research Council Epidemiology Unit, Cardiff. Main research interest: randomised controlled trials and health services research (*Effectiveness and Efficiency*, published 1972). (First president of the Faculty of Community Medicine, UK, 1972. Honorary Doctor of the University of York, 1973. Dunham Lecturer, Harvard, USA, 1974.)
1974–86	Continuing attachment to Medical Research Council Epidemiology Unit, Cardiff. Main research interests: 20- and 30-year follow-up studies of the population of the Rhondda Fach. (Honorary fellow, American Epidemiological Association, 1975. Honorary DSc, Rochester, USA, 1977. Honorary fellow, International Epidemiological Association, 1977.)

Appendix B
A L COCHRANE'S PRINCIPAL PUBLICATIONS

Cochrane A L. Elie Metschnikoff and his theory of an "instinct de la mort." *Int J Psychoanalysis* 1934; **15**: 1–14.

Cochrane A L, Campbell H W, Steen S C. The value of roentgenology in the prognosis of minimal tuberculosis. *American Journal of Roentgenology and Radium Therapy* 1949; **61**: 153–7.

Fletcher C M, Mann K J, Davies I, Cochrane A L, Gilson J C, Hugh-Jones P. The classification of radiographic appearances in coalminers' pneumoconiosis. *Journal of the Faculty of Radiology* 1949; **1**: 40–8.

Cochrane A L. Methods of investigating the connection between dust and disease. In: *The application of scientific methods to industrial and service medicine.* London: Medical Research Council, 1950: 97–100.

King E J, Wynn A H A, Nagelschmidt G, Cochrane A L. *Pneumoconiosis in Germany.* London: Ministry of Fuel and Power, Safety in Mines Research and Testing Branch, 1950. Research report no 10.

Cochrane A L, Chapman P J, Oldham P D. Observers' errors in taking medical histories. *Lancet* 1951; **i**: 1007–12.

Cochrane A L, Davies I, Fletcher C M. "Entente radiologique" – a step towards international agreement on the classification of radiographs in pneumoconiosis. *Br J Ind Med* 1951; **8**: 244–55.

Cochrane A L, Fletcher C M, Gilson J C, Hugh-Jones P. The role of periodic examination in the prevention of coalworkers' pneumoconiosis. *Br J Ind Med* 1951; **8**: 53–61.

Cochrane A L, Garland L H. Observer error in the interpretation of chest films: an international investigation. *Lancet* 1952; **ii**: 505–9.

Cochrane A L, Cox J G, Jarman T F. Pulmonary tuberculosis in the Rhondda Fach. *Br Med J* 1952; 843–53.

Garland L H, Cochrane A L. Results of an international test in chest roentgenogram interpretation. *JAMA* 1952; **149**: 631–4.

Miall, W E, Caplan A, Cochrane A L, Kilpatrick G S, Oldham P D. An epidemiological study of rheumatoid arthritis associated with characteristic chest x ray appearances in coal-workers. *Br Med J* 1953; **ii**: 1231–5.

Cochrane A L. The detection of pulmonary tuberculosis in a community. *Br Med Bull* 1954; **20**: 91–5.

Cochrane A L. Tuberculosis and coalworkers' pneumoconiosis. *British Journal of Tuberculosis* 1954; **48**: 274–85.

Miall W E, Oldham P D, Cochrane A L. The treatment of complicated pneumoconiosis with isoniazid. *Br J Ind Med* 1954; **11**: 186–91.

Cochrane A L, Cox J G, Jarman T F. A follow-up chest *x* ray survey in the Rhondda Fach. Part I. Pulmonary tuberculosis. *Br Med J* 1955; i: 371–8.

Carpenter R G, Cochrane A L, Clarke W G, Jonathan G, Moore F. Death rates of miners and ex-miners with and without coalworkers' pneumoconiosis in South Wales. *Br J Ind Med* 1956; **13**: 102–9.

Cochrane A L, Miall W E. The epidemiology of chronic disease in South Wales. *Proc R Soc Med* 1956; **49**: 261–2.

Cochrane A L, Miall W E, Clarke W G. Results of a chest *x* ray survey in the Vale of Glamorgan: a study of an agricultural community. *Tubercle* 1956; **37**: 417–25.

Cochrane A L, Miall W E, Clarke W G, Jarman T F, Jonathan G, Moore F. Factors influencing the radiological attack rate of progressive massive fibrosis. *Br Med J* 1956; i: 1193–9.

Higgins I T T, Oldham P D, Cochrane A L, Gilson J C. Respiratory symptoms and pulmonary disability in an industrial town: a survey of a random sample of the population. *Br Med J* 1956; ii: 904–9.

Miall W E, Cochrane A L. The community survey in epidemiological research. *Medical World (London)* 1956; **85**: 521–3.

Cochrane A L. *Marc Daniels memorial lecture*. London: Royal College of Physicians, 1958.

Cochrane A L, Higgins I T T, Gilson J C. Yet another industrial pneumoconiosis? *Tubercle* 1958; **39**: 399–400.

Thomas A J, Cochrane A L, Higgins I T T. The measurement of the prevalence of ischaemic heart disease. *Lancet* 1958; ii: 540–4.

Cochrane A L. The international classification of radiographs of the pneumoconioses. *Tubercle* 1959; **40**: 292–6.

Cochrane A L, Carpenter R G, Moore F. Investigation into the working of the Death Benefit for coalworkers' pneumoconiosis. *British Journal of Preventive and Social Medicine* 1959; **13**: 128–30.

Higgins I T T, Cochrane A L, Gilson J C, Wood C H. Population studies of chronic respiratory disease. A comparison of miners, foundry-workers, and others in Staveley, Derbyshire. *Br J Ind Med* 1959; **16**: 255–68.

Cochrane A L. Epidemiology of coalworkers' pneumoconiosis. In: King E J, Fletcher C M, eds. *Symposium on industrial pulmonary disease*. London: Churchill, 1960: 221–31.

Cochrane A L. Compulsory chest radiography. *Tubercle* 1960; **41**: 75–8.

Cochrane A L, Higgins I T T, Thomas J. Pulmonary ventilatory function of coal miners in various areas in relation to the *x* ray category of pneumoconiosis. *British Journal of Preventive and Social Medicine* 1961; 51: 1–11.

Cochrane A L, Moore F, Thomas J. The prognostic value of radiological classification of progressive massive fibrosis. *Tubercle* 1961; 42: 64–71.

Cochrane A L, Moore F, Thomas J. The radiographic progression of progressive massive fibrosis. *Tubercle* 1961; 42: 72–6.

Higgins I T T, Cochrane A L. Chronic respiratory disease in a random sample of men and women in the Rhondda Fach in 1958. *Br J Ind Med* 1961; 18: 93–102.

Miall W E, Cochrane A L. The distribution of arterial pressure in Wales and Jamaica. *Pathologie et Microbiologie* 1961; 24: 690–7.

Cochrane A L. The attack rate of progressive massive fibrosis. *Br J Ind Med* 1962; 19: 52–64.

Trotter W R, Cochrane A L, Benjamin I T, Miall W E, Exley D. A goitre survey in the Vale of Glamorgan. *British Journal of Preventive and Social Medicine* 1962; 16: 16–21.

Hart J T, Cochrane A L, Higgins I T T. Tuberculin sensitivity in coal workers' pneumoconiosis. *British Journal of Preventive and Social Medicine* 1963; 17: 153–65.

Higgins I T T, Cochrane A L, Thomas A J. Epidemiological studies of coronary heart disease. *British Journal of Preventive and Social Medicine* 1963; 17: 153–65.

Cochrane A L. Industrial pulmonary disease. I. The international classification of the pneumoconioses. *Br J Radiol* 1964; 37: 334–6.

Cochrane A L, Carpenter R G, Moore F, Thomas J. The mortality of miners in the Rhondda Fach. *Br J Ind Med* 1964; 21: 38–45.

Elwood P C, Cochrane A L, Benjamin I T, Seys-Prosser D. A follow up study of workers from an asbestos factory. *Br J Ind Med* 1964; 21: 304–7.

Cochrane A L. Science and syndromes. *Postgrad Med J* 1965; 41: 440–2.

Cochrane A L. Survey methods in general populations. I. Studies of a total community: Rhondda Fach, South Wales. *Milbank Memorial Fund Quarterly* 1965; iii: 43.

Cochrane A L, Thomas J, Clarke W G, Moore F. Changes in the prevalence of coalworkers' pneumoconiosis among miners and ex-miners in the Rhondda Fach, 1951–1961. *Br J Ind Med* 1965; 22: 49–57.

Cochrane A L. A medical scientist's view of screening. *Public Health* 1967; 81: 207–13.

Rees H A, Goldberg A, Cochrane A L, Williams M J, Donald K W. Renal haemodialysis in porphyria. *Lancet* 1967; i: 919–21.

Cochrane A L, Elwood P C. Iron-deficiency anaemia. In: Nuffield Provincial Hospital Trust. *Screening in medical care. Reviewing the evidence.* Oxford: Oxford University Press, 1968.

Cochrane A L, Elwood P C. Medical scientists look at screening. In:

Presymptomatic detection and early diagnosis – a critical appraisal. Oxford: Pitman, 1968.

Cochrane A L, Fletcher C M. *The early diagnosis of some diseases of the lung.* London: Office of Health Economics, 1968. (Early diagnosis paper no 6.)

Cochrane A L, Goldberg A. A study of faecal porphyrin levels in a large family. *Ann Hum Genet* 1968; 32: 195–208.

Cochrane A L, Graham P A, Wallace J. Glaucoma. In: Nuffield Provincial Hospitals Trust. *Screening in medical care. Reviewing the evidence.* Oxford: Oxford University Press, 1968.

Cochrane A L, Springett V. Pulmonary tuberculosis. In: Nuffield Provincial Hospitals Trust. *Screening in medical care. Reviewing the evidence.* Oxford: Oxford University Press, 1968.

Waters W E, Cochrane A L. An epidemiological approach to migraine. In: B M Stepanovic (ed). *Proceedings of the ?th International Scientific Meeting of the International Epidemiological Association, Primosten, Yugoslavia, 25–31 August 1968.* Belgrade: The Publishing House, 1969: 529–38.

Cochrane A L. Screening for chest diseases. Part 2. Preventive approaches to chronic diseases. *Milbank Memorial Fund Quarterly* 1969; 47: 250–5.

Cochrane A L, Elwood P C. Screening – the case against it. *Medical Officer* 1969; 71: 53–7.

Branch R A, Clark G W, Cochrane A L, Jones J H, Scarborough H. Incidence of uraemia and requirements for maintenance haemodialysis. *Br Med J* 1971; i: 249–54.

Cochrane A L, Holland W W. Validation of screening procedures. *Br Med Bull* 1971; 27: 3–8.

Cochrane A L, Moore F. Expected and observed values for the prescription of vitamin B_{12} in England and Wales. *British Journal of Preventive and Social Medicine* 1971; 25: 147–51.

Wallace J, Sweetnam P M, Warner C G, Graham P A, Cochrane A L. An epidemiological study of lens opacities among steel workers. *Br J Ind Med* 1971; 28: 265–71.

Cochrane A L. The history of the measurement of ill health. *Int J Epidemiol* 1972; 1: 89–92.

Cochrane A L. *Effectiveness and efficiency.* Nuffield Provincial Hospitals Trust, 1972.

Higgins I T T, Lockshin M D, Gilson J C, Cochrane A L, Campbell H, Waters W E, Ferris B G, Higgins M W. Coronary disease in Staveley, Derbyshire, with an international comparison with three towns in Marion County, West Virginia. *J Chronic Dis* 1972; 25: 567–80.

Bainton D, Cochrane A L, Greene J, Kilpatrick G S, Weddell J M, *et al.* Control of moderately raised blood pressure: report of a co-operative randomised controlled trial. *Br Med J* 1973; iii: 434–6.

Cochrane A L. Relation between radiographic categories of coal-workers' pneumoconiosis and expectation of life. *Br Med J* 1973; ii: 532–4.

Cochrane A L. Screening for the elderly. In: *Needs of the elderly for health and welfare services*. Exeter: University of Exeter, 1972.

Elwood P C, Cochrane A L, Burr M L, Sweetnam P M, *et al.* A randomised controlled trial of acetyl salicylic acid in the secondary prevention of mortality from myocardial infarction. *Br Med J* 1974; i: 436–40.

Waters W E, Cochrane A L, Moore F. Mortality in punctiform type of coalworkers' pneumoconiosis. *Br J Ind Med* 1974; 31: 196–200.

Cochrane A L. World health problems. *Can J Public Health* 1975; 280–7.

Cochrane A L. An epidemiologist's view of the simple relationship between pneumoconiosis and morbidity and mortality. *Proc R Soc Med* 1976; 69: 12–14.

Cochrane A L. The development of epidemiology in MRC Units in Wales, 1945–1975, a personal view. *J R Coll Physicians Lond* 1976; 10: 316–20.

Cochrane A L. Screening: the rules of the game. *T Soc Geneesk* 1978; 56: 6–8.

Cochrane A L, Moore F. Preliminary results of a twenty year follow-up of a random sample of an industrial town. *Br Med J* 1978; i: 411–12.

Cochrane A L, St Leger A S, Moore F. Health services "input" and mortality "output" in developed countries. *J Epidemiol Community Health* 1978; 32: 200–5.

Cochrane A L. 1931–1971: a critical review with particular reference to the medical profession. In: *Medicine for the year 2000*. London: Office of Health Economics, 1979: 2–12.

Cochrane A L. In: *Report to the Secretary of State for Social Services of a working group on back pain*. London: HMSO, 1979.

Cochrane A L. Forty years back: a retrospective study. *Br Med J* 1979; ii: 1662–3.

Cochrane A L, Haley T J L, Moore F, Hole D. The mortality of men in the Rhondda Fach, 1950–1970. *Br J Ind Med* 1979; 36: 15–22.

St Leger A S, Cochrane A L, Moore F. Factors associated with cardiac mortality in developed countries with particular reference to the consumption of wine. *Lancet* 1979; i: 1017–20.

St Leger A S, Cochrane A L, Moore F. Industrielander im Vergleich; Weinverbrauch und ischaemisch Herzerkrankungen. *Umwelmedizin* 1979; 2: 29–30.

Cochrane A L, Moore F. A 20-year follow-up of men aged 55–64, including coal-miners and foundry workers, in Staveley, Derbyshire. *Br J Ind Med* 1980; 37: 226–9.

Cochrane A L, Moore F. A 20-year follow-up of a population sample aged 25–34, including coal-miners and foundry workers, in Staveley, Derbyshire. *Br J Ind Med* 1980; 37: 230–3.

Cochrane A L, Moore F, Baker I A, Haley T J L. Mortality in two random samples of women aged 55–64, followed up for 20 years. *Br Med J* 1980; 280: 1131–3.

Cochrane A L. Acute myocardial infarction: place of treatment and length of stay. *Herz* 6 1981; 2: 112–15.

Cochrane A L, Moore F. Death certification from the epidemiological point of view. *Lancet* 1981; i: 742–3.

Cochrane A L, Moore F, Moncrieff C B. Are coalminers with low "risk factors" for ischaemic heart disease at great risk of developing progressive massive fibrosis? *Br J Ind Med* 1982; 39: 265–8.

Cochrane A L. NHS expectations. *Lancet* 1983; i: 154–5.

Peto R, Speizer F E, Cochrane A L, Moore F, Fletcher C M, *et al.* The relevance in adults of airflow obstruction, but not of mucus hypersecretion to mortality from chronic lung disease – results from 20 years of prospective observation. *Am Rev Respir Dis* 1983; 128: 491–500.

Cochrane A L, Moore F. Lung mechanics in relation to radiographic category of coalworkers' simple pneumoconiosis. *Br J Ind Med* 1984; 41: 284–8.

Atuhaire L K, Campbell M J, Cochrane A L, Jones M, Moore F. Mortality of men in the Rhondda Fach, 1950–1980. *Br J Ind Med* 1985; 42: 741–5.

Atuhaire L K, Campbell M J, Cochrane A L, Jones M, Moore F. Gastric cancer in a South Wales valley. *Br J Ind Med* 1986; 43: 350–2.

Atuhaire L K, Campbell M J, Cochrane A L, Jones M, Moore F. Specific causes of death in miners and ex-miners in the Rhondda Fach, 1950–1980. *Br J Ind Med* 1986; 43: 497–9.

Appendix C

The prehistory of the first Cochrane Centre and inauguration of the Cochrane Collaboration

Sir Iain Chalmers

In 1992 the first Cochrane Centre was opened in Oxford, UK, "to facilitate systematic, up-to-date reviews of randomized controlled trials of health-care." A year later a decision to form the Cochrane Collaboration was taken at a 1ˢᵗ Cochrane Colloquium convened by the Centre.

I became interested in evaluating the effects of health-care in 1969 and 1970, while working for the United Nations in a Palestinian refugee camp in the Gaza Strip. It gradually dawned on me there that some things I had been taught in medical school were probably lethally wrong.[2] This came as a very sobering realisation: how could it be that health professionals acting with the best of intentions could do more harm than good to those who looked to them for help?

After a couple of years in Gaza I returned to Britain, to train in obstetrics, in Cardiff, the capital city of Wales. As a junior obstetrician I was confused by the conflicting opinions of senior doctors about when and how to intervene

The text of Appendix C was previously published as: Chalmers I. The pre-history of the first Cochrane Centre. In Bosch X, ed. Archie Cochrane: Back to the Front. Barcelona, 2003: 242–253.

in pregnancy and childbirth. In 1972, however, a very readable little book[3] came to my rescue.[4] *Effectiveness and Efficiency: Random Reflections on Health Services* (Cochrane 1972) had been written by Archie Cochrane, the director of the Medical Research Council Epidemiology Unit in Cardiff.

Archie's book and his subsequent friendship made me a lifelong sceptic about therapeutic claims unsupported by reliable evidence. It helped me to understand why some forms of research – particularly randomized controlled trials (RCTs) – were likely to generate more reliable information than others. In addition, I could identify strongly with Archie's commitment to the decent principle of equitable access to (effective) health-care, and his emphasis on the need to provide humane and dignified (and thus effective) *care* when no effective *cure* was available.

After discussions with one of Archie's young colleagues – David Bainton – I decided to go with David to the London School of Hygiene and Tropical Medicine and the London School of Economics to learn more about evaluating health-care, by attending a masters degree course in social medicine. The first year of the course, which was the creation of Jerry Morris, was the most stimulating twelve months of formal education I had ever experienced, partly because we were actively encouraged to challenge authority! The second year of the course involved doing research at the Department of Medical Statistics at the Welsh National School of Medicine, in collaboration with two statisticians (Robert Newcombe and Hubert Campbell) and two obstetricians (Alec Turnbull and James Lawson), to assess the effects of obstetric care.[5-8] Although we had access to a wonderfully rich database of observational data – the Cardiff Births Survey – the main lesson I learned was that it was impossible, without randomisation, to be confident that our analyses had controlled all the relevant biases sufficiently to allow us to draw confident conclusions about the effects of care.

SYSTEMATIC SEARCHES FOR REPORTS OF CONTROLLED TRIALS

Through David Bainton I came to know Archie Cochrane as a friend and mentor, and, as a result of his influence and the influence of his book, I started in 1974 to search systematically for reports of controlled trials. Archie tried to help this endeavour by seeking funding support from the Nuffield Provincial Hospitals Trust and the Milbank Memorial Fund. I think that his lack of success may have been one of the factors that prompted his now famous call for a critical summary, updated periodically, of all relevant RCTs.[9] In spite of the lack of formal funding, however, it was possible to make some progress in developing a register of perinatal controlled trials.[10] Steve Pritchard, a librarian at the Welsh National School of Medicine, designed a MEDLINE search for RCTs, and a few generous volunteers – including a general practitioner, Ann McPherson, and my wife, Jan – began the task of handsearching journals for relevant reports. A few years later the Maternal and Child Health Division of WHO provided funds to support handsearches of scores of journals. This helped to create a register that was used by Kay Dickersin and her colleagues to reveal the limitations of MEDLINE searches.[11]

In the mid-1970s, women in the UK were beginning to criticise the maternity services,[12] and researchers who agreed with many of their criticisms were preparing a book entitled *Benefits and Hazards of the New Obstetrics*.[13] One of the editors, Martin Richards (a professor of psychology in Cambridge), invited me to prepare a chapter on causal inference in obstetric practice. This showed the wide variation in obstetric intervention rates within and across countries, indicating that uncertainties must exist about the circumstances in which interventions did more good than harm.[14] In 1976, while working on this chapter, I outlined in a letter to Martin a plan for addressing these uncertainties in a systematic review of controlled trials in pregnancy, childbirth and early infancy. The plan suggested that it would be worth exploring whether the results of similar trials could be combined to yield statistically more robust estimates of treatment effects.

In 1978, an institutional base to develop these ideas became available when I was asked by the Department of Health to establish a national perinatal epidemiology unit in Oxford. The same year an opportunity arose to test my tentative plans when I was invited to review evidence of the effects of alternative ways of monitoring fetal wellbeing during labour for the European Congress of Perinatal Medicine in Vienna. After I had identified the four relevant RCTs (one of which had not been published), I contacted the investigators for clarifications and additional information, and assembled the data. Klim McPherson, a medical statistician in Oxford, helped me with the analysis. This suggested that the distribution of 13 cases of neonatal convulsions among just over 2 000 babies was unlikely to reflect chance: compared with intermittent auscultation, continuous fetal heart rate monitoring with an option to assess fetal acid-base status seemed to reduce the rate of convulsions.[15] This observation informed the design of a randomized trial involving over 13 000 mothers and their babies, which confirmed the effect suggested by the meta-analysis.[16]

ASSEMBLING A PREGNANCY AND CHILDBIRTH SYSTEMATIC REVIEW TEAM

From that year on, a team began to emerge, coordinated from the National Perinatal Epidemiology Unit, for taking forward the plans for a systematic review of the effects of care in pregnancy and childbirth. The first key members to join with me in the team were Murray and Eleanor Enkin – an obstetrician and a library assistant, respectively – from McMaster University in Canada. They coded over 3 500 reports of RCTs, subsequently made publicly available in an indexed bibliography.[17]

As this raw material for systematic reviews emerged, Murray Enkin and I drew on it to edit a book on the effects of antenatal care.[18] Because the book was well received, we were encouraged to embark on a far more ambitious project, and recruited another key member of the team, Marc Keirse, a Belgian obstetrician working at Leiden in the Netherlands. With administrative support from Jini Hetherington and Sally Hunt, and computing support from Malcolm Newdick and Mark Starr, Murray, Marc and I set about extending the team to involve about a hundred contributors, to prepare systematic reviews on most aspects of care during pregnancy and childbirth.

In the 1980s there was a rapid growth in the application of scientific principles to the process of synthesizing the results of clinical research. These syntheses were mainly in the fields of cancer and cardiovascular disease, along with our work in the perinatal field. One of the perinatal reviews[19] was an early version of the meta-analysis that subsequently formed the basis of the logo of The Cochrane Collaboration (http://www.cochrane.de/cochrane/cc-broch.htm#LOGO).   This activity began to throw up methodological challenges that had not been dealt with by traditional approaches to reviewing research evidence. Publication bias was one of these challenges, and Jini Hetherington and I became involved in investigations of this phenomenon in collaboration with Kay Dickersin and Curt Meinert at the Johns Hopkins School of Public Health, and Tom Chalmers at the Mount Sinai Medical Center in New York.[20, 21]

By 1987, the compendium of systematic reviews of the effects of care in pregnancy and childbirth was beginning to take shape, and Murray, Marc and I spent May of that year working on the manuscripts at the Rockefeller Foundation's Study Centre in Bellagio, on Lake Como in Italy. While there, we met Kenneth Warren, the director of the Foundation's medical programme. When he learned that we wanted to ensure that the results of our research were disseminated to women using the maternity services, Ken provided a grant to support the preparation of a paperback summary of our findings. Later that year, our work was greatly helped by Andy Oxman, a masters student (already qualified as a physician), who had designed at McMaster University what was probably the first course on research synthesis for health professionals.[22]

PUBLISHING SYSTEMATIC REVIEWS ON PAPER AND ELECTRONICALLY

The pregnancy and childbirth books – a 1500-page, 2-volume monster entitled *Effective Care in Pregnancy and Childbirth (ECPC)*[23] and a 370-page paperback summary called *A Guide to Effective Care in Pregnancy and Childbirth (GECPC)*[24] – were published in 1989, the year after Archie Cochrane's death.[25] When it became clear that the project would be completed, we asked Archie to contribute a Foreword for *ECPC*. We were pleased that he withdrew "the slur of the wooden spoon" which he had previously awarded to obstetrics for being the medical specialty that had the worst record of rigorous evaluation of its work.[9] But we were even prouder when he declared the systematic review of the randomized trials of obstetric practice presented in the book to be "a new achievement" and "a real milestone in the history of randomized trials and in the evaluation of care", which he hoped would be "widely copied by other specialties".[26] In fact, replication was already underway: Jack Sinclair and Mike Bracken, while on sabbatical leave at the National Perinatal Epidemiology Unit in Oxford, had developed their plans for *Effective Care of the Newborn Infant (ECNI)*,[27] which were able to draw on the register of perinatal trials we had assembled for their raw material.

Like many books, ours were out of date in some important respects by the time they were published. Although updating the paperback book was a practical proposition (it is now in its 3rd edition, and has been translated into many languages), nobody had the energy or time for the task of updating the 1500 pages of the main work. Some years previously, however, in a letter to *The Lancet* in 1986, I had signalled an alternative response to Archie's challenge to publish periodic updates of systematic reviews of RCTs.[28] This had been conceptualised on a Sunday afternoon walk in Oxford with Muir Gray, a public health doctor. We had discussed how electronic media might be exploited to make up-to-date information inexpensively available in remote parts of the world (we used Juba, in the south of Sudan, as our example). The systematic reviews that were then being prepared for the pregnancy and childbirth books seemed ideal candidates for piloting this idea.

Malcolm Newdick and Mark Starr did the programming necessary to assemble and display all the hundreds of analyses being prepared for the books. At the end of 1988, these were published electronically, together with structured abstracts, and then regularly updated in an electronic journal called *The Oxford Database of Perinatal Trials (ODPT)*,[29] which also contained the register of controlled trials we had assembled. Between 1988 and 1992, *ODPT* was distributed every six months on floppy diskettes. Under Mark Starr's guidance, *ODPT* evolved first into the *Cochrane Pregnancy and Childbirth Database* and then into the pregnancy and childbirth module of *The Cochrane Database of Systematic Reviews*.[30]

In 1989 and 1990 these three outcomes of our collaborative work – *ECPC*, *GECPC* and *ODPT* – received a good deal of favourable attention.[31] We were particularly pleased by the reception given to our work by women using the maternity services and by the organisations endeavouring to represent their interests. It was even more fortunate that one of the people who approved of our work was Michael Peckham, an oncologist who had been appointed to establish and direct a Research and Development Programme for the National Health Service.[32]

ENVISIONING A *COCHRANE COLLABORATION*

In May 1991, a few months after Michael Peckham had taken up his post, I was thinking while walking soon after sunrise by the Thames, north of Oxford. It occurred to me that it would be worth attempting to initiate an international collaboration to build on the methods that we had used and explored in the pregnancy and childbirth work, with a view to extending them to other specialties – as Archie Cochrane had hoped would happen. On my return home, I prepared a synopsis of the idea on one side of a sheet of paper, and asked Michael Peckham if I could discuss it with him. A couple of weeks later we met, and he was encouraging. He sent me away to draft a full proposal for 'a Cochrane Centre, to facilitate the preparation, maintenance and dissemination of systematic reviews of randomized controlled trials of health-care'.

Michael Peckham's main advisory committee considered a first full proposal for the Cochrane Centre in October 1991, then a redrafted proposal in February 1992. I gather it received a mixed reception. Some people familiar with the pregnancy and childbirth work knew that there had been some successful pilot experience. Others simply saw the proposal as too risky. Still others thought that it was not worth investing resources to find out what, in theory, was known already. I had applied for 5 years' support, with an external assessment after 3 years. In view of the ambivalence among his advisers, Michael Peckham offered me 3 years' support, with just 20 months to show that progress towards agreed targets was occurring. As a contract researcher, who had never had any job security, this seemed like a risk worth taking. 'The Cochrane Centre' was opened later that year by the minister of health – Tom Sackville – and drawn to the attention of the outside world in editorials published in the BMJ[33] and The Lancet.[34]

Over the previous two decades, I had come to know many individuals who felt then and continue to feel that the results of research could be exploited more systematically for the benefit of those using and working in health services. During 1992, after the proposal to establish the Cochrane Centre had been given the go-ahead, I contacted many of these colleagues and friends. I thought they should know that the NHS Research and Development Programme had provided an opportunity to show that the vision that we shared could be translated into reality, but that this would not happen

without wholehearted, generous-spirited international collaboration. The most important initiative of the first Cochrane
Centre was to invite these people to participate in 'a
colloquium' to discuss whether, and if so how, an international collaboration could be established to take forward this
work. In October 1993, a year after the first Cochrane Centre
had opened, they met in Oxford and agreed to establish The
Cochrane Collaboration.

NOTES

1 Dickersin K, Manheimer E. The Cochrane Collaboration: evaluation of
health-care and services using systematic reviews of the results of
randomized controlled trials. Clin Obstet Gynecol 1998; 41: 315–331.
2 Chalmers I. Why we need to know whether prophylactic antibiotics can
reduce measles-related morbidity. Pediatrics 2002; 109: 312–315.
3 Cochrane AL. Effectiveness and Efficiency: Random Reflections on
Health Services. London: Nuffield Provincial Hospitals Trust, 1972.
4 Chalmers I. Foreword to the new edition. In: Cochrane AL. Effectiveness and Efficiency: Random Reflections on Health Services. London:
Royal Society of Medicine Press and Nuffield Trust, 1999: xiii–xvi.
5 Chalmers I, Zlosnik JE, Johns KA, Campbell H. Obstetric practice and
outcome of pregnancy in Cardiff residents, 1965–1973. BMJ 1976; 1:
735–738.
6 Chalmers I, Lawson JG, Turnbull AC. Evaluation of different
approaches to obstetric care I. Br J Obstet Gynaecol 1976; 83: 921–929.
7 Chalmers I, Lawson JG, Turnbull AC. Evaluation of different
approaches to obstetric care II. Br J Obstet Gynaecol 1976; 83: 930–
933.
8 Newcombe RG, Chalmers I. Changes in distribution of gestational age
and birth weight among first born infants of Cardiff residents. BMJ
1977; 2: 925–926.
9 Cochrane AL. 1931–1971: a critical review, with particular reference to
the medical profession. In: Medicines for the year 2000. London: Office
of Health Economics, 1979, pp 1–11.
10 Chalmers I, Hetherington J, Newdick M, Mutch L, Grant A, Enkin M,
Enkin E, Dickersin K. The Oxford Database of Perinatal Trials:
developing a register of published reports of controlled trials. Contr Clin
Trials 1986; 7: 306–324.
11 Dickersin K, Hewitt P, Mutch L, Chalmers I, Chalmers TC. Perusing the
literature. Comparison of MEDLINE searching with a perinatal trials
database. Contr Clin Trials 1985; 6: 306–317.

12 Chalmers I. British debate on obstetric practice. Pediatrics 1976; 58: 308–312.
13 Chard T, Richards MPM, eds. Benefits and Hazards of the New Obstetrics. Clin Dev Med No. 64. London: Spastics International Medical Publications/William Heinemann Medical Books, 1977.
14 Chalmers I, Richards MPM. Intervention and causal inference in obstetric practice. In: Chard T, Richards MPM, eds. Benefits and Hazards of the New Obstetrics. Clin Dev Med No. 64. London: Spastics International Medical Publications/William Heinemann Medical Books, 1977: 34–61.
15 Chalmers I. Randomized controlled trials of fetal monitoring 1973–1977. In: Thalhammer O, Baumgarten K, Pollak A, eds. Perinatal Medicine. Stuttgart: Georg Thieme, 1979: 260–265.
16 MacDonald D, Grant A, Sheridan–Pereira M, Boylan P, Chalmers I. The Dublin randomized controlled trial of intrapartum fetal heart rate monitoring. Am J Obstet Gynecol 1985; 152: 524–539.
17 National Perinatal Epidemiology Unit. A classified bibliography of controlled trials in perinanal medicine, 1940–1984. Oxford: Oxford University Press (for the World Health Organization), 1985.
18 Enkin M, Chalmers I, eds. Effectiveness and Satisfaction in Antenatal Care. Clin Dev Med Nos 81/82. London: Spastics International Medical Publications/William Heinemann Medical Books, 1982.
19 Crowley P, Chalmers I, Keirse MJNC. The effects of corticosteroid administration before preterm delivery: an overview of the evidence from controlled trials. Br J Obstet Gynaecol 1990; 97: 11–25.
20 Hetherington J, Dickersin K, Chalmers I, Meinert CL. Retrospective and prospective identifitation of unpublished controlled trials: lessons from a survey of obstetricians and pediatricians. Pediatrics 1989; 84: 374–380.
21 Chalmers I, Adams M, Dickersin K, Hetherington J, Tarnow-Mordi W, Meinert C, Tonascia S, Chalmers TC. A cohort study of summary reports of controlled trials. JAMA 1990; 263: 1401–1404.
22 Oxman AD, Guyatt GH. Guidelines for reading literature reviews. CMAJ 1988; 138: 697–703.
23 Chalmers I, Enkin M, Keirse MJNC, eds. Effective Care in Pregnancy and Childbirth. Oxford: Oxford University Press, 1989.
24 Enkin M, Keirse MJNC, Chalmers I, eds. A Guide to Effective Care in Pregnancy and Childbirth. Oxford: Oxford University Press, 1989.
25 Peto R, Chalmers I. Obituary: Archie Cochrane (1909–1988). Contr Clin Trials 1989; 16: 193–195.
26 Cochrane AL. Foreword. In: Chalmers I, Enkin M, Keirse MJNC, eds. Effective Care in Pregnancy and Childbirth. Oxford: Oxford University Press, 1989, p viii.
27 Sinclair JC, Bracken M. Effective Care of the Newborn Infant. Oxford: Oxford University Press, 1992.

28 Chalmers I. Electronic publications for updating controlled trial reviews. Lancet 1986; 2: 287.

29 Chalmers I, ed. The Oxford Database of Perinatal Trials. Oxford: Oxford University Press. 1989–1992.

30 Starr M, Chalmers I. How electronic publishing can help people to do more good than harm in health-care: the story of The Cochrane Library (available at www.update-software.com/ history/clibhist.htm).

31. Milbank Quarterly Special Issue. 1993; 71: 405–532.

32 Peckham M. Research and development for the National Health Service. Lancet 1991; 338: 367–371.

33 Chalmers I, Dickersin K, Chalmers TC. Getting to grips with Archie Cochrane's agenda: a register of all randomized controlled trials. Br Med J 1992; 305: 786–788.

34 Sackett D. Cochrane's legacy. Lancet 1992; 340: 1131–1132.

ACKNOWLEDGEMENTS

I am grateful to Jan Chalmers, Murray Enkin, Kay Dickersin, Jini Hetherington, Marc Keirse, Andy Oxman, Michael Peckham, Mark Starr and Jan Vandenbroucke for helpful comments on an earlier draft of this memoir, and to the many people who made important contributions to the pre-history of the first Cochrane Centre, particularly Frank Hytten and William Silverman.

© Appendix C: Sir Iain Chalmers

Index